DISHES FROM THE WILD HORSE DESERT

NORTEÑO COOKING OF SOUTH TEXAS

DISHES FROM THE WILD HORSE DESERT

NORTEÑO COOKING OF SOUTH TEXAS

MELISSA GUERRA

WILEY

JOHN WILEY & SONS, INC.

Photographs © Ignacio Urquiza

Published by John Wiley & Sons, Inc., Hoboken, New Jersey

Published simultaneously in Canada

For general information about our other products and services, please contact our Customer Care Department within the United States at (800) 762-2974, outside the United States at (317) 572-3993 or fax (317) 572-4002.

Wiley also publishes its books in a variety of electronic formats. Some content that appears in print may not be available in electronic books. For more information about Wiley products, visit our web site at www.wiley.com.

Library of Congress Cataloging-in-Publication Data

Guerra, Melissa.
  Dishes from the wild horse desert : Norteño cooking of South Texas / Melissa Guerra.
       p. cm.
  Includes bibliographical references and index.
       ISBN-13: 978-0-7645-5892-4 (cloth)
       ISBN-10: 0-7645-5892-7 (cloth)
  1. Cookery, American–Southwestern style. 2. Mexican American cookery. 3. Cookery–Texas. I. Title.
  TX715.2.S69G843 2006
  641.5979–dc22   2005026352

MANUFACTURED IN THE UNITED STATES OF AMERICA

10 9 8 7 6 5 4 3 2 1

Dedicated to those who have cooked for me . . .

CONTENTS

ACKNOWLEDGMENTS

I HOPE I AM GRANTED THE OPPORTUNITY and privilege of writing another book in the future. I am so very thankful to the following people:

Dianne Jacob, my writing coach and now good friend: She helped me shape the initial idea into a proposal that would be taken seriously. She advised me as I submitted my proposal to agents, stood by me while I waited for their responses, and consoled me after complete rejections. After six months of self-imposed exile from writing, I submitted more proposals to agents, and I could hear her smile over the phone as I told her about the seven agents who called me back.

Martha Kaplan and Judith Riven, my agents: Simultaneously, they pulled my proposal out of their slush pile. They decided to be my co-agents, which I took as an omen that they were women of character. They have proved this to be true, and I thank them for championing this book.

John Wiley and Sons, publishers: Thanks to Anne Ficklen and Susan Wyler, for grooming this project and giving me guidance. A very sincere thank-you to my editor Adam Kowit, who always asked for more and encouraged me to write from my heart. His patience is boundless. Thanks to production editor Michael Olivo and to Vertigo Design.

Photographer Ignacio Urquiza, and his wife, food stylist Laura Cordera: This regional cuisine could be defined by only one photographer, and happily, Nacho agreed to the job. I literally stalked him and brought him to the ranch to see what I wanted to capture. He was immediately enthusiastic. I am one of his biggest fans, and now we are good friends. Laura, quiet and lovely, defines professionalism, grace, and charm. I am looking forward to shopping for shoes with her in New York City for years to come.

George and Virginia Gause: They shared my enthusiasm and helped me find the resources that I needed.

My parents and in-laws: They gave me many insights into ranch life during their generation, and the generations before them. I also want to thank our grandparents and great grandparents, who made available to me their notes, recipes, and memories. And I want to thank my sisters, brother, *cuñados y concuños,* for their support and constructive criticism of my test recipes.

Thanks to my girlfriends, who understood when I didn't return phone calls, or accept invitations while I wrote this book.

Thanks to recipe testers Valerie Calvillo, Kristen Gaston, Cati Gomez, Nancy Ladewig, Katherine Martin, Lisa May, Tina Mendez, Paula Moxely, Cari Olea, Yolanda Pedraza, Pat Schwab, John Smedley, and May Vance.

More than anything, I want to thank my husband Kiko and my sons, Henry, Diego, and Lorenzo, who ate anything I cooked and gave me the time to write this book.

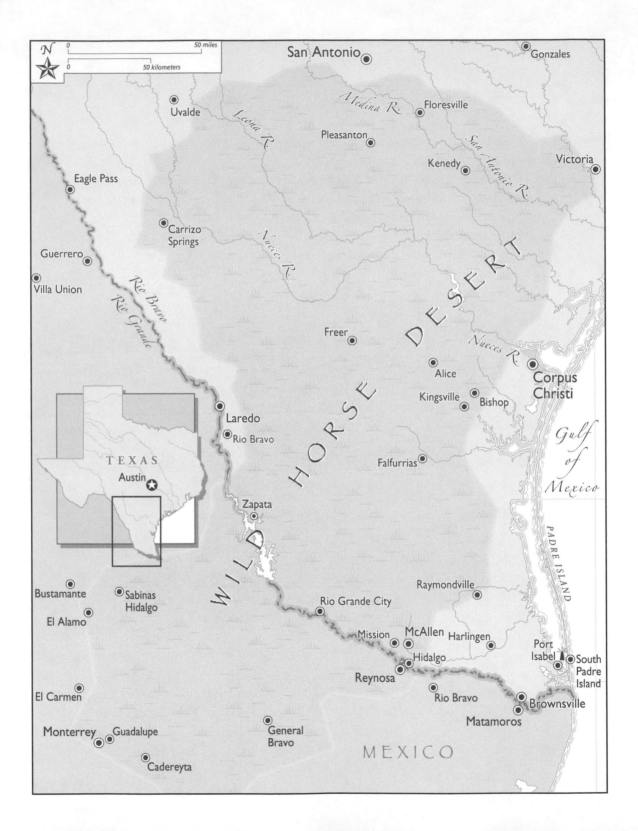

INTRODUCTION

"It would be desirable to remain in Texas. It is just the kind of country Julia that we have often spoken of in our most romantic conversations. It is the place where we could gallop over the prairies and start up Deer and prairie birds and occasionally see droves of wild horses or an Indian wigwam."

ULYSSES S. GRANT, TO HIS FIANCÉE JULIA DENT, OCTOBER 10, 1845, CORPUS CHRISTI, TEXAS

The lonely second lieutenant wrote to his beloved Julia from the plains of the Wild Horse Desert. Perhaps he was writing at sunrise, as he sipped his coffee, gazing at the blue morning mist hovering in the clumps of *sacahuiste* grass. Maybe he was writing in the evening, when the heat from the day rises from the red dirt, filling the air with the scent of earth. Was he listening to the distant shots of his fellow soldiers as they hunted wild turkey for the camp's dinner? I wonder.

I wonder, because from my kitchen window I see the same brushland that the young soldier saw. I wonder how he, and others before him, survived in the rugged terrain of the Wild Horse Desert. Where did they find their food? What dishes did they crave? What recipes did they bring with them? What could they recreate with the food they found, and what recipes did they invent?

Texas has been inhabited by natives, colonized by Spain, desired by the French, claimed by Mexico, promoted in turn-of-the-century German publications, became its own independent republic, and at last became one of the United States. The war with Mexico was to determine the southern border of Texas, and the territory between the disputed boundaries was the area that is called the Wild Horse Desert. To understand this region is to delve into the politics of Europe and its race to claim the New World.

Horses are not native to the New World: they were brought to the Americas by the Spanish *conquistadores* and used as beasts of burden, to transport goods and people across the vast territory. Domesticated horses and cattle made existence possible for settlers in the New World. However, South Texas became famous for the enormous droves of wild cattle and horses that roamed its dry, dusty plains.

The first wild herds were formed of livestock that had run away or been abandoned. The reason for a majority of the abandonment was the U.S.–Mexican

War in 1846, a dispute that involved the establishment of the international boundary between Mexico and the U.S. Each country recognized the boundary that afforded them more acreage: for Mexico it was the Nueces River in the north, for the U.S. it was the Rio Grande, toward the south. The swath of land between these two rivers is known as the Nueces Strip. Our lonely soldier's regiment was placed in the Nueces Strip to make sure Texas kept her desired southern boundary of the Rio Grande.

With the signing of the treaty of Guadalupe Hidalgo in 1848, the official international border was established at the Rio Grande. Many of the Mexican citizens that lived within the Nueces Strip fled the disputed territory, as they were no longer considered citizens on their own property. Much of the land and livestock were abandoned. With no one to care for them, huge herds of donkeys, cattle, and horses wandered across the plains in search of food and water. Horses and cattle that accidentally escaped from their owners would join these large herds. The herds wandered beyond the river boundaries of the Nueces Strip, from present day Eagle Pass, east toward the Gulf Coast, and down to the Rio Grande. Thus, South Texas became known as "The Wild Horse Desert."

Flat, barren, and hot, the Wild Horse Desert was the perfect safe haven for escaped animals. The wide open plains made it simply impossible to recapture them. They ran everywhere. However, with no mountains, few hills, and sparse vegetation, the land was uninviting to humans. The landscape was so bare that cowboys carried special loop-ended steel augers that screwed into the ground, giving them a secure place to tie their horses in the evenings, as there were no trees. Over time, wild and domestic cows and horses seeded the plains with cactus and mesquites, bringing in their bellies the plant life from distant, verdant areas. The wild horses and livestock changed the landscape.

Before the horses arrived, however, there were native tribes that lived in South Texas. These tribes were master survivalists, existing on precious little water and the meager food offerings of the desert. My personal belief is that the harsh environment made them fierce and warlike, as they consistently defeated the campaigns from the south conducted by Spanish explorers. Many of the parties of settlers met their death at the hands of the unwelcoming tribes. Spanish explorer Jose de Escandon was the leader of the first successful colonizing effort in South Texas, and in 1749 set up over 24 settlements along the Rio Grande.

Eventually, more settlers came to South Texas in search of their fortune. Many immigrants came to obtain a portion of the plentiful land for farming and raising livestock. Scotch-Irish immigrant Richard King amassed over 825,000 acres in South Texas, building the legendary cattle empire of the King Ranch.

The largest ethnic group from Europe in Texas is the Germans. Actively recruited by land impresarios in the 1830s, the Germans came to farm in Texas, and brought with them their love of beer, knowledge of sausage making, and accordion musical traditions, which have all become popular elements of South Texas culture and cuisine. Other immigrants that settled in Texas were the Mexicans, Irish, Czechs, Poles and Greeks.

My dad speaks of the bus ride to school when he was growing up in the 1940s—there was a local Polish farming community as well as the Hispanic and Anglo ranchers and ranch workers who sent their children into town every morning. At each stop, the children entering the bus would bring their breakfast: Some brought *tacos de chorizo con huevo,* some brought peanut butter sandwiches, others brought *polska keilbaska* (Polish sausage). Each child spoke the language that corresponded with their breakfast, many speaking all three languages as they greeted their friends entering the bus.

I come from a family of Texas historians, and much to their chagrin, I never shared their enthusiasm. History has always seemed to me a recitation of names, dates, battles, and deaths. But, through my love of cooking, I have become fascinated with the daily chores of the folks that lived in South Texas. And because we live at the crossroads of two cultures, the recipes I find tell as much, if not more, about the people who settled here.

I wanted to write this book because the Wild Horse Desert is the part of Texas where I grew up; it is where I live and raise my children, and where someday my ashes will be scattered. I love the Wild Horse Desert; I am one of her people. My family has lived here for 8 generations, dedicating their lives to caring for the land and raising cattle. My parents, grandparents, and all the generations before them woke up every morning to the same horizon I see, and walked the same red sand that I do. Many of these recipes are my family recipes, some are from neighbors, but all are authentic and traditional of the ranchlands of South Texas.

You may find the recipes in this book an eclectic mix, which, I assure you, is a fair representation of who we are. But I will explain how these recipes arrived in this area, and therein lies the story of this book. Far more than listing of ingredients, we will look very closely at this unique American culture through its food.

Ideals nourish the spirits, but food sustains the body that houses that spirit. Food keeps the spirit alive. The Wild Horse Desert provided very little for the people who roamed and settled this harsh, hot land. Yet, they survived, and in time, they flourished. Their dreams tamed the desert.

So, although this is a cookbook, this is also the story of a land and a people that I love dearly. Hopefully, it will inspire you to look at your own land, your own family, your own story, and your own recipes. I have written down the stories that my grandparents shared with me, the stories of their love for the land and people, which communicate the essence of what their grandparents told them. And, just as I write to tell you of my love for the land, maybe we will come to understand the romantic sentiments of a man writing to his sweetheart, as he tells her about the land for which he is fighting, to which he wished someday to return.

A NOTE ON THE NORTEÑO

The music and cuisine of northern Mexico are many times referred to as *norteño*, a term that simply means "northern." Although the Rio Grande serves as an international boundary for the United States and Mexico, South Texas is considered part of *norteño* culture.

Chiles

CHILES, OR HOT PEPPERS, form the basis of flavor for *norteño* cuisine. Every meal, even breakfast and snacks, features some type of chile, whether presented in spicy salsa or serving as the binding flavor in a rich *guisado*, or stew. We shop for chiles as commonly as the rest of the United States would shop for apples and oranges. Although we celebrate the chile for its flavor, it also adds a good dose of vitamin C to our rather beefy diet and is an aid in preserving food (see Chile con Carne recipe, page 120).

Each chile has a specific way in which it should be prepared before using it in a recipe. Below is a quick index of the chiles you will encounter in this book and what you should do with them. I have also given them a heat factor number, which will give you a general idea of each chile's spiciness level: Level 1, the mildest, comparing to that of a bell pepper; to Level 10, the hottest, comparing to our wild little piquín chile.

FRESH CHILES

There is no visual clue to tell you how hot a chile will taste. Each variety has a certain expected "heat" range. But each crop is subjected to different levels of rain, different fertilizers, and different soil qualities—all of which determine the flavor and heat of any chile. Make sure the fresh chiles you select are firm and evenly colored, with no soft spots on the body of the chile or at the stem.

CHILE PIQUÍN—HEAT LEVEL 10: The piquín chile is the original wild chile. All peppers are hybrids of this chile. The size of a pea, these small green chiles are also known as bird peppers in English. In Mexico, there are myriad names for them—*tepin, petín, pitín, piquín*—and there are as many shapes as there are derivative names. The fresh variety can be very hot and have a sharp green biting flavor. When the chile turns red and matures, it is usually dried (see page 4).

CHILE POBLANO—HEAT LEVEL 3 TO 4: Look for large shiny chiles with no soft spots or cracks. Check the stem end, as sometimes mold and dirt can hide in the deep indentation. Poblano chiles that have a slight reddish cast might be a little hotter than the green ones. Poblano chiles are always roasted before use, as it not only enhances their flavor but also helps to loosen their thin bitter skin.

CHILE SERRANO—HEAT LEVEL 6 TO 7: This is a very basic chile, with a fresh green flavor and a piquant bite. Serrano chiles remind me of the shape of a pinky finger; slim and smooth, they should be firm, without black spots or sunken places. No special preparation is required for these chiles, no roasting as for the poblano chile. Just wash the serrano chiles well before using as directed in your recipe.

CHILE JALAPEÑO—HEAT LEVEL 5 TO 6: Fresh jalapeños are rather lackluster and mild, but once they are seasoned and pickled in vinegar, they are terrifically flavorful, revealing the true reason for their popularity. If they are allowed to mature on the plant, then dried and smoked, they become chipotle chiles (see page 4). Their name derives from the olden days, when fresh jalapeños were first grown in Xalapa, also spelled Jalapa. Jalapeños are known sometimes as *chile cuaresmeño* in Mexico. They reached their peak of ripeness during the season of Lent, *La Cuaresma,* thus the reason for the chile's other name.

BELL PEPPER—HEAT LEVEL 1: Not a trace of heat is left in this pepper hybrid, only the fresh grassy flavor. Bell peppers do not require roasting, although they are always delicious when grilled on a mesquite fire.

TO ROAST POBLANO CHILES

WASH THE CHILES THOROUGHLY. If you have a gas stove, you can put the chiles directly on the flame to roast. Place 1 or 2 chiles directly on the burner over a medium flame and turn them periodically with tongs so that they roast and blacken evenly. Be careful that they don't burn and develop an ashy layer of skin, as this will give them a bitter flavor. You can also roast the chiles in your oven by placing them directly underneath a heated broiler. Turn the chiles occasionally so that they roast evenly. Roasting the chiles should take around 5 minutes on the stove, 10 minutes in the oven.

After the chiles are well roasted, place them in a plastic or paper bag, fold or twist the bag to seal in the steam, and allow them to sweat for 15 minutes. I like to further insulate my sweating chiles by wrapping the filled bag in a kitchen towel. After 15 minutes, remove the chiles from the bag and begin to peel off the outer charred layer of skin. You can remove the stem or leave it on if you are preparing Chiles Rellenos (see page 106).

Now cut a slit in the chile starting at the stem end and remove the cluster of seeds. Rinse the chile under cold water to remove any straggling seeds or flakes of charred peel. Your chile is now ready for use. For best flavor, use the roasted chiles immediately, but if necessary, you can store them overnight in the refrigerator.

DRIED CHILES

Select chiles that are whole and that don't appear dirty or buggy or have webs. The chiles should not be matted together, torn, or dull in color.

CHILE ANCHO—HEAT LEVEL 3 TO 5: These are poblano chiles that have been left on the plant to redden and mature; once harvested and dried, they are called ancho chiles, also known as *chile de color*. Mild in heat but robust and deep in flavor, this is the chile that gives the familiar reddish cast to so many Mexican and border dishes. The word *ancho* means "wide," which reflects the large triangular shape of these chiles.

CHILE DE ARBOL—HEAT LEVEL 3 TO 5: Dry, fruity, and very hot, this chile is my favorite for Salsa de Chile de Arbol (see page 100). I prefer to toast these chiles in the oven for 1 to 2 minutes to deepen their flavor, which can otherwise be overshadowed by the addition of tomatoes. Spiky and dark red in color, these chiles are approximately 3 inches long, with straw-colored stems.

CHILE CHIPOTLE—HEAT LEVEL 6 TO 8: The chipotle chile is a dried red jalapeño that has usually been smoked over a mesquite fire. There are several varieties, such as the spicy dark purple *morita* and the dark golden brown *dorado,* which are sweeter and smokier in flavor. The purée of any type of chipotle chile makes an outstanding salsa. Although the purée can be added as a flavor base to a soup or stew, it can quickly surpass most people's tolerable heat level.

CHILE PIQUÍN—HEAT LEVEL 8: This dried chile is most commonly ground into a powder for salsas (see page 99), although plenty of folks eat them whole as a condiment between forkfuls of food. It is not unusual to walk into a kitchen in South Texas and find platefuls of these chiles drying. Many folks harvest fresh mature red piquín chiles from their yards before the birds get to them and dry them to supply their pantry. The heat level seems to mellow a bit when piqín chile is dried.

CHILE PASILLA—HEAT LEVEL 3 TO 5: Reminiscent of raisins both in color and in flavor, the pasilla chile is a long, sweet mild pepper used mostly for flavoring and coloring stews. Pasilla chiles add lots of flavor without adding heat, which makes it a favorite addition to the meat filling for tamales.

CHILE GUAJILLO—HEAT LEVEL 2 TO 4: Dry and tannic in flavor, the long, wide, dark red guajillo chile is often mistakenly labeled cascabel chile in South Texas. The guajillo chile is often added to balance the sweetness of pasilla chiles as a flavoring for a tamale filling and provides excellent flavor without adding too much heat.

TO RENDER CHILE PURÉE FROM DRIED CHILES

ONE OF THE SIMPLEST WAYS to master South Texas and Mexican cuisine is to learn how to render chiles. Rendering chiles is the process of boiling the dried chiles, then grinding them into a paste for use in salsas or stews. No French sauce can match the depth of flavor in a chile purée, and yet the purée is easy to prepare and store.

TO PREPARE THE CHILES FOR PURÉEING: Always use a large cooking vessel for rendering chiles, as the dried peppers have a tendency to float and jump out of the pot if the water level is too high. If you have never worked with chiles before, start by purchasing 1 pound of ancho chiles. They are mildly spicy and have limitless uses. In an 8-quart stockpot, bring 4 quarts of water to a boil. Add the chiles. When the water returns to a boil, partially cover and boil for 30 minutes.

The chiles are ready when they are soft and have changed from a raisin color to dark red. Drain, reserving the cooking water. Using rubber gloves (to avoid skin irritation), remove the stems, seeds, and veins.

TO MAKE CHILE PURÉE: Put the chiles in a blender. (You may want to do this in 2 batches.) Add about 1 cup of water to facilitate blending, and purée. Don't worry about being precise with the amount of water.

Pour the purée into a mesh strainer (see note) to remove any seeds or skin particles and discard the seed pulp. You should have 4 to 5 cups of purée. It freezes very well and can be conveniently packed in freezer bags in 1- or 2-cup portions. Chile purée is a great flavor base for almost anything and is always a welcome find when you are digging through the freezer, looking for inspiration. You can turn leftover shredded pork or chicken into a terrific taco filling, or turn your regular chicken soup into tortilla soup. See other creative uses on page 101.

NOTE: I have become quite a fan of my chinois strainer. It is cone-shaped with a wooden pestle, which quickly separates the pulp from the usable purée. Compared with a mesh strainer, it is sports-car fast.

Cooking with Cast Iron

I HAVE A CAST-IRON *COMAL*—a flat griddle—that is always on my stove. It belonged to my mother, but when she bought a newfangled stove with a built-in griddle, she put her comal into storage. So I took it. It is a lovely American-made cast-iron griddle with a low, sloping edge and over thirty years of seasoning built up on its surface. Seasoning is the process of continually coating the iron surface with cooking oil, and as the cast iron heats, the oil melds with the metal to produce a nonstick surface. Cast iron browns foods better than any other metal used for cookware and the browning quality, combined with the advantage of a nonstick surface, makes this material a favorite with chefs. I use my comal every day, and sometimes I travel with it when I do cooking demonstrations. I love it.

Cast-iron cookware, including skillets, Dutch ovens, cornbread molds, and comals, made up the basic *batterie de cuisine* in the Wild Horse Desert. Used by itinerant cowboys, bandits, and settlers, cast iron didn't break on the trail like pottery; abuse and insufficient washing (remember, no water here in the desert) actually seasoned it, improving its performance; and cast iron has always been amazingly inexpensive.

I presume that, because the indigenous tribes here on the border (namely the Coahuiltecans and Karankawas) were nomadic and did not forge metal, they made their comals out of clay, simply making new ones when they arrived at a new campsite. Gathered clay would be shaped into a disk and fired in a mesquite fire, similar to the way clay pottery is still made in Mexico today. Cast iron would have been brought by European settlers and traded with the native tribes.

Although the primary use for cast iron here in the Wild Horse Desert is stovetop baking, such as making tortillas and *gorditas,* it is quite versatile. A cast-iron griddle will last for many years as long as you give it a little special care. I don't clean my comal often, as I use it mainly for making tortillas and roasting chiles for salsa. The tortillas and chiles have no fat and leave behind no liquid residue, so once they have cooled, I simply season the comal by wiping the iron surface clean with a paper towel dipped in vegetable oil.

However, if you use your cast iron for stovetop grilling of meats, I recommend a good scrub in your sink. Use a plastic woven cloth or scrubber made for Teflon pans, but never steel wool, as that would remove your precious seasoning layer. Whether you clean with soap or not is up to you. I use soap, although some cast-iron enthusiasts would cringe at this notion. Next, dry it well, then season it by rubbing it with a paper towel soaked in oil, inside and out, before storing. Vegetable sprays don't work as well, as they seem to char and leave a sticky film on your pan. Never put cast iron in the dishwasher.

Seasoning must happen every time you use a piece of cast iron in order to build up a nice, slick surface. The first time you season a pan, wash the cast iron thoroughly, completely yet lightly coat with oil, and bake in a 300°F oven for 30 to 60 minutes. Old cast iron can be revived and reseasoned using the same technique. I have bought several cast-iron skillets at rummage sales. They are terrific bargains, and with a little tender care, they become faithful friends in the kitchen.

Corn and Flour Tortillas

FOR MILLENNIA, WOMEN HAVE been making corn tortillas. Every night, the corn was put to boil, and every morning, the grinding process would begin. Using a *metate,* a three-legged sloped stone table, the women would kneel for hours at a time, grinding the *nixtamal,* or boiled and prepared corn, until there was enough *masa*—cornmeal dough—to make tortillas for the family. Today, instant tortilla mix has freed legions of women (and everyone else) from this daily grind. These mixes are now readily available, and many of my tortilla recipes call for it. But as a nod to tradition, and for anyone seeking to replicate the old recipes, I have also included directions for the orginal grinding processes. As much as I value tradition, I am rather glad that we have advanced beyond stone grinding masa every day. See pages 11–13 for both traditional recipes and versions using instant tortilla mix.

TO PRESS CORN TORTILLAS: In order to make *tortillas de maiz* in the modern fashion, using instant corn tortilla mix (sometimes called *masa harina*), or corn masa made in the traditional way, you will need a tortilla press. They are usually made out of cast aluminum and are coated with tin. The dough is pressed between the two large metal plates that arc compressed with a lever.

In order to extract the tortilla from the press, you will need a liner. Fifty years ago, these liners would have been made of a linen cup towel or a smooth banana leaf. Today, most cooks fashion a liner out of a plastic bag. Use a heavy plastic bag, like a ziplock bag. Cut a circle the same diameter as your press, which should give you two circles. When you press the tortilla, place the ball of masa between the layers of plastic. Once the tortilla is pressed, simply peel off the plastic from both sides of the tortilla and place the uncooked tortilla on the hot griddle.

Only corn tortillas are made with a tortilla press. I can't tell you how many times I have opened a kitchenware catalog to see a bright shiny tortilla press, with a flour tortilla placed on top as a prop!

Flour tortillas are more popular in the north of Mexico, and therefore are seen more often on the U.S. border. Some believe that flour tortillas were developed by Germans, who preferred wheat to corn flour, and who settled in northern Mexico to farm wheat, barley, hops, and sorghum. Others believe that flour tortillas were developed by the Middle Eastern families who settled in northern Mexico and were attempting to replicate pita bread. Heavy use of cumin and the popularity of roasted kid goat *(cabrito)* in *norteño* cuisine are also attributed to Middle Eastern influence, reinforcing the pita bread theory.

Other sources indicate that Sephardic and Ashkenazic Jews who settled around Monterey and in South Texas invented flour tortillas as a replacement for matzo, the traditional Jewish unleavened bread. The Ashkenazic Jews could not eat corn during Passover and were forced to invent alternative breads to the corn tortilla. However, I am not quite sure how the traditional lard with which the flour tortillas were made fits with the Jewish diet. See page 18 for the recipe for flour tortillas.

TO ROLL FLOUR TORTILLAS: In contrast to corn tortillas, flour tortillas must be rolled out by hand. Rolling out a round flour tortilla can be tricky, but here are a few guidelines:

- ❖ Don't knead your dough too much. Allow it to rest at least 20 minutes, covered with a damp cloth, before you roll it out. I let it rest for a few hours if I have time. In fact, you can make the dough one day in advance and store it in the refrigerator.

- ❖ Make *textales* before you roll out the tortillas. Textales are the divided pieces of dough that are each rolled with your hands into balls. Pat it into a thick circle, then push a depression into the center of each circle of dough, without making a hole. When you roll out a flour tortilla, your hands are applying pressure at the far ends of your rolling pin, not the center. Therefore, you are pushing out the edges of the dough, not rolling out the dough from the middle. This divot establishes a thin center thickness for the tortilla, and helps keep an even thickness throughout.

◆ If you can, use a thin rolling pin, like a large dowel. This helps you apply less pressure than with a heavy pastry rolling pin and rolls the dough more evenly. Many people use old broom handles that have been cut and sanded.

◆ As you roll out the tortillas, give each textal a quarter-turn with each pass of the rolling pin. This ensures that the dough rolls evenly in each direction. Use plenty of flour to keep your tortilla from sticking to the work surface.

◆ It is easier to roll out all of your tortillas before you cook any of them. This shortens your entire cooking time, as you won't have to pause to roll out another tortilla. Also, the *comal* (iron griddle) can get very hot as it waits, and can raise the temperature in your work area.

COOKING TORTILLAS

There is one cardinal rule in making any tortilla, whether flour or corn: A tortilla has three sides. The first side, when you put the raw pressed-out dough onto your hot *comal,* is what I call the "setting" side. This seals the shape of the tortilla and should cook for about 20 seconds. Using a metal spatula, you then flip the tortilla onto the other side, called the "cooking" side. This has the longest cooking time, about 2 minutes, depending on the heat of your griddle. Occasionally lift up the tortilla briefly to see if toasted brown dots are forming.

When you see these dots, flip the tortilla again, back onto its third and final side, the "inflating" side. Since you sealed your tortilla on the first side, and then again on the second side, you have trapped the moisture inside the tortilla, and as it turns to steam it inflates when cooking on its third side. The inflating step makes beautifully light and tender tortillas. Once your tortilla has fully inflated, let it cook for 20 seconds more, then remove it from the griddle and place it in a clean towel to keep warm.

CORN TORTILLAS
MAKES 24 TORTILLAS

The word tortilla *is the diminutive Spanish word for a cake. The indigenous Aztec name was* tlaxcalli, *which means "bread of maize." This is a simple, basic recipe for making corn tortilla dough using instant tortilla mix (masa harina).*

4 cups instant corn tortilla mix

PLACE the instant corn tortilla mix in a large mixing bowl. Slowly add up to 4 cups warm water while kneading the mixture. Add only enough water to make a cohesive dough. Knead for 1 minute.

BREAK off a golf-ball-size piece of dough and roll into a ball. Using a clapping motion with your hands, pat it out into a flat circle about ½ inch thick.

PRESS the dough in a tortilla press and cook, following the pressing and cooking instructions on pages 7–9.

TO MAKE YOUR OWN TORTILLA CHIPS, cut cooked tortillas into quarters and fry in hot (350°F) vegetable oil. Drain on paper towels and sprinkle with sea salt.

CORN TORTILLAS WITH CILANTRO

MAKES 24 TORTILLAS

I am not usually a fan of the nouvelle *tortillas made with spinach, eggplant, tomato, and other flavors, but this variation of traditional tortillas actually shows up sometimes in the more inspired taco stands in Mexico. Artistic in presentation, these tortillas present the delicate leaves of cilantro as green silhouettes on a pale yellow corn background.*

4 cups instant corn tortilla mix
¾ cup chopped cilantro

COMBINE the instant corn tortilla mix and cilantro in a large bowl. Slowly add up to 4 cups warm water while kneading the mixture. Add only enough water to make a cohesive dough. Knead for 1 minute.

BREAK off a golf-ball-size piece of dough and roll into a ball. Using a clapping motion with your hands, pat it out into a flat circle.

PRESS the dough in a tortilla press and cook, following the pressing and cooking instructions on pages 7–9.

RED CHILE CORN TORTILLAS

MAKES 24 TORTILLAS

The added chile *purée imparts only a hint of flavor, but rich depth of color. Substitute red chile corn tortillas in any recipe calling for regular corn tortillas, such as quesadillas, enchiladas, flautas, or even tortilla chips. I love making flautas with a colorful mix of regular and red chile corn tortillas, and topping them off with handfuls of freshly chopped cilantro.*

4 ounces dried ancho chiles or your favorite type of dried chile
2 cups instant corn tortilla mix

RENDER a purée from the dried chiles according to the instructions on page 000.

COMBINE the corn tortilla mix, chile purée, and $1\frac{1}{2}$ cups of warm water in a large mixing bowl. Knead ingredients together with your hands until well combined. If the dough sticks to your fingers, add a little more tortilla mix. If the dough feels too stiff, add a little more water. Your dough should be soft, yet firm enough for working.

BREAK off a golf-ball-size piece of dough and roll into a ball. Using a clapping motion, pat it out into a flat circle, about $\frac{1}{2}$ inch thick.

PRESS the dough in a tortilla press and cook, following the pressing and cooking instructions on pages 7–9.

FRESHLY GROUND CORN MASA FOR TORTILLAS AND TAMALES

MAKES 2 POUNDS OF MASA

Fresh masa *is quite different from masa made with instant tortilla mix: The texture will be less elastic, with more toothsome graininess to it, and it will have a much more intense corn flavor. Although it is more laborious to make, fresh masa has a rustic honesty that cannot be replicated.*

You need to grind and prepare your nixtamal *within 24 hours, as it will sour if left. Hand-cranked corn-grinding mills are available in many Mexican markets. (Some electric kitchen mixers come with grain-grinding attachments, although I have never experimented with these.) You cannot substitute a food processor for the corn mill.*

2 pounds freshly made Nixtamal (see page 16)

GRIND the nixtamal according to the manufacturer's directions, adjusting the grinding disks for fine or coarse texture. Enlist the help of friends and family members to grind the nixtamal, as it can be a laborious task. Store for up to 24 hours in your refrigerator before use.

TO USE MASA to make tortillas, follow the instructions on page 7 for pressing corn tortillas and 9 for cooking tortillas. To use masa to make tamales, follow the instructions on pages 75–79.

TRADITIONAL MASA

GRINDING INGREDIENTS was how most women spent their time in the days before electricity, so here it is worth mentioning the *metate*. A metate is a three-legged stone table that was used for grinding masa, chiles, chocolate, or any other food substance that needed processing before consumption. The rolling pestle used on this sloping table is called the *metlapil*. The metate and metlapil have almost disappeared from use, except in remote regions in Mexico. Occasionally, farmers and ranchers will dig up metates in fields here in the Wild Horse Desert. They were buried and left behind by nomadic tribes, who would return to dig them up and use them again as they traveled the same routes every year.

CORN VARIETIES

THERE ARE five different varieties of corn:

- Dent: field corn, this has a higher starch content, is recognized for the dented exterior. It is soft, used for tortillas and tortilla products like chips and taco shells.

- Flint: field corn, this is similar to dent corn in its starch content. Hard and gritty with a tough outer hull, it is also known as Indian corn and mostly used for animal feed.

- Sweet: sugary and juicy, this is the fresh corn we buy in the United States to be eaten boiled or roasted.

- Pop: a special kind of flint corn whose internal moisture expands rapidly enough when heated to explode its starchy core. It's our favorite movie snack that was also enjoyed by early tribes.

- Flour: starchy, soft, and favored because it is easily ground, this is one of the older types of corn grown for food. It was widely grown by Native Americans as was flint corn.

- Pod: Some add this other variety to this list, which is the original wild, unhybridized grasslike corn plant, known as *teosinte*.

NIXTAMAL PREPARED CORN FOR MASA

MAKES 2 POUNDS

Few people make their own nixtamal *for tortillas and* tamales. *However, I felt that a recipe should be included in this book for those who cannot find a* molino *in their neighborhood, and for those (like myself) who like to cook using the freshest ingredients possible.*

Nixtamal is dried corn that has been boiled in anticipation of being ground for masa. The process of preparing corn to be ground is called nixtamalizaicion. *The result is nixtamal, whose name comes from the Aztec term* nextli, *meaning "ashes," and* tamlli, *which means "tamal." For millennium, dried corn was boiled and soaked in water mixed with wood ashes in order to make the corn tender and to loosen and dissolve the hulls. The wood ash, which contained sodium hydroxide, or lye, was later replaced with calcium oxide or lime (known in Spanish as* cal) *as the soaking agent. Slaked lime, or calcium hydroxide, works as a soaking agent as well and can be found in the canning section of most grocery stores, labeled "pickling lime." In addition to loosening the hull of the corn kernel, the sodium or calcium hydroxide improves the nutritional value of the corn, rendering the niacin contained in the kernel more easily assimilated by human beings.*

The nixtamal must be prepared the night before it is ground into masa.

1 pound dried white or yellow corn
2 teaspoons pickling lime (calcium hydroxide)

PLACE the dried corn in a colander and rinse well under running water. Pick through the corn to remove any foreign matter. Pour the cleaned corn in a 4-quart saucepan and cover with water. Place on the stove and bring to a boil.

MIX the pickling lime with 1 cup of fresh water in a separate bowl. Add the pickling lime solution to the corn and stir to distribute in the water. Allow the corn to boil for about 30 minutes, until the corn is cooked. You will need to test the corn for "doneness" by extracting one kernel from the pot and breaking it in half. If the center of the kernel is still white, then it is not cooked thoroughly. Boil for another 10 minutes and test again. When corn is cooked, there should be little to no white color in the center of the kernel. (This is similar to testing pasta for doneness—the corn must be *al dente*.)

REMOVE the pot from the heat, cover, and allow to cool and soak overnight at room temperature. The next day, drain and discard the water from the cooking pot. Using a colander, in batches rinse the nixtamal thoroughly under running tap water. Rub the kernels to remove any loose hulls. (You can store the prepared corn for 24 hours in your refrigerator before you grind it. Once ground (see following recipe), the masa should be used immediately for best flavor.)

TORTILLAS DE HARINA FLOUR TORTILLAS

MAKES 24 TORTILLAS

Over the years I have made thousands of tortillas simply by eyeballing the ingredient quatities (see "Tortillas by the 'Guelita Method"). It works every time, or follow the recipe below, where I have measured and explained everything completely. Actually, I am rather proud that I can make them without a recipe. And if I can do it, you can, too.

4 cups all-purpose flour, plus more for rolling the dough
1 tablespoon salt
1 cup vegetable shortening (see Note)

COMBINE the flour and salt thoroughly in a large bowl. Knead in the shortening with your hands. Add up to 2 cups warm water in small amounts, continuing to knead. Once the dough is smooth, cohesive, somewhat firm and elastic, gather it into a ball and let it rest in the mixing bowl for at least 20 minutes, covered with a kitchen towel. (You can let the dough rest overnight in the refrigerator as well. The elasticity of the dough will change dramatically during the resting period, as the dough "relaxes," which makes it easier to roll out.)

DIVIDE the dough into 24 equal pieces and shape into round patties. Heat a comal (griddle) on the stove. Press a divot into the center of each patty to make a slight depression.

ON A FLOURED SURFACE, roll out a tortilla until very thin. Place the tortilla on the comal for 30 seconds, then flip to cook on the other side for 2 minutes. Flip again and cook until the tortilla balloons with steam. Remove the tortilla from the comal and keep under a kitchen towel until all the tortillas are finished. Cooked flour tortillas will keep for 1 week in the refrigerator.

◆ **TORTILLAS DE HARINA INTEGRAL (WHOLE WHEAT TORTILLAS):** Whole wheat tortillas are made exactly like white flour tortillas, however use 2 cups all-purpose flour mixed with 2 cups whole wheat flour. Also, with whole wheat tortillas, the resting period before rolling out the tortillas should be a bit longer. I leave my whole wheat dough in the fridge overnight, wrapped in plastic, and it is in prefect condition early the next morning to be rolled out to make our breakfast taquitos.

NOTE: Traditionally, flour tortillas are made with pork lard, but we use cholesterol-free vegetable shortening in this recipe. If you would like to experiment with pork lard, just use the same amount as you would shortening.

TORTILLAS BY THE 'GUELITA METHOD

I HAVE HEARD the story many times. "My grandmother never measured anything when she made flour tortillas" and consequently, as the recipes were unwritten and unmeasured, not many folks these days know how to make them from scratch. I call this method of making flour tortillas the *'guelita,* or granny, method, a method that is pretty much lost with the passing of the years and generations.

Neither of my grandmothers made flour tortillas. But I was determined to learn on my own. I asked my friends' grandmothers for their secrets, read recipes, and made up my own techniques. In the early years of my marriage, my flour tortillas were terrible. Hard, tough, and thick, they were inedible (although my husband gallantly tried—he was a gracious newlywed). I gave up, thinking I would join the legions of breakfast taco lovers who surrendered to the convenience of gluey-textured tortillas that came from the store in a plastic bag.

Then, I met Claudia, a young neighbor from the ranch across the road. She made the lightest, thinnest tortillas I had ever eaten. While cooking, they ballooned with steam, seeming to rise off the surface of the hot iron griddle. They practically floated in midair. With a flash of a spatula, they were swept up into a straw basket.

Deflating and sighing a toasted and buttery-scented steam, the tortillas were covered with a hand-embroidered dishtowel to keep them warm. And best of all, they melted into crisp yet tender flakes in your mouth. Heaven!

I asked Claudia for her secret recipe, and she politely explained to me that she didn't measure anything exactly, but that she had a method that she learned from her mother and grandmother. "The 'guelita method," I thought to myself. But I watched her and listened on several occasions, and now I can also make flour tortillas without measuring. Claudia had cracked the 'guelita code. Only 23 years old, Claudia was a 'guelita ahead of her time.

Her method? Five mixing spoonfuls of white flour, 2 half-spoonfuls of shortening, a pinch of salt, and enough warm water to make a cohesive dough. No baking powder. That's it. The proportions are not exact, but the results are consistent. I am not sure why this recipe works, however, it does.

If you want to try Claudia's recipe or the 'guelita method, choose a mixing spoon to be your measuring spoon, and try to use the same spoon every time you make tortillas. Use the same spoon when you are measuring the flour and the shortening, and the proportions should work.

Dairy Products

SOME OF THE RECIPES will call for *crema,* Mexican-style sour cream, which is actually closer to *crème fraîche.* It is thinner than American sour cream and pours easily. If you can't find Mexican crema in your supermarket, you can substitute crème fraîche or American-style sour cream that has been thinned with a little milk. However, the cultures in American sour cream will cause the thinned cream to thicken again, so thin with milk right before you use it.

Queso fresco was the typical cheese made on the ranches across the Wild Horse Desert. The abomasum, or fourth stomach of a calf or goat, known in Spanish as the *cuajo,* was collected at the time of slaughter, salted and air dried, then used for cheese making. The cuajo contains digestive enzymes, which thicken milk and cause the formation of curds that are strained out, mixed with salt, gathered into cheesecloth, and drained to form cheese. Similar to Greek feta cheese, queso fresco is eaten in wedges or crumbled over beans, eggs, and the like. It is easy to make, and like all cheeses, it provided a way to preserve large quantities of milk that might otherwise go bad.

Other cheeses you can use to make authentic border-style food would be *queso cotija, queso panela, queso de Oaxaca,* or even Monterey Jack. Generally speaking, all of these cheeses are used to top off a dish or as a filling for tacos or *enchiladas.* Unfortunately, these days American-style processed cheese is the predominant cheese found in restaurants in this region. Restaurants, as well as lower prices, have influenced home chefs, and processed cheeses sell well in the supermarkets, outselling the natural cheeses. I feel compelled to mention this to give a completely accurate description of our regional fare today. However, for my taste, a natural cheese is preferable in any dish calling for cheese. Check out the offerings in your local supermarket, and see what is available.

Herbs

MANY OF THE HERBS used in the Wild Horse Desert, while hard to find outside the region, were curative and are mentioned briefly throughout this book. Cooking herbs are becoming more popular throughout the country. Check your local supermarket; if they're not there, you'll probably be able to find them at a Mexican grocery. Three of the most common cooking herbs are the following.

CILANTRO (CORIANDRUM SATIVIUM): Originally from the Mediterranean, this is one of many flavors brought to the New World by the *conquistadores*. It's best when used fresh; the flavor tends to mellow when cooked.

EPAZOTE (CHENOPODIUM AMBROSIODES): This herb is used to flavor beans and is sometimes added to *quesadillas*. Many curative traits are attributed to epazote—it was a digestive aid, a relief to asthmatics, a relief for toothaches, an amenogogue; the seeds were used to rid oneself of internal parasites. Known in English as worm-seed or goosefoot, epazote imparts a fresh, green, almost minty flavor.

MEXICAN OREGANO (VARIOUS SPECIES): In her research, Diana Kennedy found that there were over 30 varieties of Mexican oregano. *Lippiaberlandieri* is the variety commonly considered to be Mexican oregano, but our local variety is *L. graveolens H.B.K.* Also known as *hierba dulce* and *oregano cimmaron*, Mexican oregano is woodier and sweeter than Greek oregano, *Origanum vulgare hirtum*, the more common oregano in the United States. However, even I can't get wild-growing local oregano sometimes, so use the fresh variety of whatever oregano is available.

Lard and Oil

WHEN THE INDIGENOUS TRIBES roamed the vast open Wild Horse Desert, the cooking techniques they employed were either roasting, boiling, or steaming. The Spanish explorers, *conquistadores,* and missionaries brought with them the technique of heating and melting the fats of domestic animals (known as rendering) and using this melted fat for cooking. Corn oil arrived on the scene later, around the turn of the century. Today, cooking with lard and oil typifies Mexican border cooking.

LARD: For most folks, lard is a four-letter word. They would rather smoke, talk on a cell phone while driving, or bungee jump before they would cook with or even eat a food containing lard. However, on the small *ranchitos* of the Wild Horse Desert there were no other fats used for cooking other than animal fats. And even then, a fattened hog would be killed only once a year, so even though the traditional recipes used lard, they would have been prepared only at holiday time. Fats were used on special occasions, with everyday cooking techniques limited to boiling, steaming, stewing, and grilling. We consider ourselves health conscious and informed, but the *ranchito* dweller consumed far less fat than we do today.

Lard gives a rich and satisfying flavor and an unctuous, silky consistency to *tamales,* baked goods, and other recipes. Substitute vegetable shortening if you wish, but a small amount of lard once or twice a year is definitely safer than bungee jumping.

CORN OIL: Corn oil did not enter the market until 1910, when the technique for extracting oil from corn was developed. Initially, it was used as a cheap alternative to olive oil for packing sardines, but soon it was discovered that corn oil was a better frying medium than animal fats, producing a golden crispness without masking the flavor of the food. You will notice that I have a definite preference for corn oil in my recipes. I feel you get better results frying with corn oil, rendering golden corn tortillas and producing crisp crust on both breads and meats.

Molcajetes

I CALL FOR pre-ground spices and advocate using blenders and food processors in this book—modern conveniences. Not everyone wants to take the time to hand-grind spices and salsas. Both the blender and the *molcajete* have their place in a Mexican kitchen, each having distinct advantages and disadvantages.

In my kitchen, as in my mother's and grandmother's kitchens, I use a molcajete, the traditional hand-carved lava rock mortar and pestle used in Mexico and the Americas since prehistorical times. Roughly the size of a soup bowl, a molcajete can grind only a small amount of spices and ingredients. Freshly ground spices, gently ground by hand, impart superior flavor to any dish. Salsas made in a molcajete are chunkier, with a more pleasing texture. Anyone who wants to "connect" with Mexican cuisine should acquire a molcajete.

If you do choose to use a molcajete, here are some general instructions for how to use it. If I am grinding spices, I grind the dried spices first along with salt and garlic, then combine this with a small amount of water to make a flavorful liquid that is then added to my dish. For instance, every time I make a small pan of rice, I grind peeled cloves of garlic, whole black peppercorns, and sea salt into a paste, add a tablespoon of water, and grind for another minute until the paste is smooth. The pestle is gripped in your fist, and the ingredients are scraped across the surface of the rock bowl. The paste is then mixed into the simmering rice. Usually, I rinse the molcajete bowl with some of the cooking liquid and return the liquid to the simmering pan, making sure all the freshly ground flavor goes into the rice.

When making a salsa, I employ a similar technique, first grinding the chiles with salt and garlic. However, once this paste is made, I add quartered chunks of tomato, or *tomatillo* instead of water, and grind them with the pestle. The flesh of the tomato picks up all the flavors that have been ground into the surface of the stone mortar.

Molcajetes need to be cured before the first time they are used. The traditional method is to add uncooked rice to the bowl with a few tablespoons of water and grind the rice using the *ajolote*, or pestle. The rice should sand the interior smooth and extract any sand or rock particles from the surface pores. It may take several grinding sessions and several changes of rice to smooth the interior surface. As the interior becomes clean, each change of rice will be less dirty and remain increasingly white.

Traditionally, women would expend up to 20 hour-long sessions using this traditional curing method. As I am an impatient, modern woman, I once bought a brass fiber brush with a 2-inch square head at the hardware store. I briskly scrubbed the interior surface of the bowl of the molcajete in the sink, occasionally rinsing the loosened grit away with running water. Eventually, the water flowed clean and clear from the molcajete, indicating that my job was done. My molcajete was perfectly cured within 20 minutes.

Many people have switched from grinding salsas in the traditional molcajete to using a blender or food processor. Many of my students ask me which I prefer, and the answer is simple: For a stew that requires large amounts of freshly puréed tomatoes or tomatillos, I always use a blender. It's fast and easy. For a salsa that I am going to serve on the table along with tacos or a good steak, I would use a molcajete, without exception. The texture and flavors can be better controlled by hand-grinding your salsa ingredients in a molcajete. See page 99 for specifics on which chiles and salsas I like to make in a molcajete, and which I'm happier making in a blender or food processor.

NOTE: If you don't have a molcajete, there are plenty of ways to get that fresh spice flavor. Pepper mills are always great to have on hand (look for the Peugeot brand), as well as garlic presses (I like Zyliss). Coffee grinders are perfect for grinding large amounts of spices, but you may want to buy one specifically for your spices, as some may object to the flavor of cumin and anise in their morning cup of java.

Nopalitos

THE WORD *NOPALITOS* is a diminutive name of *nopales,* or prickly pear cactus. It refers to the dethorned pads that are chopped, boiled, and added to many traditional dishes here in the Wild Horse Desert. In the past, nopalitos were the only green vegetable available on a ranch, providing an excellent source of vitamin C. Many supermarkets now carry cleaned and dethorned whole and chopped nopalitos in the produce section. Also, there are wonderful jarred nopalitos, which are cooked and ready for use. Picking and cleaning nopales from the field is not an unpleasant task, however, if you happen to live where nopales grow. Around Easter, when the tender new pads appear, you often see families on the side of the road, tongs in hand, harvesting a few of the nopalitos that strayed over a rancher's fence.

To pick wild nopalitos, with one hand grip the cactus pad with a pair of tongs. Using a knife in your other hand, while still gripping the pad with the tongs, cut the pad at its base and place it in a metal pan. Place a paper towel or branches from a nearby tree between the layers of cactus pads, as their thorns will cause them to stick together. Once you have picked all the nopalitos that you need (about a dozen pads), the thorns must be removed carefully. Holding a pad with the tongs, trim the perimeter of the pad with the knife, removing the thorny outer edge. Nick the thorny pores from the surface the sides. Rinse well under running water and inspect for any remaining thorns. Place the cleaned pad well away from the other pads, as loose thorns could attach themselves to a clean nopalito. Once all the pads are cleaned, discard all of the loose thorns and trimmings.

If you buy fresh nopalitos at the supermarket, you are spared the chore of removing the thorns. Many times, the cactus leaves are already chopped and so they just need to be boiled, as indicated in the procedure below. If you purchase jarred nopalitos, they are already boiled and ready for immediate addition to any recipe.

There are thornless varieties of prickly pear, which some gardeners enjoy propagating in their gardens. However, they are not completely thornless, as hybridizing has reduced their thorns to mere hairs. They must be de-thorned as well.

TO PREPARE FRESH NOPALITOS

CUT THE CLEANED PADS into strips or cubes, about $1/4$ -inch dice and boil in water until they turn from bright green to dull olive in color. Some people like to add a pinch of baking soda to the boiling nopalitos in order to reduce the gooey liquid exuded from the pad. Drain and rinse briefly under running water.

Piloncillo

TRADITIONALLY SOLD IN CONE SHAPES, *piloncillo* is an unrefined form of sugar. In days of old, refined, granulated sugar was very expensive and was often adulterated with cheap fillers, such as sawdust or iron filings. Only pure sugar can crystallize, so buying one's sugar in a crystallized cone or loaf form was proof of its purity. Grudgingly, I could suggest brown sugar as a substitute. However, nothing quite compares to the smoky sweet sugarcane flavor of piloncillo. It has become quite common in most supermarkets, although most people don't know how to use it.

There is no standard size for a cone of piloncillo, nor does it come in any other form other than a loaf or cake, so in the recipes I refer to the amount of piloncillo by weight. There is no English translation for piloncillo that I am aware of. Cane syrup or turbinando sugar (such as Sugar in the Raw®) are not substitutes. Piloncillo is sometimes referred to as *panocha, panela,* or *tacha.*

Usually, the piloncillo is melted with water into a syrup before adding to a recipe. I love to add a small chunk when boiling my morning oatmeal, along with dried cherries.

Tomatillos

TOMATILLOS (PHYSALIS IXOCARPA) are small, green berrylike fruits that resemble a tomato, yet have a papery outer husk. They have a sweet, tart flavor similar to regular green tomatoes. The origin of the plant is Mexico and tomatillos are commonly used for salsas.

To use fresh tomatillos, you must first remove the outer husk and wash the fruit well to remove the sticky outer coating. Once cleaned, tomatillos should be boiled for about 20 minutes, until they turn olive drab in color. When shopping for tomatillos, look for fruit that is covered with an intact, golden husk; that way the fruit contained therein will be bright green, occasionally with a purplish cast to the skin, devoid of soft spots or cracks.

Canned tomatillos are exported from Mexico to U.S. supermarkets. There is hardly any flavor difference between canned and fresh tomatillos, but the canned variety are incredibly convenient. No husking, or washing; just open the can, drain, and use. A 10-ounce can will substitute for ½ pound of fresh tomatillos called for in a recipe.

Salt

I PREFER TO USE sea salt in the recipes in this book, as it most closely resembles the salt gathered from the local salt lakes (see page 169 for a discussion of salt in the Wild Horse Desert). Kosher salt and regular table salt work just as well, however.

Spices

IF YOU HAVE BEEN staring at a spice rack so old the spices were acquired during a prior presidential administration, I encourage you to dispose of these and start fresh. Even though the recipes in this book use commercial, pre-ground spices, I also urge you to use only whole spices and to freshly grind them in a molcajete or coffee grinder every time you cook (see "Molcajetes," page 22). The difference in flavor is vast. As with coffee beans, the delicious and delicate oils in a spice are released when ground, but then dry and fade when exposed to air.

Avoid extending the shelf life for your spices. Many markets are now selling spices in bulk, so you can buy small amounts. Keep seldom-used spices in the refrigerator.

BLACK PEPPER: Freshly crack whole black peppercorns for best results.

CHILE POWDER: This is usually ground ancho chiles, although it can be a blend of several different dried chiles, depending on the manufacturer. Look for bright red chile powder, which indicates freshness. Discard old chile powder, which may be buggy or dull in color. To keep your supply fresh, buy in small amounts and store in the refrigerator.

CUMIN: Believed to have been popularized in northern Mexico by Middle Eastern immigrants, cumin is usually added to rice, *tamales*, stews, and salsas. It should be used in moderation, as the flavor can overwhelm a dish.

GARLIC: Although not technically a spice, garlic has a definite presence in our kitchen. Brought by the *conquistadores*, garlic is included in salsas, stews, marinades, and dressings. Use only fresh garlic, as opposed to powdered or garlic salt.

MEXICAN CINNAMON: Also known as soft Ceylon cinnamon, Mexican cinnamon has a flaky appearance and a floral citrus aroma that gives our regional desserts their distinctive flavor. The hard sticks of conventional cinnamon that you see in the supermarket are actually cassia bark, which has a sharper, more acidic flavor and aroma. An electric coffee grinder is a must for grinding fresh cinnamon.

STAR ANISE AND ANISE SEED: Although from different plants, both types of anise impart a licorice flavor, which goes beautifully with the smoky sweet flavor of *piloncillo,* the raw loaf sugar used in traditional Mexican sweets (see page 26). Both types of anise are used in regional pastries and beverages, especially at Christmas. Star anise is simmered in a liquid to extract its flavor; anise seeds are sprinkled into dough recipes to add a hint of spice.

CHAPTER ONE

BEVERAGES

I REMEMBER the way my grandfather would prepare his water cooler for a long day of working cattle. The old, ribbed five-gallon canister was always trussed to the inner left corner of the pickup bed, right behind him as he bumped down the road. Of course, his old green truck had no air-conditioning, so the windows were down, his khaki-covered elbow cocked outside.

On the morning of the cattle drive, as he was preparing his vaccine kit, he would take a frozen cardboard milk carton that he had previously washed and filled with water, peel back the red-and-white checkered paper, and dump the block of ice into his filled cooler. There it would float and bounce underneath the sealed lid of the cooler until the midday break. The cowboys would line upto take their turn pushing the small white tap that released the icy water into the wire-handled tin can that served as the community cup. I still remember drinking from it and tasting the raspy metallic feel on my lips. Sometimes someone would take off his cowboy hat, bend over, and let the stream douse his head— but, never too much, as the water was too precious to be wasted. The thought of a cool drink was what made the day bearable.

Everyone has habits and rituals regarding what he or she will drink. Rising early to fix morning coffee, brewing tea to be chilled and ready for lunch, freezing beer mugs for a perfectly chilled draught—these are routines that people follow to have the beverages ready when they want them. People will wait as dinner simmers, but everyone wants his or her drink right there, on hand.

The traditional beverages of the Wild Horse Desert had everything to do with survival. Of course, we have our drinks for festive occasions, but the daily drinks hydrate, cool, and nourish. Commercial beverages on the market give us the convenience of not having to plan ahead what we'll drink and offer us so many choices that the homemade beverages have fallen out of favor. Still, I think they are very much worth the effort. Drinks are not difficult to prepare, and they lend completeness to any meal.

A little bit of extra planning and care can even make memorable a drink of water from an old tin cup.

Tea

TO TALK ABOUT TEA IN SOUTH TEXAS is to delve into all that is curative and mysterious in the early ranch kitchen. Of course, there is the simple delight of a tall, frosty glass of iced tea, and I will share a recipe for our local Sweetened Iced Tea. However, tea for many here goes beyond the mere cup.

A hundred years ago, the brushy wilderness served as a vertiable variety store for the little ranches scattered across the Wild Horse Desert—it was their strongest ally for survival. The brush plants were what the ranchers had on hand to cure ailments, and the best way to extract their medicinal properties was by making a tea from them. Many homes today still have gardens dedicated to growing curative herbs.

Tea can be made two ways: either by infusion, which is pouring boiling water over the ingredients, steeping for a few minutes, then straining out the spent material; or by decoction, which is simply boiling the ingredients in water, then straining out the spent material. Infusions are generally made with leafy ingredients; decoctions are usually made of hard woody ingredients such as stems and bark.

Loose tooth? Try a decoction of *sangre de drago,* which tightens the gums. Stomach problems? Boil comancha root for a curative tea. Puffy eyes? Try a compress soaked in tea of mesquite leaves. Any ailment could be cured with the right plant and a little faith.

Other teas were simply refreshing drinks. Store-bought coffee and oriental teas were scarce; instead, ranchers brewed refreshing teas, or *tisanes* ("healthy teas"), from cinnamon sticks, lemon or orange leaves, eucalyptus leaves, or other garden herbs.

TE DE MANZANILLA CHAMOMILE TEA

SERVES 4

Herbal remedies should be administered with caution, as the concentrated extracts of some plants can prove hazardous. However, there is one recipe that even doctors recommend for colic in babies: te de manzanilla, or chamomile tea. A good strong infusion, barely warm, quiets and soothes a child's tummy and demeanor. Right next to the diapers in almost every South Texas supermarket are long cardboard displays hung with hanks of manzanilla. My babies certainly got their share of te de manzanilla, and I still make it for my kids whenever they need a little extra care and comfort.

4 bags te de manzanilla (chamomile tea)

PLACE the tea bags in a 4- to 6-cup teapot. Bring 4 cups of water to a boil, pour over the tea bags, and allow to steep for 5 minutes. Remove bags from the water and allow tea to cool to warm.

SWEETENED ICED TEA

SERVES 8

When brewing the tea, allow tea to cool to room temperature before chilling in the refrigerator, to avoid clouding.

2 quarts freshly brewed black tea, chilled

1 cup sugar

6 to 8 Mexican limes, cut in half (see page 36)

STIR TOGETHER the tea and sugar. Squeeze in limes, and add the spent lime rinds. Stir well and serve over ice in tall glasses.

✦ **LEMON ICED TEA:** Lemons can be substituted for the Mexican limes, but discard the lemon rind after squeezing. When packed for shipping, most lemons are coated with wax, which will leave a film on the surface of the tea.

ICED TEA

AFTER DINNER AT MY GRANDMOTHER'S HOUSE, I would always head back to the kitchen to visit the housekeeper to see what she was having. Of course, she would be eating basically the same meal as the rest of the family, but I always thought the way she fixed her plate was more interesting. She always mixed Mexican and American traditions: roast beef we were eating with fresh salsa, barbecued ribs with pickled carrots and *chile del monte* (wild chile). One thing I always begged from her was a sip of her sweetened iced tea. Loaded with freshly squeezed limes picked from the tree in the yard, the icy glasses always had long spoons in them to stir up the settled sugar. Eating with my family, I never got to have my own glass. Tea was for grown-ups. But that just made the stolen sips taste all the better.

MEXICAN LIMES

THERE ARE TWO SPECIES OF LIMES: the large fruited limes and the small fruited limes. Mexican limes (*Citrus aurantifolia*), also known as Key limes or West Indian limes, are small fruited limes and are usually smaller than a Ping-Pong ball. They have a sweet, tart flavor and are terrifically aromatic. I prefer to use Mexican limes in place of lemons, especially since we have a lime tree in our garden.

Aguas Frescas

AN *AGUA FRESCA* IS JUST THAT: water that has been "freshened" with fruit flavor. The evolution of the agua fresca is similar to that of *atole* (see page 49). Seasonal fruits were ground into a pulp on a *metate* (stone mortar), combined with water, and sweetened with sugar. Nowadays, blenders do the same work in a fraction of the time. Making an agua fresca is a snap.

Sugar plays an important role in making an agua fresca, although most recipes call for too much. Commercial aguas frescas are way too sweet to be refreshing. But imagine a cold glass of lemonade with half the sugar of a commercial agua fresca but plenty of lemon flavor, served over cracked ice; bracing, without a cloying aftertaste—the perfect agua fresca.

Also, the fruit you use will dictate the amount of sugar you use. Many times I make *agua de sandia* (watermelon water) without adding any sugar; the fruit is sweet and ripe enough that I don't want to mask its flavor. Other times, the fruit flavor may be improved with a small amount of sugar. It's something you have to decide when you taste the fruit. And, similar to the adage about never cooking with bad wine, you can't make a great agua fresca from old or flavorless fruit.

AGUA FRESCA DE FRUTA

SERVES 8

2 cups fresh fruit peeled, seeded, and chopped (pineapple, mango, watermelon, cantaloupe, honeydew are most common—use whatever you like)

¼ cup sugar, or to taste

PLACE the fruit in the container of a blender or food processor. Add 2 cups of water or enough to make a smooth purée. Blend until smooth, then pour through a wire strainer to remove the pulp. Pour the strained "water" into a pitcher, and add about 6 cups more water and stir in the sugar. Serve chilled over ice.

TEPACHE PINEAPPLE WINE

SERVES 8

Tepache, *a type of pineapple* agua fresca, *is still served on many ranches and sold on the streets out of large barrels in Border towns. The slight fermentation of the sugars in the pineapple rind, paired with the mingled flavors of black pepper, cinnamon, and cloves, gives it a pleasing bite. Even though pineapple is not native to the Wild Horse Desert, the fruit is widespread throughout Mexico, and the drink is quite popular in our hot climate.*

1 pineapple rind, washed, plus any leftover pineapple bits or core (not the leaves)

6 black peppercorns

1 stick cinnamon (Mexican if possible; see page 29)

6 whole cloves

2 ounces piloncillo (unrefined sugar; see page 26)

PLACE the pineapple rind and pieces of core in a 1-quart glass or ceramic container. Add 4 cups water and the spices, seal tightly, and allow to ferment at room temperature for 72 hours. Using a mesh strainer, filter the liquid into a pitcher and discard the pineapple remains. Add the piloncillo and stir to completely dissolve. You may want to dilute the drink further with up to 4 cups more water. The tepache should have a distinct winey flavor. Serve over cracked ice, and store any leftover tepache in the refrigerator.

AGUA DE JAMAICA HIBISCUS FLOWER WATER

SERVES 8

Deep scarlet in color and tart in flavor, the juice of the hibiscus flower, or flor de jamaica (Hibiscus sabdariffa), *will remind you of cranberry juice. Originally from India and Malaysia, flor de jamaica can be a bit expensive, as the blossoms are harvested by hand, but you need only a small amount to make enough of this* agua fresca *for a crowd. You can find flor de jamaica in your local Latin American market; however, there are several brands of cranberry teas that combine hibiscus flowers with dried cranberries and other herbs. These make a fine substitute—just check the ingredients on the label to make sure the tea contains hibiscus flowers to achieve the same refreshing flavor.*

½ **cup dried flor de jamaica (hibiscus flowers)**
¾ **cup sugar**

COMBINE the flor de jamaica and 4 cups water in a 2-quart saucepan. Bring to a boil, reduce the heat, and simmer for 5 minutes, then remove from heat. Allow to cool.

STRAIN the cooled liquid into a 2-quart pitcher. Add the sugar and enough water to make 2 quarts, stir well, and chill. Serve chilled over ice.

HORCHATA RICE REFRESHMENT

SERVES 8

Even though the recipe is ancient, horchata, *a sweet, cold rice beverage, is still quite popular in the taco stands of the Wild Horse Desert. Also considered an* agua fresca, *horchata has a light, sweet creaminess perfect for cooling your mouth down after a fiery salsa. Commercial horchata mixes are always disappointing; homemade is infinitely better.*

½ **cup rice**
2 **cinnamon sticks (Mexican if possible; see page 29)**
½ **to 1 cup sugar, or to taste**

COMBINE 2 quarts water, the rice, and cinnamon sticks in a 4-quart saucepan and bring to a boil. Cover, reduce the heat, and simmer for 30 minutes, until rice is tender. Remove from heat and cool to room temperature.

REMOVE the cinnamon sticks. Place the rice and liquid in the container of a blender or food processor (you may have to do this in a couple of batches). Purée well until there are no visible particles. Pour the purée into a pitcher. Stir in the sugar and add enough water to make 2 quarts of horchata. Chill well, and serve over ice.

HORCHATA

HORCHATA CAME TO MEXICO by way of the Spanish colonists, who brought with them the European technique of making beverages from starchy ingredients such as grains and nuts. Originally, in Spain, horchata was made from the chufa nut, a starchy tuber that was brought to Spain from the Middle East by the Moors. As the chufa nut was unavailable in the New World, the Spanish colonists adapted their recipe to the starchy ingredients they were able to obtain. Rice was an inexpensive grain, and became the traditional choice for making horchata.

There are two possibilities for the origin of the name; one has to do with the legend of a little girl who presented a glass of *leche de chufa* (chufa milk) to the visiting King of Aragon and Catalunya. He asked what this marvelous drink was called, and she responded that it was leche de chufa, to which he replied *"Este no es leche, es oro, chatal,"* meaning "This is not milk, this is gold, my pug-nose girl!"

The other possibility is that the word *horchata* comes from the Latin *hordeum,* or "barley," which was also used to make starchy yet refreshing restorative beverages. In fact, barley water is still quite popular in England, and is made the same way as our rice horchata. And even in Mexico, horchata is made not only from rice but also from oatmeal or almonds, even melon seeds.

AGUA DE TAMARINDO TAMARIND WATER

SERVES 8

Agua de tamarindo *always needs to be stirred* right before serving, as it has a tendency to separate. You can use a blender to better combine the pulp with the water, but the drink becomes somewhat foamy. Instead, I serve agua de tamarindo with a long spoon left in the pitcher, to give it an occasional stir.

1 pound tamarind pods
¾ to 1 cup sugar

CRACK the outer peel of the tamarind pods to separate and pull out and discard the stringy interior veins (don't worry about the seeds yet). Place the peeled tamarind pods in a 2-quart saucepan and cover with water. Bring to a boil, reduce the heat, and simmer for 25 minutes, or until the tamarind pods are soft. Drain.

PLACE a mesh strainer over a 2-quart mixing bowl. Press the cooked pods through the mesh strainer, breaking up the pods and scraping the pulp against the mesh to remove the seeds. The pulp will drop into the bowl. You may have to do this in batches to accommodate all the pods. Discard the seeds. You should have about 1½ cups of pulp.

PLACE the pulp in a 2-quart pitcher. Add 2 quarts of water and the sugar to taste. Stir well to combine. Serve chilled over ice.

TAMARIND

NATIVE TO ASIA AND AFRICA, tamarind is grown throughout Mexico and is a favorite candy and beverage flavor. Tamarind can be found in its whole-pod form in Latin American and Indian markets. Make sure the tamarind pods are fresh, are moist, and that the shell breaks cleanly away from the fruit, showing no mold or bugs (if you can, test one at the market before buying).

CAFÉ DE OLLA CLAY POT COFFEE

SERVES 4

Early in the morning, between November and December, when the wind blows cold outside and the misty rain clutters the view from the kitchen window, that is the exact moment when I make café de olla. Originally boiled in a traditional clay pot called an olla, this coffee has a rich, strong flavor, sweetened with spices and the raw sugar flavor of piloncillo. Comforting like a grandmother's hug, the aroma of the spices wraps itself around my kitchen and makes the world right.

This is an old recipe, enjoyed in cow camps across the Wild Horse Desert.

4 whole cloves

1 stick cinnamon (Mexican if possible; see page 29)

½ orange, unpeeled

2 pieces star anise

2 ounces piloncillo (unrefined sugar, see page 26) or 2 tablespoons brown sugar, tightly packed

3 to 4 tablespoons ground coffee

POUR 4 cups of water into a 2-quart saucepan and add the cloves, cinnamon, orange, star anise, and piloncillo. Bring to a boil, reduce the heat, and simmer for 2 minutes. Add the coffee, simmer for 1 minute more, then remove from the heat. Allow the mixture to steep for 2 minutes. Remove the orange and whole spices, then strain the café de olla into a serving pot. Serve hot.

MEXICAN HOT CHOCOLATE

The cacao plant, from which chocolate is made, is native to Mexico, where chocolate is highly celebrated, but if you visit the country you might notice that there is nary a chocolate candy bar to be found. Chocolate is consumed mainly as a beverage. Montezuma, the Aztec emperor, enjoyed his chocolate in a golden cup. Drinking chocolate was the original way it was served. Aside from its indescribably delicious flavor, the aroma of a steaming mug of chocolate, as well as the warmth of the mug in your hands, is part of the complete chocolate experience.

1 cup milk
1 ounce Mexican chocolate, broken into pieces (see Notes)

HEAT the milk and chocolate together in a 1-quart saucepan over low heat. When the chocolate is melted and the milk is well heated, blend with an immersion blender (see Notes), or transfer the liquid to a blender and process to achieve a properly frothy mug of chocolate.

NOTES: Mexican chocolate is flavored with cinnamon and ground almonds, and sweetened with sugar. Most Latin American groceries will carry it, but if you can't find Mexican chocolate, substitute 1 ounce of unsweetened chocolate, add ½ teaspoon of ground cinnamon, and sweeten to taste.

The drink is traditionally beaten with a *molinillo,* a wooden whisk carved out of a single piece of wood that is used for frothing chocolate in Mexico. It is long and thin, with a flared bulb on its end, with rings of wood that spin as the top handle is rubbed quickly between your hands. My grandmother had several, but I think she would have enjoyed using an electric immersion blender, as it is infinitely more efficient.

CACAO

THEOBROMA CACAO is the plant from which cacao, the unprocessed predecessor of chocolate, is derived. Cacao grows throughout southern Mexico, where raw chocolate is still roasted and ground in many households. Most families have their preferred *molienda,* or grinding recipe, which dictates the proportion of cacao to cinnamon, almonds, and sugar that fits that family's tastes.

Spirits of the Wild Horse Desert

THE KARANKAWAS ROAMED THE COASTAL PLAINS OF SOUTH TEXAS, around what is now known as Corpus Christi and South Padre Island. They were fierce, cruel warriors with tattoos, their lips and chests pierced with pieces of cane; they were seven feet tall and known to eat their enemies. Cabeza de Vaca, the famed Spanish explorer who was their captive, observed them as they often binged on a yellow brew of yaupon leaves, drinking themselves into a torpor, until they were only blinking, barely breathing.

I think if I were Cabeza de Vaca, I would have needed a drink myself.

With the exception of the above-mentioned yaupon brew, almost all the alcoholic drinks enjoyed in the Wild Horse Desert were brought in by the settlers, from either the United States, Europe, or Mexico. And, even though we share much of the food culture of Mexico, *tequila* was a rare commodity. The agave plant, although present in this area, was not exploited or cultivated as it was in Central Mexico. The native tribes of our area were nomadic hunter/gatherers, not farmers. In addition, climatic conditions were not optimum for the agave plant. From time to time, you will hear of local folks making home-brewed *mezcal* from an agave plant in their backyard, but these occurrences are anecdotal and in no way compare to the full-scale production seen in the Mexican states of Jalisco and Oaxaca.

Beer is very much the libation of choice in Texas and northern Mexico. One reason might be that the Wild Horse Desert is surrounded by some of the most notable breweries in the world. The largest brewery in Latin America is Cerveceria Cuauhtémoc, established in Monterrey, Nuevo Leon, and is only 140 miles south of the Rio Grande. Brands such as Carta Blanca, Tecate, Sol, Superior, Dos Equis, Indio, Bohemia, and Noche Buena are produced by this one company. North of the Rio Grande, breweries flourished, especially among the clusters of German immigrants in the Texas Hill Country and in San Antonio. In 1876 there were 58 known breweries in Texas, almost 30 of which were in and around San Antonio. The largest was William A. Menger's Western Brewery, which was located directly across from the Alamo in San Antonio. Mr. Menger constructed a hotel adjacent to the brewery, with a cellar built with three-foot-thick limestone walls. The Alamo Madre, an irrigation ditch dug by the Spanish in 1745 that diverted water from the San Antonio River, flowed in front of the hotel and kept the cellar humid and chilly, a perfect storage solution for the beer.

MARGARITAS DE TUNA PRICKLY PEAR MARGARITAS

SERVES 2

My friend Stephan Shearer gave me this recipe, which was inspired by a few
poor days of dove hunting. Having had no luck with bird hunting, he collected some of the
prickly pears from a cactus plant as he ambled through the goatweed. Once home, he puréed
the prickly pear (tuna) into a cocktail with a South Texas signature. The sweet raspberry-like
flavor of the puréed tunas and the bracing tang of tequila naturally go together. I can just
imagine his serving these to his hunting buddies and laughing about that day, as they watch
the doves dart across the clear orange October sky.

You'll need two prepared glasses for this recipe.

Salt for rims of glasses, plus a piece of cut
lime (optional)

4 ounces tequila

4 tablespoons cactus pear purée (see below)

4 tablespoons fresh lime juice

2 tablespoons sugar

2 ounces orange-flavored liqueur, such as
Cointreau

SALT the rims of your glasses if you wish: fill a saucer with salt; rub the cut lime
around the rim of each glass, then dip the rims in the salt.

FILL a cocktail shaker with 2 or 3 ice cubes, or ½ cup crushed ice. Pour in the
tequila, purée, lime juice, sugar, and orange liqueur, and cap the shaker. Shake
for about 15 seconds. Strain the cocktail into your prepared glasses.

❖ CACTUS PURÉE: You'll need about two fresh prickly pears. You need to peel the cactus pears by using a fork and knife, never touching the skin of the cactus pears with
your bare hands (invisible thorns!). To do this, hold the pear in place with the fork
and cut off one end of the pear, then the other. Lay the pear on its side and slit the
pear vertically. With the fork, pull the skin of the pear down and hold the skin against
the cutting surface with the fork as you roll the fruit out of the skin with the knife.
Place the whole skinned fruits in a blender with enough water to facilitate blending,
about ¼ cup. Purée well and strain out seeds with a mesh strainer. The purée is now
ready for use.

You can make a larger quantity of purée simply by increasing the number of prickly pears and the water. Store the extra purée in the freezer by pouring it into ice cube trays. When you need it, you can pop out a cube of frozen purée, which is approximately 2 tablespoons.

MICHELADA SPICY PREPARED BEER BEVERAGE
SERVES 1

The word michelada *is composed of the separate words* mi *("mine"),* chela *(slang for* cerveza, *or beer), and* helada *("icy cold"). A michelada is a beer prepared with zippy seasonings, namely Tabasco, lime, and salt, and is enjoyed throughout Mexico. Because we are mainly beer drinkers here on the border, micheladas show up at many backyard barbecues. It's incredibly refreshing—your lips will buzz.*

½ Mexican lime (see page 36)

2 dashes Tabasco

2 dashes Maggi liquid seasoning (available in most supermarkets, near the bouillon cubes)

2 dashes soy sauce

Pinch salt and pepper

12 ounces beer, icy cold, preferably a dark Mexican beer such as Bohemia

SQUEEZE the lime into a cold glass and add the spent rind. Add the remaining ingredients, pouring the cold beer in last.

Atole

OTHER THAN WATER, *atole* (pronounced ah-TOH-leh) is one of the two oldest beverages enjoyed here in the Wild Horse Desert (the other being herbal tea). Atole is a thin porridge made from a starchy grain such as corn, rice, oats, or mesquite beans. It is drunk hot, traditionally from an earthenware mug. The original inhabitants of this area, the nomadic tribes of Karankawas (who in the early nineteenth century were declared by pirate Jean Lafitte, when he was stranded in Galveston Island, as "demons from Hell") and Coahuiltecans (a more peaceful nation of small tribes, with whom Cabeza de Vaca lived in 1533), made atole by grinding mature dried mesquite beans (long sweetish pods produced by the mesquite tree) in large stone mortars called *molcajetes,* along with dried berries, prickly pear pulp, chiles, herbs, and even dirt (which was very filling in times of poor hunting or harvest). Many of these stone mortars have been found along the tribes' travel routes, suggesting that the heavy objects were left there for future use. The powder would be mixed with water, possibly sweetened with wild honey, and heated over a mesquite fire. Atole of mesquite beans is still consumed by the indigenous Coahuiltecan tribes of northern Mexico.

Atole was truly a food of convenience. As it was made of dried ingredients, the powder could easily be carried by travelers. The amount of water could be increased to stretch the most meager ration as far as possible. The ingredients changed depending on the season and what was found en route, such as wild grains or fruits. Atole made a nourishing pap for babies, as well.

Ground corn generally served as the base for atoles, and was used even more frequently after the arrival of early Spanish settlers from Mexico, as these settlers were more proficient farmers than the nomadic hunters of the local tribes. In the mornings, when corn was being ground into masa for making tortillas, a bit would be reserved for making atole, which was then sweetened with *piloncillo* (unrefined sugar; see page 26) or wild honey. If the corn was first toasted and then ground, the resulting atole was known as *pinole,* and had a toasted corn flavor; this form was convenient for travelers—toasting dried out the corn and gave it a long shelf life. The addition of ground chocolate to the corn atole produced *champurrado,* a satisfying chocolate and corn porridge. Atole, pinole, and champurrado are still enjoyed today, although they are mostly found south of the border.

Using cornstarch instead of corn produces a different atole. In this case, milk is thickened with a mixture of cornstarch and water, then sweetened with sugar; different flavorings are added, such as strawberries, blackberries, cinnamon, and the like. This type of atole is frequently called by the brand name of the cornstarch used in Mexico: *Maizena.*

Later, as oats and rice made their way to the Americas, they too became popular grain bases for atole. Atole is still consumed in the homes of the Wild Horse Desert, albeit rarely. With the array of bottled sodas, teas and coffees, and prepared beverage mixes available to the modern consumer, the humble atole is a recipe from yesteryear, enjoyed mostly by an older generation.

ATOLE DE ARROZ RICE ATOLE

SERVES 4

Comforting and warm, this drink is especially nice on blustery December afternoons. *Like a warm rice pudding you can drink,* atole de arroz *has a creamy cinnamon flavor that makes it a favorite with kids and adults alike.*

1 stick cinnamon (Mexican if possible; see page 29)
¼ cup white rice

1 cup milk
¼ cup sugar

BRING 4 cups of water and the cinnamon to a boil in a 2-quart saucepan. Add the uncooked rice, reduce the heat to medium, and simmer for 30 minutes, until the rice is tender. Remove from the heat and remove and discard the cinnamon.

REMOVE the cooked rice from the saucepan using a slotted spoon, reserving the cooking liquid; place the rice in the container of a blender or food processor, add a few tablespoons of the cooking liquid, and process the rice for 1 full minute, until very smooth, adding more liquid if needed. Return the purée to the saucepan with the cooking liquid. Stir until well combined. Add the milk and sugar, and warm over medium heat. Once the atole is piping hot, serve immediately in big mugs.

Pan de Campo (*page 85*)

Cooking Pan de Campo

Turcos *(page 240)*

Cordinoz en Escabeche *(page 221)*

Asado de Puerco *(page 184)*

Salsa Roja (page 96)

Tortillas de Harina (page 18)

Nopalitos con Camarón (page 193)

ATOLE DE MAIZ AND CHAMPURRADO I
CORN ATOLE AND CHOCOLATE-FLAVORED CORN ATOLE
(FROM FRESHLY GROUND DRIED CORN)
SERVES 4

This recipe is for the hard-core history buffs out there. Granted, it calls for grinding the corn using a blender instead of a metate, *the stone table-like mortar used in Latin America since pre-Hispanic times. Regardless, this is an excellent approximation of the food that kept people alive for millennia throughout the Americas. Its deep corn flavor is made even better when chocolate is added, which converts the atole into* champurrado.

1½ cups dried corn (see Note)

1 stick cinnamon (Mexican if possible; see page 29)

3 ounces piloncillo (unrefined sugar; see page 26) or 2 tablespoons brown sugar, tightly packed

COMBINE the dried corn with 4 cups of water in a 2-quart saucepan. Bring to a boil, reduce the heat, and simmer for 20 to 30 minutes, until the corn is al dente, or tender when bitten. Drain the corn.

PURÉE the corn with 4 cups of fresh water in a blender or food processor until very smooth, about 1 full minute. Using a mesh or chinois strainer placed over a bowl, strain the liquid, pressing to extract any remaining liquid; this liquid is the atole. Strain the atole two or three more times, cleaning out the chinois/strainer between strainings. Discard the remains of the ground corn.

RETURN the atole to the saucepan, add the cinnamon and piloncillo, and simmer for about 15 minutes over medium-low heat, stirring to keep the atole from burning on the bottom of the pan. The atole is ready when it has reached the degree of thickness you desire. Serve warm.

❖ CHAMPURRADO: When simmering the atole, add 3 ounces of Mexican chocolate or semisweet baking chocolate and 1 teaspoon of ground cinnamon.

NOTE: Look for dried corn at Latin American or health food stores. Any dried corn except popcorn will work.

ATOLE DE MAIZ AND CHAMPURRADO II

CORN ATOLE AND CHOCOLATE-FLAVORED CORN ATOLE
(FROM INSTANT TORTILLA MIX)

SERVES 4

If you can't find dried corn, you can always use instant corn tortilla mix for making atole *and* champurrado.

3 ounces piloncillo (unrefined sugar; see page 26) or 2 tablespoons brown sugar, tightly packed

1 stick cinnamon (Mexican if possible; see page 29)

1 cup instant corn tortilla mix

2 cups milk or water

COMBINE 2 cups of water with the piloncillo and cinnamon in a 1-quart saucepan. Simmer until the piloncillo is completely dissolved. Do not remove the cinnamon sticks yet.

COMBINE the corn tortilla mix and 2 cups water in a 2-quart saucepan. Stir well to dissolve any lumps. Add the piloncillo syrup with the cinnamon sticks. Simmer over medium-low heat until the atole is thickened, about 5 minutes, stirring constantly. Stir in the milk; add extra water if the atole is too thick. Remove the cinnamon sticks before serving. Serve warm.

❖ **CHAMPURRADO**: When simmering the atole, and add 3 ounces of Mexican chocolate or semisweet baking chocolate and 1 teaspoon of ground cinnamon.

ATOLE DE ZARZAMORA BLACKBERRY ATOLE
SERVES 6

The color of this atole *is dazzling* and always catches the attention of my kids. It's a great way to get them to drink their milk. Fruity and creamy, this is a terrifically nutritious breakfast, with no artificial ingredients.

You can also make this drink with strawberries.

1 cup blackberries, fresh or frozen

4 cups whole milk

2 tablespoons cornstarch

1 vanilla bean (optional) or 2 teaspoons vanilla extract

¼ cup sugar

COMBINE the blackberries and 2 cups of the milk in the container of a blender. Blend until smooth, then strain through a mesh strainer to remove any seeds. Pour the strained mixture into a 2-quart saucepan and stir in the cornstarch. Add the vanilla bean, if using (do not add vanilla extract yet, if using). Simmer the mixture over medium heat, stirring constantly, until it starts to thicken, about 10 minutes. Add the sugar and remaining 2 cups milk, and continue to stir constantly until atole is slightly thick and well heated, about 10 more minutes. Remove the vanilla bean and scrape in the seeds (or add vanilla extract, if using). Stir to combine well. Serve immediately in big mugs.

WILD FLAVORINGS FOR ATOLE

BLACKBERRY CANES grow wild in many parts of the world, rambling around the countryside. Although they do not grow wild in the Wild Horse Desert, the flavor of the blackberry is a good approximation of the berries that do grow in the brush country of South Texas with names like *granjeno, coma, filigrana, duraznillo, clepe, manzanita, anacahuita, chapote, agarita,* and *brasil.* These berries would have been gathered, ground into a paste, and incorporated into atoles. Prickly pears and the fruit of the strawberry pincushion cactus (or *pitaya*) are other natural sweet fruits that would have been foraged in the wild, and may have been used in a recipe similar to this one.

CHAPTER TWO

CORN AND FLOUR DISHES

"**WOULD YOU LIKE CORN OR FLOUR** with that?" the waitress asks. In the Wild Horse Desert, we have always had two types of tortillas on our table. We take their daily appearance for granted, but to understand their separate journeys to the tortilla basket is to understand the history of European settlement in the New World.

Corn is native to the Americas; it is believed to have originated in present-day Mexico. In fact, the world's oldest recorded mention of the cultivation of corn was found in Tamaulipas, the Mexican state that shares the Rio Grande with South Texas. From where I sit, this archeological find is only three hours away by car.

It would be impossible to overemphasize the importance of corn in the Americas. Corn was the basis of tribal economy and survival. It served as money, food, and religion. For example, in their legends of the creation of the universe, the ancient tribes of Mexico believed that man was made of corn—more specifically, of corn dough or *masa*, the same dough used to make tortillas.

"After that they began to talk about the creation and the making of our first mother and father; of yellow corn and of white corn they made their flesh; of corn-meal dough they made the arms and the legs of man. Only dough of corn meal went into the flesh of our first fathers, the four men, who were created."

POPOL VUH, PART III, CHAPTER 1

Hernán Cortés, who founded New Spain in 1519 (as present-day Mexico was originally named), reported seeing vast fields of corn, some of which his troops could not cross owing to their impenetrable growth. When Cortés eventually returned to Spain, he brought with him a supply of seed corn, introducing corn to the European continent.

In 1621, farther north, a Pawtuxet Indian named Squanto, of the Wampanoag tribe, taught the Pilgrims who arrived on the *Mayflower* how to plant corn, using fish as fertilizer. The Pilgrims were grateful for Squanto's instruction and their flourishing corn crop. Without corn to eat, they would have perished.

However, not all of the New World settlers enjoyed corn. Some felt that it was coarse, offensive in flavor, and fit only for livestock and native peoples. The corn was sufficient to keep them alive, but it wasn't what they hungered for. They longed for the bread of home—bread made with wheat flour.

Legend has it that the first grains of wheat arrived in the New World by accident. An African slave of Hernán Cortés named Juan Guerrero found three grains of wheat in a bag of rice he was cleaning. Supposedly, those three grains formed the seed stock for all future plantings of wheat in Mexico.

Wheat was grown in the New World for the exclusive use of European settlers, from the military to the missionaries. In many ways, wheat represented the separation of the two peoples. The conquered natives, who believed the gods had made them of corn masa, were now encouraged to convert to Christianity, and partake of the body of Christ, which was made of unleavened wheat bread.

Eventually, the people of New Spain desired freedom from Spanish rule, and they sought to establish their own government. In order to keep European supremacy in place, in 1863 Napoleon III installed the Archduke of Austria, Maximilian, as the Emperor of Mexico. Maximilian's wife, the Empress Carlota, is credited with bringing European taste and style to Mexico. Her presence accelerated the desire for European sophistication among the common folk, which increased the demand for wheat flour. The market for European-style yeast breads flourished, and wheat bread became a staple in everyone's diet, although it never took the place of the corn tortilla.

Much of the development of baked wheat breads in Mexico can also be attributed to the influence of the monasteries and convents. Within these cloistered societies, European descendents followed recipes from the Old World, eventually incorporating local ingredients and creating many of the breads and sweets we see in Mexican bakeries today.

Corn tortillas existed before the birth of Christ, but flour tortillas developed much later, in the northern wheat-growing states of Mexico. So, in our tortilla basket we see the tradition of the indigenous people paired with the tradition of the European settlers. Corn tortillas and flour tortillas—both cooked over the same flame, on the same *comal,* filled with the same *guisados.*

What would you like, corn or flour?

MIGAS CON HUEVO CRUMBS WITH EGGS

SERVES 2

Migas con huevo, *or torn-up bits of toasted corn tortillas added to scrambled eggs, is one of those lazy Sunday night comfort foods, a soul-satisfying favorite for my kids. This dish appears in our kitchen like a childhood friend, unpretentious, humble, presented with little fanfare, but it brings with it a welcome sense of nostalgia; it is a reliable, simple pleasure.*

Ranch folks have also long known the early morning pleasure of a steaming plate of migas con huevo. Served with a little salsa, hot coffee, and a side of refried beans, it's about the most traditional breakfast around.

2 tablespoons corn oil	4 eggs
2 corn tortillas (see Note)	Pepper
Salt	

HEAT the oil over medium heat in an 8-inch skillet. Cut or tear the tortillas into ½-inch-square pieces and add them to the pan. Stir to coat well with oil, and toast in the pan until golden and crunchy, about 5 minutes. Add salt to taste as the tortillas are browning.

WHISK the eggs in a small bowl until combined. Pour the eggs into the hot pan over the tortilla bits, and stir until the eggs are scrambled. Season with pepper. Serve immediately.

NOTE: Stale tortillas work best for this recipe, as they are extra crunchy when cooked in oil. The grains of salt are added during cooking so they will cling to the tortilla bits, intensifying the flavor of the corn. But the pepper is added after the eggs, so that the delicate oils in the pepper do not burn.

ENTOMATADAS TACOS IN FRESH TOMATO SAUCE

SERVES 6-8

What could be more inviting than the aroma of crispy corn tortillas filled with tender chicken, bathed in a garlicky tomato broth, and topped with salty cheese and fresh cilantro? You should use the freshest tomatoes for this recipe, as the focus here is on the tomato flavor (the name entomatadas *literally means "that which has been tomatoed"). So make this during the height of tomato season, when you have vine-ripe tomatoes from the garden.*

3 pounds ripe tomatoes (about 12)

1 to 2 garlic cloves

2 to 3 tablespoons corn oil

Salt and pepper to taste

32 (8-inch) corn tortillas

3 cups cooked, shredded chicken, either white or dark meat

4 ounces crumbled queso cotija or shredded Monterey Jack cheese

¼ cup chopped cilantro

BRING a large pot of water to a boil. Plunge the tomatoes into the water for 1 minute or until the skins have split. Remove the tomatoes from the water and allow them to cool. The tomato skin should slip off easily. Cut the tomatoes in half, and squeeze out seeds.

PLACE seeded tomatoes and the garlic in the container of a blender or a food processor and purée well. If necessary, add ½ cup of water to facilitate blending.

HEAT the corn oil in a large skillet over medium heat. Add the tomato purée and season with salt and pepper. Bring the sauce to a simmer, then reduce over low heat until thick, about 25 minutes. Keep warm while preparing the tortillas.

WRAP half of the tortillas in a damp dishtowel and heat in the microwave on high for 2 minutes. Remove from the microwave and take out one tortilla; keep the remaining tortillas wrapped. Fill the tortilla with 2 tablespoons of the chicken and fold in half. Place on a serving platter and keep warm. Fill the remaining tortillas.

SPOON a generous amount of warm tomato sauce over the tacos, then sprinkle with the cheese and garnish with the cilantro. Serve immediately.

FLAUTAS FLUTE-SHAPED CHICKEN TACOS

SERVES 6

Flautas, *or flute-shaped fried tacos,* are what I consider my specialty when feeding large numbers of guests.

24 (8-inch) corn tortillas	1 small onion, cut into thin rings
2 cups shredded cooked chicken, white or dark meat	1 cup crumbled queso cotija or shredded Monterey Jack cheese
Corn oil for frying	¼ cup Mexican-style sour cream or crème fraîche
1 cup chopped, seeded tomato	
2 cups shredded iceberg lettuce	Salsa Chimichurri (see page 102) or other hot sauce (see "Sauce Ideas" on page 61)

WRAP the corn tortillas in a damp kitchen toweland heat in the microwave for 1 to 2 minutes, until the tortillas are flexible. Remove one tortilla from the damp towel and fill with 1 to 2 tablespoons of the shredded chicken. Roll up the tortilla like a flute or cone, and set aside while you continue to stuff the remaining tortillas.

PREHEAT the oven to 200°F.

HEAT 2 to 3 cups of oil in a large, heavy skillet until very hot. Using tongs, carefully place the rolled tacos, one at a time, in the hot oil, seamed side down. Place the tacos close to each other (as many as can fit in one layer), so they maintain their shape while frying. Fry the tacos for about 2 to 3 minutes, then flip them over to fry on the other side for about 1 minute. Remove the fried tacos from the hot oil and drain on paper towels. Place in a casserole dish and keep tacos warm in the oven until all the tacos are done.

TOP the flautas with the chopped tomato, shredded lettuce, onion rings, and cheese. Drizzle the sour cream over the top. Serve with Salsa Chimichurri or other hot sauce.

NOTE: Cooking flautas for a crowd: If you are having guests, make the flautas in advance. Store the unfried tacos in the freezer (without their toppings) and use them as needed. Or, you can fry the tacos in advance and keep them warm in the oven until you are ready to serve them—just add the toppings at the last minute.

SAUCE IDEAS

SALSAS WITH A SOUR EDGE go very well with flautas—they cut through the fat. I've suggested using the Chimichurri Sauce because it has a vinegar base. Another sauce I like is a *tomatillo*-avocado sauce. To make it, you will need 2 cups of cooked tomatillos (see page 27 for cooking instructions, or use a 28-ounce can of tomatillos) and one ripe avocado. Purée the ingredients in a blender and add salt to taste. The fruity tang of the tomatillo is delicious when paired with the buttery flavor of avocado.

TACOS DE ACELGAS SWISS CHARD TACOS

SERVES 6-8

Swiss chard, known as acelgas *in Mexico, is often overlooked in the produce aisle. It is mild in flavor and pairs nicely with garlic and onion. The fresh tomato sauce is the same as that prepared for the* Entomatadas *(page 59). This is a beautifully satisfying dish for vegetarians.*

3 pounds ripe tomatoes (about 12)

3 to 4 garlic cloves, 2 minced

4 to 6 tablespoons corn oil, plus more for frying

Salt and pepper

1 pound Swiss chard, red or white, washed and chopped into ½-inch-wide ribbons

½ cup chopped onion

32 (8-inch) corn tortillas

3 ounces crumbled queso cotija or shredded Monterey Jack cheese

BRING a large pot of water to a boil. Plunge the tomatoes into the water for 1 minute or until you see that the skins of the tomatoes have burst. Remove tomatoes from water and allow to cool. The skins should slip off easily. Cut tomatoes in half and squeeze out seeds.

PLACE the tomatoes and 2 or 3 of the whole garlic cloves in the container of a blender or a food processor and purée until smooth. If necessary, add ½ cup water to facilitate the blending.

HEAT 2 to 3 tablespoons corn oil in a large skillet over medium heat. Add the tomato purée and season to taste with salt and pepper. Bring the sauce to a simmer and reduce until slightly thickened, about 25 minutes.

PREPARE the chard while the tomato sauce is reducing. Fill a 4-quart pot with water and bring to a boil. Add the chard, boil for 20 minutes, and drain. In a 9-inch skillet, heat another 2 to 3 tablespoons corn oil over medium heat. Add the onion, and sauté until translucent, about 5 minutes. Add the chard, 2 minced garlic cloves, and salt and pepper to taste. Sauté about 10 minutes to blend flavors.

WRAP 8 of the corn tortillas in a clean, damp dishtowel. Heat the wrapped tortillas in the microwave for 1½ to 2 minutes on high, until they are steamy and pliable. Remove one tortilla from the bundle, and keep the rest wrapped in the towel. Fill the tortilla with 1 to 2 tablespoons of the chard and roll up like a flute or cone. Place the rolled taco in a baking pan with the curved open edge underneath. Preheat the oven to 200°F.

CONTINUE to shape the remaining tortillas into tacos in this fashion. Heat about 2 or 3 cups of corn oil in a large, deep skillet until very hot. Remove tacos from baking pan, and place one by one in the hot oil, with the open edge again facing down. Fry for 2 minutes, then gently turn over with tongs to fry the other side for about 2 minutes. Remove from the oil and drain on paper toweling. Keep warm in the oven until all the tacos are fried, and you are ready to serve your meal.

PLACE all the cooked tacos on a serving platter, pour warm tomato sauce over the top, and sprinkle with the cheese.

ENFRIJOLADAS TORTILLAS IN BEAN SAUCE

SERVES 6-8

Enfrijoladas *get their name* from the frijoles *used for their sauce. Hearty and easy, this recipe can be adapted for vegetarians by substituting cheese or beans for the chicken filling. The* epazote *gives a fresh herbal flavor to this dish.*

3 cups cooked beans (either black or pinto beans, canned or homemade)

2 to 3 tablespoons corn oil

32 (8-inch) corn tortillas

3 cups shredded cooked chicken

½ cup crumbled queso cotija or grated Monterey Jack cheese

1 cup chopped tomato

Thin slices of onion, for garnish

Epazote leaves for garnish (optional)

PURÉE the beans until smooth in a food processor.

HEAT the oil in a large skillet. Add the bean purée, and stir in 1 cup of water. Heat the purée and simmer until it reaches the consistency of a thin cream soup; add more water as needed. Stir occasionally so the bean sauce will not scorch.

WRAP half of the tortillas in a damp dishtowel and heat in the microwave on high for 2 minutes. Remove from the microwave and take out one tortilla. Keep the remaining tortillas wrapped. Fill the tortilla with 2 tablespoons of the chicken and fold in half. Place the taco on a heatproof serving platter and keep warm in a low oven while you make the remaining tacos, using the rest of the chicken.

POUR the bean sauce over the tacos, then sprinkle with the cheese and garnish with the tomato, onion slices, and epazote, if using.

ENCHILADAS NORTEÑAS ENCHILADAS, NORTHERN STYLE
SERVES 8

The ancho chiles that form the basis of the sauce give this dish its depth of flavor. No chili powder or packet mix can compare. The flour used to make the sauce is a dead giveaway that this dish comes from north of the border, since wheat flour is rarely used in Mexican sauces.

3 dried ancho chiles

1 pound ground beef

½ cup chopped onion and ½ cup minced onion

¼ cup all-purpose flour

1 garlic clove, minced

2 teaspoons salt, or to taste

1 teaspoon pepper

Pinch ground cumin

32 (8-inch) corn tortillas

6 cups shredded Cheddar cheese

FILL a 2-quart saucepan with water and bring to a boil. Add the chiles and boil until they are soft and dark red. Drain the chiles, remove the stems, and purée in a blender with 2 cups of fresh water. Strain the purée though a mesh colander or chinois to remove the seeds and skins. Reserve the purée and discard seeds.

HEAT a large Dutch oven over medium heat, then cook the ground beef and chopped onion until well browned, about 10 minutes. Add the flour and stir until it is absorbed. Then add the chile purée, 3 cups of water, the garlic, salt, pepper, and cumin. Simmer the sauce until it thickens, about 10 minutes.

WRAP 8 of the corn tortillas in a damp dishtowel, and microwave for 1 minute on high, until the tortillas are flexible. Remove one tortilla from the towel, leaving the rest wrapped so that they stay warm. Place a couple of tablespoons of cheese on one side of the tortilla and fold it over (or roll it up into a flute) and place on an ovenproof platter. Fill the remaining tortillas in this fashion, using 5 cups of the cheese and heating more batches of tortillas in the damp towel if necessary. Once the tortillas are all filled and together on the platter, pour the sauce over the tortillas and top with the remaining 1 cup cheese and the minced onion.

PREHEAT the broiler. Place the platter of tacos under the broiler until the cheese melts. Serve piping hot.

ENCHILADAS SUISAS SWISS ENCHILADAS
SERVES 8

Enchiladas suisas, *or "Swiss Enchiladas,"* are a recent development in Mexico, but they have quickly established their place as standard offering on most Mexican restaurant menus. Because they are made with cream cheese, shredded cheese, and sour cream, they are named for the country famous for its milk products, Switzerland. However, their origin can be traced to the Sanborn's chain of restaurants, familiar throughout Mexico. This dish is still quite popular on their menu, and has also become famous on the Texas side of the border.

Around here, enchiladas suisas tend to show up at ladies' luncheons and potluck dinners. The rich cream cheese filling and tangy tomatillo sauce make them a hit with every crowd.

3 pounds fresh tomatillos or 2 (28-ounce) cans tomatillos, drained (see page 27)

2 garlic cloves

Salt and pepper

3 tablespoons corn oil

½ cup chopped onion

3 cups shredded cooked chicken, either white or dark meat

1 (8 ounce) package cream cheese

32 (8-inch) corn tortillas

2 cups shredded Monterey Jack cheese

½ cup Mexican style sour cream or crème fraîche

IF USING FRESH TOMATILLOS, clean and boil them according to instructions on page 27. Using a food processor or blender, purée the tomatillos and garlic. Add salt and pepper to taste.

HEAT the oil over medium heat in a 12-inch skillet. Add the onion and sauté until transparent, about 5 minutes. Add the chicken and stir to mix with the onion. Add the cream cheese and continue to cook until cheese is completely melted. Remove from the heat. Correct seasoning.

PREHEAT the oven to 350°F. Wrap 8 of the tortillas in a damp kitchen towel, and heat in microwave on high for 1 to 2 minutes, until the tortillas are soft and pliable. Keep the tortillas wrapped in the hot towel. Remove one tortilla at a time and fill with 2 tablespoons of the chicken mixture. Roll up the tortilla into a cylinder and place in a large ovenproof casserole (you can also use 2 smaller dishes or 4 individual gratin dishes). Continue filling the other warmed tortillas in this fashion, then heat the remaining tortillas in the microwave, and fill them. When all of the filled tortillas are in the baking dish, pour the tomatillo sauce over the top and sprinkle with the cheese.

BAKE until the cheese is melted, about 20 minutes. Remove the casserole from the oven, and drizzle the sour cream over the top.

ENCHILADAS

IN THE BORDER REGION, enchiladas are the classic blue plate special, a truck-stop favorite. Folks who venture beyond our fair state usually reminisce about Texas enchiladas, as they peruse the paltry offerings in Tex-Mex-themed restaurants around the country.

In restaurants, the enchiladas are filled and the sauce is prepared in advance. When enchiladas are ordered, they are placed on the plate along with the requisite rice and beans, then covered with sauce and topped with cheese and onions. There's a quick trip to the broiler, and they are on their way to your table, bubbling and steaming with a deep red aroma. "Careful, *mi hija* [my daughter], that's a hot plate!" are some of the sweetest words ever put together. These are so simple and good you'll want to make them every week.

PUFFY TACOS

SERVES 6-8 (24 TACOS)

A "puffy" taco is regional fare in South Texas (as is its relative, the puffy nacho—*see variation*). *To make it, a raw tortilla is deep-fried instead of being baked on a comal,* then filled with chicken or beef, shredded lettuce, onions, and tomatoes. *Puffy tacos are enjoyed in Mexico, but they are not celebrated as they are here in South Texas. I have seen many restaurants around here claim to be the originator of the "puffy" taco.*

TORTILLAS

2 cups instant corn tortilla mix

1 teaspoon salt

Corn oil or vegetable shortening for frying

FILLING

2 tablespoons corn oil

½ cup chopped onion

1½ pounds ground beef

1 garlic clove, minced

Pinch ground cumin

Salt and pepper to taste

½ cup seeded and diced tomato

½ cup chopped onion

1 cup shredded lettuce

COMBINE the tortilla mix and salt in a large bowl. Add 1 cup of warm water, mixing the dough with your hands. Add enough water to make a smooth, dense dough. Divide dough into 24 equal pieces.

PREHEAT the oven to 200°F. Pour in the oil to a 1-inch depth in a heavy 8- or 9-inch skillet; heat until it reaches 350°F. Using a tortilla press, shape one piece of dough into a 5-inch diameter tortilla (see page 7–8). Carefully place the uncooked tortilla in the hot cooking oil. Fry the tortilla on one side for approximately 30 seconds, or until puffed. Using tongs, flip the tortilla and fry for another 30 seconds on the other side. Remove from oil and drain in a 9 x 13-inch baking pan lined with paper toweling. Continue to shape and fry all of the tortillas in this fashion. Place the pan in the oven to keep the fried tortillas warm while preparing the filling.

HEAT the corn oil in a separate 9-inch skillet over medium heat, add the onion, and cook until translucent, about 5 minutes. Add the ground beef, garlic, cumin, salt, and pepper. Reduce the heat and simmer for 20 minutes, until the beef is completely cooked.

FILL each warm taco shell with 2 or 3 tablespoons of filling. Top each with a little chopped tomato, chopped onion, and shredded lettuce.

❖ **PUFFY NACHOS**: Puffy nachos are the quintessential border appetizer. Rarely seen in Mexico, they appear in many of the small Mexican eateries of the Wild Horse Desert. Prepare the tortilla masa the same way as for Puffy Tacos. Remove one of the plastic liners after the tortilla is shaped (see page 7–8). Using a spatula edge or a table knife, cut the tortilla into quarters while it is still on the second plastic liner. Carefully remove the quartered tortilla wedges, and place in the hot oil. Fry on each side for 30 seconds, remove from oil, and drain on paper towels. Keep the nachos warm in the oven while you are shaping and frying the remaining tortillas. Top with a dollop of guacamole, refried beans, cheese, sliced jalapeños, or whatever else you like.

NOTE: Although too small for making puffy tacos, bucket-style deep fryers are perfect for making puffy nachos.

DINNER AT CARO'S

EVERY FAMILY HAS A SPECIAL RESTAURANT that to them is as comfortable and familiar as their home. Caro's Restaurant in Rio Grande City is our family's all-time favorite. When I was little, we would load up the station wagon on Saturday night and travel the 60 miles (one way) for the best border food in Texas. The place was small and hard to find—you had to look around the corner, off the beaten path, for a tiny neon sign that simply said "Caro's." Juan Caro was always at the cash register, a black and white portrait of his mother hanging behind him, his wife Carmen overseeing the kitchen. We'd sit down, and soon hot white china plates filled with classic border fare—*enchiladas,* beans, rice, puffy tacos, puffy *nachos,* and T-bone steaks—would be placed before us. Dad would order a Lone Star draught beer, and we would dig in to our food. After we had eaten our fill, we would pile back into the station wagon, and head back across the rocky flatlands of Starr County, 60 miles back to the ranch.

SOPES TORTILLA CUPS

SERVES 4 (20 SOPES)

I think sopes *were invented* specifically to showcase a good salsa. The walled edge of the cup-shaped tortilla makes a little reservoir for the salsa and filling, giving you a good, juicy mouthful. Garnished with a drizzle of Mexican-style sour cream, thin slices of avocado, and red onion, they are hard to resist.

The technique for making sopes is different from that for making regular tortillas. You briefly cook one side of the sope, when you form the edge, then cook the other side. I find it easier to make them in batches, first browning as many tortillas as the griddle can accommodate, then cooling and forming that batch, and finally returning the formed sopes to the griddle to finish all together.

2 cups instant tortilla mix

¼ cup lard or vegetable shortening

1 teaspoon salt

1 cup refritos (refried beans, see page 139)

2 cups shredded cooked chicken, pork, or beef

1 cup crumbled queso cotija or shredded Monterey Jack cheese

¼ cup Mexican-style sour cream or crème fraîche

1 avocado, peeled, pitted, and thinly sliced

1 medium onion, thinly sliced

½ cup salsa (any recipe, see pages 94–103)

COMBINE the tortilla mix, shortening, salt, and 1½ cups of water in a large bowl. Knead together, adding enough water to make a smooth dough that does not stick to your hands. Divide the dough into 20 walnut-size pieces.

PREHEAT a griddle on the stove over medium heat.

FLATTEN the dough balls to a ¼-inch thickness using a tortilla press. Place each flattened round on the heated griddle and brown for 60 seconds. Remove the tortilla from the griddle and place on a baking sheet, uncooked side down, and allow to cool for 1 or 2 minutes. When the tortilla is cool enough to handle, pinch the edges upward until you form a small ¼-inch-high wall around the entire perimeter to make a sope. Return the sope to the griddle, with the uncooked side down and the walled side up. Brown sope on the griddle for about 3 minutes, until toasted spots form underneath. Remove from the heat and set aside. Continue cooking and shaping all the sopes in this fashion. (With practice, you will become adept at forming one batch while another cooks.)

HEAT the refried beans, and place approximately 1 tablespoon of beans on each sope. Top each sope with some chicken (or whatever cooked meat you choose), cheese, sour cream, avocado, and onion. Serve with your favorite salsa.

❖ **APPETIZER SOPES**: For an interesting appetizer, try making sopes half the size as directed above; this recipe will make 40 hors d'oeuvre-size sopes.

SOPES

THE WORDS *sope, sopa, soup, sop,* and the diminutive *sopaipilla* all come from the Mozarabic word *xupaipa,* which means "food soaked in liquid." (Mozarabic was the language that developed in the regions of Spain under Arab occupation from the early eighth century to approximately A.D. 1300.)

CHALUPAS COMPUESTAS
"COMPOSED" TOASTED TORTILLAS

SERVES 8 (24 CHALUPAS)

This recipe has a different name depending on where you come from. In central Mexico, a chalupa *is an oval-shaped fried tortilla, named for the raftlike boat it resembles. Here in the north, a chalupa is a round fried tortilla. (In central Mexico, our round chalupa would be called a tostada.) Both shapes are topped with the same ingredients, such as refried beans, shredded chicken, lettuce, tomatoes, and so on, depending on your preference. Once they've been given toppings, they become "chalupas compuestas," meaning a fried tortilla that has been "composed" or assembled.*

Corn or vegetable oil for frying

24 (8-inch) corn tortillas

2 cups refried beans, warmed (see page 139)

2 cups shredded cooked chicken

1 cup crumbled queso cotija or shredded Monterey Jack cheese

1 cup seeded and chopped tomato

2 cups shredded iceberg lettuce

1 small onion, cut into thin rings

¼ cup Mexican-style sour cream or crème fraîche

POUR the corn oil, at least 1 inch deep, into a 12-inch skillet, and heat over medium heat. Once the oil is hot, about 350°F, place a tortilla into the skillet and fry on each side for 1 minute, until crispy. Remove the tortilla from the oil and drain on a baking sheet lined with paper toweling. Continue to fry all the tortillas in this fashion. This fried tortilla is now called a tostada.

PREHEAT the oven to 200°F. Spread each tostada with 1 generous tablespoon of beans, and top with the same amount of chicken and 2 teaspoons of cheese. Keep the tostadas warm in the oven until you are ready to serve them. To serve, top the tostadas with the tomato, lettuce, onion, and a dollop of sour cream right before serving.

GORDITAS DE CHORIZO CON PAPA
FAT TORTILLAS WITH CHORIZO AND POTATOES
SERVES 6-9 (12 GORDITAS)

Gorditas *always taste better* when someone makes them for you. Maybe this sentiment hearkens back to my childhood, when I would sit at the kitchen counter and listen to the pat-pat-pat of these extra-thick tortillas being formed. Maybe it is the waiting for the gordita to be ready, while the aroma of chorizo fills the air. Maybe it is the fact that someone cares enough about you to make you one of these little sandwiches entirely from scratch and serve it hot, topped with a frizzle of crunchy lettuce, onions, and cool cubes of tomato.

We always have gorditas at my in-laws' house, on quiet Sunday evenings at the ranch. I have to admit that my favorite thing about gorditas is the way the fat from the spicy chorizo soaks into the crusty corn masa—it's sinful and delicious.

3 cups instant tortilla mix

1 cup vegetable shortening

1 tablespoon salt

12 ounces fresh chorizo sausage

1 russet potato, cut into ½-inch cubes (about 1 cup)

OPTIONAL

1 cup seeded and chopped tomato

1 cup shredded iceberg lettuce

½ cup sliced onion

Any salsa recipe (see pages 94–103)

HEAT a comal, or griddle, or skillet, preferably cast iron, on the stove until it is moderately hot.

COMBINE the tortilla mix, shortening, salt, and 2 cups warm water in a large bowl. Knead the dough with your hands until it is smooth, adding more water if necessary. Divide the dough into 12 equal portions. Roll each piece into a ball, then pat it into a round cake about 4 inches wide and ¼ inch thick.

PLACE one tortilla cake on the heated griddle and cook for 10 minutes, then flip and cook on other side for 10 more minutes. Keep the gorditas warm and soft by wrapping them in a clean dishtowel while you continue to make the remaining gorditas.

(continued)

GORDITAS DE CHORIZO CON PAPA, CON'T.

TAKE a gordita in your hand, and split it with a fork lengthwise as you would an English muffin. The center of the gordita will be uncooked and creamy. With a table knife or a narrow spatula, remove this moist center (called the *migajon,* or "big crumb") and discard. Your gordita will now be a crisp outer shell with a hollow interior. Set aside and continue to make the gorditas.

HEAT a 10-inch skillet with a lid over medium heat. Remove the casing from the chorizo (if any) and add to the skillet. Break the sausage apart with a spatula until you have small pieces. Once the fat begins to render (about 5 minutes), add the potato cubes, then reduce the heat and cover. Cook for about 10 minutes, until the steam has cooked the potatoes. When the potato is tender, remove the lid and allow to brown for another 5 minutes. Remove from the heat.

FILL each gordita with a few spoonfuls of the chorizo. If these are breakfast gorditas, they would be served as is. For lunch or dinner gorditas, top with the garnishes, as desired.

PACHUCOS BEAN AND MASA FRITTERS

MY HUSBAND GREW UP in Reynosa, Tamaulipas, along the northernmost border of Mexico, and he speaks fondly of a local street food there called *pachucos*—deep-fried 2-inch balls of corn *masa* filled with refried beans, dipped in a fiery salsa, and sold by vendors as afternoon snacks. We have tried making them several times at home, but with disastrous results. The masa balls would build up tremendous pressure in the hot oil and explode across the kitchen, spewing hot beans, masa, and oil in a 30-foot radius. I will omit the description of the burns suffered. And for your own safety, I will not share that recipe here. However, for food history's sake, pachucos are still alive and well in the streets of Reynosa. I will leave their legacy to the professionals, the pachuco street vendors.

The term *pachuco* is the name for someone from Pachuca, Hidalgo, Mexico. I can only surmise that the originator of this popular street food was from that region of Mexico.

TAMALES NORTEÑOS
NORTHERN-STYLE TAMALES
MAKES 4 DOZEN TAMALES

It is almost impossible to give exact measurements for tamales, or to follow any recipe and expect perfectly consistent results. The reason is that, if you use just a little more or less filling, or spread the masa just slightly thicker or thinner, you could produce anywhere from 3 to 5 dozen tamales. You could have extra filling at the end or run out before using all the masa. So if you end up with extra masa or extra meat at the end of your tamalada, don't worry—you didn't do anything wrong. (See variations for ways to fill leftover corn masa.)

To steam the tamales you will need a two-piece steamer pot with a lid. The tamal steamer can be any steamer that you have on hand. Some enamel steamers are available in the market, specifically made for tamales, but don't be afraid to improvise. A lobster steamer works very well, as does a stockpot with a pasta insert. I confess that I sometimes use an electric turkey roaster. I remove the inner roasting pan and place a cake rack in the bottom of the roaster, which raises the tamales slightly above the boiling water; with this method I can steam 10 to 15 dozen tamales in one batch.

MEAT

1½ pounds pork (bone-in country-style ribs work well)

¼ medium onion

1 garlic clove

1 bay leaf

Salt to taste

SEASONING

3 ounces ancho chiles (about 6)

1 garlic clove, mashed into a paste with a molcajete or garlic press

2 tablespoons pork lard

¼ teaspoon pepper, or to taste

Pinch ground cumin

1 teaspoon salt, or to taste

2½ pounds prepared corn masa (see recipe, page 78)

3 ounces dried corn shucks, soaked in warm water 1 to 2 hours before use

(continued)

TAMALES NORTEÑOS, CON'T.

PREPARE THE MEAT: Place the pork and any bones into a 4-quart saucepan. Cover with water and add the onion quarter, garlic, bay leaf, and salt, and bring to a boil. Reduce the heat and simmer the pork, partially covered, until the juices are clear when meat is pierced with a fork, about 30 minutes.

REMOVE the pork from the pot and reserve the broth. Remove any meat from the bones, and discard the bones. Mince the meat, chopping by hand or using a meat grinder. You should have between 2 and 3 cups of chopped pork.

PREPARE THE FILLING AND SEASON THE MEAT: Fill a 4-quart saucepan with water. Bring the water to a boil and add the chiles. Boil until tender, about 15 minutes. Drain the chiles, discard the stems, and add chiles to the container of a blender. Add 1 cup of the reserved pork broth and the garlic, and purée well, adding more broth if necessary to facilitate blending. Strain the purée through a wire strainer to extract any seeds. This should make approximately 2 cups of purée.

HEAT the lard in a large skillet over medium heat. When melted, add the pepper, cumin, and salt, and sauté for 10 seconds. Add the chile purée and sauté for 2 minutes. Add the chopped pork, combining well. Adjust the seasonings as desired. Simmer for 10 minutes, and then remove from heat. Set aside. (You may elect to prepare the filling a day in advance. Once cooled, you can also freeze the meat for later.)

PREPARE the masa as directed in the recipe.

DRY OFF a handful of the corn shucks and place within reach. To make a proper tamal, be sure the bottom edge of each corn shuck is around 8 inches wide. Discard those that are too narrow and tear strips off of the ones that are too wide. Take a corn shuck, and spread the bottom two-thirds of the leaf with 2 or 3 tablespoons of masa. Spread the masa thin, leaving a 1½-inch-wide area along one edge free. Along the center of this, following the direction of the corn shuck veins, form a line of about 1 tablespoon of the filling on the masa. Now fold the masa-covered edge of the shuck over the filling and roll it up toward the edge of the shuck with no masa. Fold down the top (uncovered) part of the shuck. Set aside and continue until all the tamales have been formed.

FILL the bottom of the steamer with about 3 inches of water, depending on depth of the steamer, and bring to a boil. Place the tamales in the basket of the steamer—as many as will fit. All of the tamales must be positioned with their open end straight up, folded end down. As a top layer, cover the tamales with extra corn shucks, then with a sheet of aluminum foil. Secure the lid of the steamer, using foil around the edges of the lid to prevent the escape of steam. Place the steamer over the boiling water. Steam the tamales for about 40 minutes, until the masa is firm.

❖ **VEGETARIAN TAMALES**: You can make vegetarian tamales using refried beans instead of meat in the filling. Follow the instructions for preparing the filling, using vegetable shortening instead of lard and 1½ pounds of refried beans instead of meat.

❖ **FILLING FOR EXTRA CORN MASA**: If you are making the meat tamales, refried bean can come in handy if you use up your filling and have leftover corn masa. Just switch over to refried beans—seasoned as above or simply with a little extra chile sauce.

❖ **FILLING VARIATIONS**: Concoct your own filling using leftover cooked chicken, beef, pork, or venison. Just mince or grind the meat and add spices and a little leftover chile purée. Be creative, but write down what you do so you can do it again! Or use cheese, such as Monterey jack or even a pepper jack or chopped vegetable guisado for the filling (see Tacos de Acelgas, page 62).

FRESH CORN MASA

MASA IS THE SPANISH WORD FOR "DOUGH," and usually the term refers specifically to the corn dough used for making tortillas and tamales. Dry corn tortilla mix (also known by the commercial names of masa harina and maseca) is often referred to as masa as well, although the proper name would be *harina para masa,* or "flour for masa." Good masa is very important when making tamales, as it is the dough that binds the *tamal* together. Many of the small tortilla producers here in the United States grind their own corn and sell masa on the side. Look around in your com-munity; you'll be surprised how many *molinos* can be found.

I usually make my own *nixtamal* and freshly ground masa when making tamales, mainly because I live an hour from the nearest molino, where the fresh masa is commercially produced. If you are interested in making your own masa, just follow the recipe you'll find on page 78. But buying masa is much easier, and just as good as homemade, so look around for a small tortilla shop in your community. Use freshly ground masa immediately, as older masa produces tough tamales.

PREPARED CORN MASA FOR TAMALES

MAKES 2½ POUNDS PREPARED MASA

Instant corn tortilla mix can also be used to make masa, with fair results. Tortilla mix lacks the texture and earthy corn flavor of fresh masa, but it is not a bad substitute for the real thing. Both of these recipes should produce approximately 2½ pounds of prepared masa. Notice that the quantities in each recipe are slightly different. Fresh masa is moist, and does not need as much broth or lard as the dry masa.

WHEN USING DRY MASA

1 pound instant corn tortilla mix

3 ounces pork lard

2 teaspoons sea salt

4 cups pork stock, slightly warmed

WHEN USING FRESHLY GROUND MASA

2 pounds freshly ground masa (see page 14)

3 ounces pork lard

1½ teaspoons sea salt

1 cup pork stock, slightly warmed

PLACE the tortilla mix or freshly ground masa in a large bowl. Using your hands, knead in the lard and salt. Add the pork stock a little at a time and continue to knead until the masa is cohesive, smooth to the touch. Taste for salt and add more if necessary.

❖ **VEGETARIAN TAMALES**: Use vegetable shortening and stock in place of pork lard and stock.

TAMALES

TAMALES ARE PROBABLY THE OLDEST prepared food in Mexico. Ground corn would be mixed with what foods could be gathered, chiles, crushed fruits, wild herbs, and even small animals such as frogs or minnows. The mixture would be steamed in corn husks. When the Spanish *conquistadores* arrived, they brought domesticated pigs and cattle, as well as the technique of rendering lard. Although corn and chile still constitute the base for tamales, pork and lard became standard ingredients as well. Bananas were brought from Africa to the New World by Spanish *conquistadores*, and the banana leaf became a popular alternative wrapper to the corn husk.

It is said that if you are not in good spirits when making tamales, they will feel resentful and will never cook properly. The same is said of tamales made in the presence of a crying baby. Harmony in one's home is crucial to the production of a good batch of tamales.

Making tamales is like a quilting bee or a barn raising. It's a lot of work—an affair that takes planning, several days of cooking, and a team of skilled hands to render a good yield. Large pots on the stove rattle with boiling chunks of pork or plump chickens, which will be hand-chopped for the savory filling. The sweet aroma of boiling chiles (which are puréed and added for flavor and color) lifts from another bubbling pot and brings back the memory of past tamale-making episodes.

Fretting and tasting, complaining, inspiration, and pride swirl and swell in the steam that envelops the kitchen. The crescendo of activity abruptly subsides when everyone sits down at the table to fill and roll the tamales. Time ceases to move forward and we talk of the past year, of family, friends, recipes, hair styles, shopping, weight loss, weight gain, husbands, wives, could-haves, should-haves, and would-haves. The work is hard, but the gossip is delicious.

I will confess that I never learned to make tamales until my grandmother passed away. She had always made them every year, and we, her grandkids, were never interested in helping. When she was gone, it seemed disloyal to just go out and buy tamales from a stranger, or a supermarket. So I rolled up my sleeves and taught myself how to make them. While I missed my grandmother, it was comforting to think I was carrying on her work, with the balanced flavors of garlic, chiles, corn, and meat in my memory guiding me. Continuing her tradition was a way to hold on to her, and all the family members that made tamales before her.

So now I am the *tamal* maker in the family, and from what people tell me, I make them very well. Maybe it is my recipe, but then again, maybe it is because I am just happy to be working (and gossiping) with my family, so my tamales never feel resentful. Whatever the case, the results are absolutely delicious.

SHORTY'S BISCUITS

MAKES 15 BISCUITS

Weneslado "Shorty" Perez has worked on the Santa Fe Ranch, a cattle ranch near San Manuel, Texas, for over 30 years. He makes a large batch of biscuits for the cowboys at roundup time, enough to get his crew through a morning's work. Slathered with butter and drizzled with wild honey from the ranch, and paired with a cup of Shorty's hot coffee, these are the quintessential ranch biscuits.

2½ cups all-purpose flour

2¼ teaspoons baking powder

1½ teaspoons salt

¼ cup sugar

¼ cup margarine or vegetable shortening (see Note)

¼ cup milk

2 to 3 tablespoons butter or margarine, melted

COMBINE the flour, baking powder, salt, and sugar in a large bowl. Using your fingers, cut in the margarine or shortening until the mixture resembles coarse meal. Stir in just enough milk for the dough to leave the sides of the bowl.

FORM the dough into a ball with floured hands. Place ball on a floured smooth service, and roll out into a sheet ½ inch thick. Cut out rounds with a 3-inch biscuit cutter and place on a greased baking sheet. Brush the top of the biscuits with half the melted butter and allow to rest for 20 minutes.

PREHEAT the oven to 400°F.

BAKE biscuits for about 15 minutes, then remove from the oven and brush the tops of the biscuits again with the remaining melted butter.

NOTE: Shorty prefers margarine over shortening for his biscuits. The margarine keeps the biscuits tender and prevents staleness.

BAKING BISCUITS

IF YOU WANT to make more biscuits, here is a conversion chart for the ingredients. Follow the baking procedure as noted above:

INGREDIENTS	FOR 30 BISCUITS	FOR 60 BISCUITS
Flour	5 cups	10 cups
Baking powder	1½ tablespoons	3 tablespoons
Salt	1 tablespoon	2 tablespoons
Sugar	½ cup	1 cup
Margarine or shortening	½ cup	1 cup
Milk	1 cup	2 cups
Melted margarine or butter	About ¼ cup	About ½ cup

THE BIRTH OF THE BISCUIT

SCOTCH-IRISH IMMIGRANTS who arrived in the U.S. territories in the early 1800s brought with them a raised bread called a *scone*. The leavening agent was baking soda, not yeast, which proved a convenience. (Traveling or overworked immigrants were unlikely to dedicate any of their precious spare time to the care of live yeast cultures, nor to the lengthy process of raising yeast breads.)

Baking soda had its limitations, however, in that it needs an acidic ingredient (such as vinegar or buttermilk) with which to react to work as a leavening agent, and that it needs a precise balance of acid to produce optimum results. Too much or too little would leave a baker with unpredictable results. Double-acting baking powder, a more controllable leavening agent (it reacts twice, first with acid, then with heat, in order to start the leavening process), eventually replaced baking soda in many baked goods.

Scones quickly became popular throughout the South, but at some point the name for this food changed from *scone* to *biscuit,* the latter word derived from the French term *bis cuit,* or "twice cooked." (Today, scones have crossed the Atlantic again, appearing in supermarket bakeries, and in high-end coffeehouses.) As settlers from the southern states moved into Texas (tempted by the availability of land), they brought with them their basket of biscuits.

The word *scone* is believed to come from the "Stone of Destiny," also known as the "Stone of Scone": a rock that has been used in the coronation of Scottish kings since time immemorial. The legend is that the stone was used at the coronation of King David of Israel. It was believed that, since then, the presence of the Stone during a coronation ceremony imparted divine authority and complete sovereignty to the new king. For this reason, the Stone of Scone was moved from kingdom to kingdom, carted off to the current dominant monarchy. Eventually the Stone made its way to Westminster Abbey, where it resided for 700 years; it was recently returned to the Scots in 1996.

In 1983, when I visited England, I toured Westminster Abbey. I remember seeing the "Stone of Destiny" and, yup, it looked like a biscuit.

CACTUS CORNBREAD

SERVES 8

Cornbread was a staple among the Anglo settlers who migrated from the southern United States to the Wild Horse Desert. Although Mexico is the birthplace of corn, Southern-style cornmeal is unavailable there. Southern cornmeal and Mexican corn masa are processed differently, and cannot be used interchangeably.

In South Texas, however, both versions of ground corn are available. Corn pone, corn fritters, hush puppies, and cornmeal-battered seafood are all common foods in South Texas. The simultaneous presence of cornmeal and corn masa exists only at the cultural crossroads of the Wild Horse Desert.

Cactus cornbread is an excellent accompaniment for Chile con Carne (see page 120).

1 cup yellow cornmeal

1 cup all-purpose flour

1 to 2 tablespoons sugar (optional)

1 tablespoon baking powder

½ teaspoon salt

1 egg, beaten

1 cup milk

¼ cup corn oil, melted shortening, or drippings

¾ cup fresh or canned corn kernels

¾ cup diced nopalitos (cooked cactus pieces; see page 24)

PREHEAT the oven to 425°F. Grease and flour an 8-inch square baking pan.

COMBINE the cornmeal, flour, sugar, baking powder, and salt in a large bowl. Add the egg and milk; combine well. Add the corn oil and mix well. Stir in the corn kernels and nopalitos. Pour the batter into the prepared pan and bake for 20 to 25 minutes, or until the cornbread is golden brown and a wooden pick inserted in the center comes out clean. Serve warm.

❖ **CORNBREAD MUFFINS OR CORNSTICKS**: Pour the batter into greased or paper-lined muffin tins or into well-greased cornstick forms. Bake for 15 to 20 minutes or until golden brown.

PAN DE CAMPO CAMP BREAD

SERVES 4-6

Pan de campo *is a bread* usually baked over an open campfire. Here, in its home version, it is baked in an oven. But just as meats are better when grilled over an open fire, I encourage you to experiment making your pan de campo over live coals, using a Dutch oven (see variation). Kids especially love to help make the bread and tend the fire—it's a great activity for your next camping trip.

4 cups all-purpose flour, plus more as needed

4 tablespoons sugar

2 teaspoons baking powder

1 tablespoon salt

¼ cup vegetable shortening

¼ cup vegetable oil

About 2 cups milk

PREHEAT the oven to 450°F. Sift together the dry ingredients into a large mixing bowl. Stir in the shortening and oil, and work the dough with your hands until it resembles coarse meal. Add 1½ cups of the milk, and stir. The dough should be sticky but workable. If the dough is too stiff, add more milk; if the dough is too thin, add more flour.

TURN the dough out onto a counter dusted with flour and knead it hard for about 1 minute, but don't overwork it. Pat it out or gently roll it into a 9-inch circle that is ¼- to ½-inch thick. Using a fork, prick the dough all over. Place it on an ungreased baking sheet, and bake for 20 minutes. When done, pan de campo should be golden brown on the outside and have a biscuit texture on the inside.

◆ **TO BAKE PAN DE CAMPO OVER A FIRE:** The mesquite wood that we use in Texas for all our outdoor cooking burns hotter and smokier than almost any other wood and gives the bread extra crispiness and just a hint of mesquite flavor. If you are inclined to make pan de campo over a wood fire, follow the instructions on page 150 for starting an outdoor wood fire. Once your fire has burned for about 30 minutes (so that it has steady, yet calm heat), you are ready to bake. Using a shovel, transfer some of the coals to a separate spot a few feet away from your fire. Arrange the coals in a small bed about 2 feet square. Remove the lid and grease the interior of your Dutch oven generously with vegetable shortening. Replace the lid and put your Dutch oven

(continued)

CORN AND FLOUR DISHES

PAN DE CAMPO, CON'T.

in the center of the coals, and allow it to heat for about 10 minutes. Now remove the lid and place the rolled-out pan de campo dough in the Dutch oven. Replace the lid, and using your shovel, pile a small amount of live coals on the top of the lid so that the Dutch oven is entirely surrounded with gentle heat. Cook for about 10 minutes on each side to produce a golden-brown pan de campo. Use a spatula to flip the pan de campo to the other side to bake evenly.

NOTE: Your Dutch oven must fit certain requirements to be useful for making pan de campo. The lid must be flat, so that you can pile coals on top. Underneath, there must be three or four small legs attached so that the bottom surface does not sit directly on the live coals. Other Dutch ovens made for kitchen stovetop use (i.e., domed lids and no legs) will not work.

The skill in making pan de campo over live coals is in controlling the temperature of the Dutch oven. Too hot and the bread will burn; too cold and it will not cook properly. Remember that you need a 450°F oven to bake pan de campo successfully in your home oven, so your Dutch oven needs to be maintained at the same temperature. Using a thermometer with a live fire is a bit difficult, so judgment and experience will eventually become the tools on which you will rely for perfect pan de campo.

JAMES'S PRIZE-WINNING PAN DE CAMPO

PAN DE CAMPO is a flat, dense round bread baked outdoors in a Dutch oven over a mesquite fire and usually served with honey or molasses, or alongside a savory *guisado,* or stew. The texture and flavor remind me of a large white biscuit, only a bit crisper and thinner. It is a simple bread, as you can see from the ingredients, and has been prepared on the small ranches of the Wild Horse Desert ever since white flour has been available. Both the mesquite-flavor and the nostalgia of this bread make it a popular cook-off dish, with almost a cult following.

My brother James is the champion pan de campo cook in my family. He has won just one trophy, but he is the only one of us who has mastered the art, so he is the undefeated (albeit unchallenged) champ.

James wasn't born knowing how to make pan de campo, and he didn't pick it up from his dad or grandfather. His interest was piqued by watching men from other ranches make the bread at local cook-offs. Men in the Wild Horse Desert pride themselves on their pan de campo skills. I believe the appeal has something to do with a primal instinct for building and cooking over fires—the same can be said for *carne asadas* or barbecues. James learned by trial and error, spending hours bent over the mesquite fire grilling loaves, burning his face as well as his bread. His first few attempts, black and convex, were great for skeet shoots.

One of the secrets of his eventual success was a piece of sheet metal cut to fit the bottom of his Dutch oven. It gave his bread a cushion of air above the bottom of the skillet, reducing the risk of burning.

So here's to James, who has spent countless hours perfecting the ancient art. A Dutch oven can produce only one round pan de campo every 20 minutes. By tending several Dutch ovens at once, James can bake 70 batches of bread in a day at community fundraisers—no small feat.

SPINACH DUMPLINGS IN CHICKEN VEGETABLE BROTH

SERVES 4-6

My earliest memory of dumplings is watching my grandmother carefully peek into the pot through the steam as she lifted the cover. Sometimes she smiled at the plump dumplings bobbing in the boiling salty broth, but most memorable were the winces, grimaces, and frowns when her dumplings failed. Sadly, she gave up making them.

I found this old recipe, and it reminded me of the soups my grandmother used to serve. The fresh, earthy flavor of spinach combines nicely with the rich flavor of chicken stock and the tangy bites of fresh tomato.

8 ounces fresh spinach, washed and chopped, or ½ cup canned or frozen

3 tablespoons vegetable shortening

1½ cups all-purpose flour

1 teaspoon salt

½ cup milk

2 quarts Basic Soup Stock—chicken (see page 112)

2 carrots, peeled and chopped

1 medium tomato, seeded and chopped

1 celery stalk, chopped

BLANCH the spinach if you are using it fresh: Boil it for 5 minutes, until wilted. Using a slotted spoon, remove the spinach and allow to cool, about 20 minutes. Squeeze any excess liquid out of the cooked spinach and chop the spinach again so that it is a fine pulp. (For canned or frozen spinach, squeeze any excess liquid out of the spinach and chop to a fine pulp.)

CUT the shortening into the flour and salt. Add the milk and stir until you have a smooth batter. Add the spinach and combine well.

BRING the chicken stock to a boil in a 4-quart stock pot. Add the vegetables and boil for 5 minutes. Add the dumpling batter in half-teaspoon amounts, then cover the pot and allow to boil for 5 more minutes (see Note). Serve immediately.

NOTE: Do not be tempted to lift the lid of your boiling pot! Your dumplings need all the steam pressure they can get in order to be firm but fluffy.

WHOLE WHEAT PANCAKES WITH FRESH PEACH SYRUP

MAKES ABOUT A DOZEN 6-INCH PANCAKES

This recipe puts fresh peaches to good use; the pancakes soak up every drop of their perfumed sweetness. Peaches have such a nostalgic aura about them; I don't think any of us waxes poetic about a banana or a kiwifruit. But we all remember that perfect peach we enjoyed as a kid, with the juice streaming down our face. Even the pleasure of eating an overripe peach over the sink, late at night in your kitchen, cannot be denied.

1 pound fresh ripe peaches, sliced	2 teaspoons baking powder
³⁄₄ cup plus 1 tablespoon sugar	Pinch salt
1 stick cinnamon (Mexican if possible, see page 29)	2 tablespoons vegetable oil
1½ cups all-purpose flour	1 egg
½ cup whole wheat flour	1 cup milk
	Butter for serving

COMBINE the peaches, ³⁄₄ cup of the sugar, the cinnamon, and ½ cup water in a small saucepan. Bring to a boil, then reduce the heat to low and simmer for 20 to 30 minutes, stirring occasionally. Skim off any foam that may form on the surface of the syrup. Remove from the heat, but keep warm.

PREHEAT a griddle over medium heat. Sift together the flours, baking powder, and salt in a large bowl. Stir in the remaining 1 tablespoon sugar, the oil, and egg, then slowly whisk in the milk, breaking up any lumps.

DROP batter by large spoonfuls, one at a time, onto the griddle; pancakes should be about 6 inches in diameter. Holes should form as the pancake cooks. When the holes cease to bubble, flip the pancake and cook for another minute or so. Remove the pancake from the griddle and keep warm while you make the remaining pancakes. Serve warm, with warm peach syrup and butter.

NOTE: Remember that you want the pancakes to be fluffy. Do not press down on pancakes as they cook, and do not flip them more than once.

TEXAS PEACHES

IN 1910, it was reported that there were over 10 million peach trees of producing age in Texas. Most of this peach production was in the center of the state, in an area known as the Hill Country. German immigrants farmed the Hill Country, and still today the area is known for its peaches and German culture.

Up near Fredricksburg, Texas, around the northernmost borders of the Wild Horse Desert, little fruit stands of clapped-together scrap wood suddenly come alive in April, when peach season begins. The farming families set up for business, gently piling the blushing ripe peaches in red baskets and selling them to passing motorists.

CHAPTER THREE

SALSAS AND CHILES

I GREW UP BELIEVING that there was only one kind of chile, namely *chile piquín*, the wild variety of chile that grew in our yard. We would pick them whether they were young and green or mature and red. We'd grind them into a paste in my mother's *molcajete* with garlic, salt, and pepper, then add puréed tomato and serve the salsa in a small glass dish on the table. A small dab was the requisite condiment at every meal, on every plate.

Although the piquin chile is the signature chile we enjoy here on the border, there are many other types of chiles that we use in our regional cuisine (see Chiles, page 2, for a full description of different types). A purée made from reconstituted dried red *chile ancho* gives our local *enchilada* plates their characteristic color. Bowls of pickled *jalapeños* are common condiments on most dining tables here. Each chile has its own personality and function, just like the myriad herbs and spices commonly employed in the kitchen. Some of these chiles are used only for salsas, some are pickled and eaten whole, others add color to stews or soups.

In this chapter, I will describe the uses of the most common chiles enjoyed in the Wild Horse Desert, and share with you my favorite family recipes.

SALSA CRUDA DE CHILE PIQUÍN

UNCOOKED PIQUÍN CHILE SAUCE

MAKES 1¹/₂ CUPS

We have wild chiles that grow in the yard, and as they are always on hand, *that is what we use for making our everyday salsa. This is the recipe for the standard salsa that always appears on my mother's table. Breakfast, lunch, and dinner, this is the condiment of choice.*

The term salsa cruda *means a sauce that is not cooked after it is made. The fresh, mild flavor is a great accent for fish and is terrific when served beside a mesquite-grilled steak, as it is in Salsa de Chile Chipotle Ahumado (see page 103).*

½ pound ripe tomatoes (about 2 medium)

1 teaspoon salt

½ teaspoon whole black peppercorns

¼ teaspoon piquín chile, dried or fresh

1 garlic clove

ROAST the tomatoes on a very hot griddle until the skins blister and blacken in patches, 7 to 10 minutes. Remove them from the griddle, allow them to cool, then peel with your fingers. Cut the tomatoes in half, squeeze out the seeds, chop into quarters, and set aside.

GRIND the salt with the peppercorns, chile, and garlic using a molcajete or a stone mortar and pestle. When you have a fine paste, add the tomatoes and crush just until no large chunks remain. Serve immediately. Store leftover salsa in the refrigerator. I like to give it a quick zap in the microwave before serving it again, so that it is barely warm.

CHILE PIQUÍN

PIQUÍN CHILES ARE WILD CHILES. They cannot be cultivated; they grow only where the seeds are casually deposited by a bird after they have passed through the bird's digestive tract. On our land, the chiles grew in the strangest places—near the gutter spout, next to the garage, behind the tool shed. There was no telling where one would pop up. But once growing, they were protected and became the daily destination for the household chef. And others who came by wanted them, too. You could always tell when a repairman had visited our house: the next day, we would find our piquín chile plant stripped of its fruit.

Salsa Roja and Salsa Verde

THESE TWO SALSAS ARE SEEN TOGETHER on almost every table in border restaurants. These are the absolute basic recipes for red and green salsas. The red sauce, or *salsa roja,* has a tomato base, while *salsa verde,* or green sauce, has a tart *tomatillo* base. Unlike red or white wine, there is no designation for which sauce goes better with which dish; it depends on your personal preference or on the ingredients you have on hand.

SALSA ROJA RED SAUCE

MAKES ¾ CUP

Roasting the tomatoes and chiles caramelizes their natural sugars and adds a distinctive depth of flavor to this salsa. For a more intense roasted flavor, leave the charred skins on the tomatoes when grinding.

½ pound ripe tomatoes, about 2 medium
1 ounce serrano chiles (about 4)
½ teaspoon salt

½ teaspoon whole black peppercorns
1 garlic clove

HEAT a cast-iron griddle or regular skillet over medium-high heat until it is very hot. Add the tomatoes and chiles and roast until they have several blackened areas, 10 minutes, turning occasionally so they blister evenly. Remove them from the griddle and allow to cool. Peel the skins from the tomatoes with you fingers, and remove the stems from the chiles. Slice the tomatoes in half and squeeze out the seeds. Separately, roughly chop the tomatoes and chiles.

GRIND the salt, peppercorns, and garlic to a paste in a molcajete or a stone mortar and pestle. Add the chiles and continue to grind until the paste is smooth. Add the tomatoes, and continue to grind until the salsa is smooth and well blended. Serve immediately. The salsa can be stored in your refrigerator for up to one week.

❖ **HOTTER OR MILDER SALSA**: Do you like your salsas mild? Simply double the amount of tomato. Do you like them really hot? Double the chiles. After making a few batches, you will develop your own recipes and techniques.

SALSA VERDE GREEN SAUCE

MAKES ³/₄ CUP

½ pound tomatillos (see page 27)

1 ounce serrano chiles (about 4)

½ teaspoon salt

½ teaspoon whole black peppercorns

1 garlic clove

2 tablespoons minced cilantro

FILL a 2-quart saucepan with water and bring to a boil. Meanwhile, remove the husks from the tomatillos and wash thoroughly to remove the stickiness from the skins. Place the washed tomatillos in the boiling water and boil until the tomatillos turn from bright green to olive drab, 7 to 10 minutes. Drain the tomatillos in a colander.

HEAT a cast-iron or regular skillet over medium-high heat until it is very hot. Add the chiles and roast until they have a few black areas (10 minutes). Remove from the griddle and let cool, then remove the stems and roughly chop.

GRIND the salt, peppercorns, and garlic to a paste in a molcajete or a stone mortar and pestle. Add the chiles and continue to grind until the paste is smooth. Add the tomatillos, and continue to grind until the salsa is smooth and well blended. Stir in the cilantro. Serve immediately. The salsa can be stored in your refrigerator for up to one week.

GRINDING CHILES FOR SALSA

ALL SALSAS CONSIST OF A CHILE PURÉE, either served by itself or combined with tomatoes, garlic, or other ingredients. Every chile has a particular way that it should be ground before it is to be consumed. *Molcajetes,* the prehistoric stone mortars and pestles traditionally used for grinding ingredients, are still used in many parts of Latin America and here in South Texas. Even though we have modern appliances that make the job easier, they can lessen the quality of your salsa. The character of each chile must be understood before you begin to prepare your salsa.

FOR SALSAS MADE WITH FRESH CHILES AND TOMATOES: I strongly encourage you to use a molcajete. Although you can get fair results using a food processor, the flavors of freshly stone-ground garlic and peppercorns, paired with the uneven chunky texture of stone-ground tomatoes and zesty chiles, beats all of the machine-processed salsas by miles. Salsa made in a molcajete is a hand-crafted food and imparts a dash of human artistry and care to the steak or quesadilla with which it is served. Using a blender for fresh table salsa is unacceptable, as a blender turns the tomato into a runny, foamy purée.

FOR SALSA MADE FROM PIQUÍN CHILES AND TOMATOES: Because of their extreme heat and small size, a few piquín chiles can easily be ground into a powder (if dried) or paste (if fresh) in a molcajete for a salsa. The added tomato, when ground in the molcajete, picks up every last drop of chile flavor from the stone bowl.

FOR SALSA FROM ARBOL CHILES: These dried chiles are crisp.. They don't need to be boiled and can be hand-ground in a molcajete for a table salsa. However, they are not as spicy as piquín chiles, and it would take awhile to pulverize the amount you would need for a salsa. So instead I usually remove their stems and grind them in the blender with a little water. And as there is no tomato added to this salsa, there is no unwanted foamy texture when made in the blender.

FOR SALSA MADE FROM LEATHERY-SKINNED DRIED CHILES: Ancho, dried chipotle, pasilla, and other soft and leathery-skinned dried chiles should be boiled to soften them so they can be more easily ground into a purée. Follow the instructions for boiling and puréeing ancho chiles on page 5. You can then further refine the purée by straining it in a colander to remove any seeds or large pieces of skin. Although food processors work well for making purées, blenders liquefy food particles better. Food processors produce a more granular-textured sauce.

Generally speaking, I prefer to use my molcajete for table salsas that are served as condiments. The quantity will be fairly low, and it doesn't take that long to grind up a couple of chiles and a tomato. Blenders are terrific when you need a lot of chile purée for use in a soup, in *tamales,* or a stew. Not many of us have the time to hand-grind several pounds of chiles. Also, hand-grinding a lot of chiles can be very irritating to your skin, so a blender can save your hands from some serious pain.

SALSA DE CHILE DE ARBOL ARBOL CHILE SAUCE

MAKES ABOUT ½ CUP

This salsa is my favorite. *I always have a few* chiles de arbol *stashed away in my spice cupboard for last-minute dinners. The toasty, tannic flavor of arbole chiles is so good on its own that this salsa needs no tomatoes or other flavor enhances beyond a little garlic and salt. Guests are forever intrigued as they watch me toast the chiles for a seemingly insignificant amount of time, then blend the toasted chiles to produce a hot, yet intensely flavorful salsa.*

1 ounce dried arbole chiles
2 garlic cloves
2 tablespoons corn oil
Salt

PREHEAT the oven to 350°F. Place the chiles on a baking sheet and toast in the oven for 1 to 2 minutes. Be vigilant, as the chiles will burn quickly. Allow the chiles to cool, then remove the stems. Place the chiles in the container of a blender with the garlic. Add 1 cup of water and purée well until you have a smooth sauce.

ADD the corn oil to an 8-inch skillet and heat on the stove. Add in the chile purée and simmer until the sauce is reduced, about 15 minutes, or until it reaches the degree of thickness you desire. Stir occasionally and add salt to taste. The salsa can be stored in your refrigerator for up to one week.

INTERESTING USES FOR SALSA

ADD A SPOONFUL OF SALSA to any of the following:

- Bloody Mary mix
- Pesto or spaghetti sauce
- Scrambled eggs
- Bread, biscuit, or cornbread dough
- Salad dressing, either homemade or storebought

- Marinades
- Cocktail sauce for seafood
- Chicken soup
- Beer (see Michelada, page 48)
- Chocolate frosting for a spicy twist!
- Meatloaf or meatballs
- Cranberry sauce

SALSA CHIMICHURRI

MAKES 4½ CUPS

Grill your favorite steak or toast a quesadilla *and serve it with this tangy, hot salsa. Your friends will beg for the recipe.*

About ⅓ cup garlic cloves

20 dried arbol chiles

1½ cups apple cider vinegar

2 teaspoons salt

¼ cup chopped parsley

Approximately 3 cups olive oil

PLACE the garlic, chiles, vinegar, salt, and parsley in the container of a blender and purée well. While the blender is running, add the olive oil in a very slow, thin stream through the feed hole in the lid. The olive oil should be poured directly into the vortex of the mixture. Continue to add the oil until the vortex closes completely, then stop the blender. Pour into a serving dish and serve with roasted meats or quesadillas. The sauce will keep in the refrigerator for about 60 days.

ORIGINS OF CHIMICHURRI

AFTER SPEAKING WITH SEVERAL Argentinean chefs, I have determined that this is not really an authentic Argentinian chimichurri sauce. The original sauce contains parsley and garlic but no chile, and is not made in a blender. Somehow the recipe traveled to South Texas and morphed into this recipe. South Texas and Argentina are both famous for their grilled meats and their gauchos, or cowboys, so it can be assumed that some creative chef understood the appeal this sauce would have in the Wild Horse Desert. Today, this version of the Argentinian chimichurri sauce is served in most of our better restaurants.

SALSA DE CHILE CHIPOTLE AHUMADO
SMOKED CHIPOTLE CHILE SAUCE
MAKES ABOUT 1½ CUPS

Jalapeño chiles were the flavor darlings a few years ago in the United States. Now, it seems that all the food manufacturers are focused on chipotle chiles, or smoked red mature jalapeños. Although there are plenty of canned chipotle chiles on the market, the dried variety seems to have a more intense mesquite flavor, as the chiles are dried slowly over densely smoky mesquite fires.

You can use this sauce as a condiment for tacos, but be creative. Add a couple of tablespoons to mayonnaise, and you have a superb sandwich spread. Add a roasted puréed tomato to the salsa, and serve it over a broiled chicken breast. Combine a spoonful of the salsa with sour cream for a terrific topper for salt-crusted baked potatoes. The salsa's tangy smokiness gives it a complex flavor, yet it's easy to prepare.

2 ounces dried chipotle chiles
1 garlic clove

1 teaspoon salt
1 tablespoon corn oil

FILL a 2-quart saucepan with water and bring to a boil. Add the dried chiles and boil for 15 minutes, until chiles are tender. Drain the chiles and discard the cooking water. Remove stems from chiles, and place chiles in the container of a blender. Add the garlic, salt, and 1 cup of water, and purée until well blended, adding more water if necessary.

HEAT the oil in an 8-inch skillet. Add the chile purée, stir, and simmer to reduce for at least 15 minutes, until the sauce reaches the degree of thickness you desire. Taste and adjust amount of salt, if necessary. The salsa can be stored in your refrigerator for up to one week.

NOTE: The aroma of the chiles can tickle the back of your throat and make you cough a bit. Stand back from the blender or from the path of the steam, as the aroma can sometimes be overpowering.

PICO DE GALLO CON AGUACATE
FRESH VEGETABLE RELISH WITH AVOCADO
MAKES 2½ CUPS

This fresh relish is always on the table at my in-laws' house. Pico de gallo, which means "rooster's beak," is a nice, piquant dash of flavor that pairs well with anything from roasted meats to a late-night supper of eggs.

Pico de gallo is a terrific condiment for tacos, accompanied with lime wedges.

1 cup minced white onion

½ pound ripe tomatoes, seeded and chopped (about 2 medium)

½ avocado, peeled, pitted, and cubed

1 ounce serrano chiles (about 4), stems removed, minced

2 tablespoons minced cilantro

Salt to taste

COMBINE the onion, tomatoes, avocado, chiles, and cilantro in a medium mixing bowl. Taste and add salt. Pico de gallo is best when freshly made. Leftover pico de gallo can be added to soup stock or beans.

❖ **FRESH UNCOOKED TOMATILLOS**, which have a flavor reminiscent of green grapes or green tomatoes, make an excellent substitute for the red tomatoes.

RAJAS DE CHILE SLICES OF CHILE

SERVE 6-8

The spicy green, herbaceous flavor of the poblano chiles pairs beautifully with grilled meats, making this an interesting vegetable side dish. The flavor of the roasted peppers is deep and satisfying—could a side of broccoli compare?

2 pounds fresh poblano chiles (about 8 medium)

¼ cup corn oil

1 medium onion, cut vertically into strips

2 medium carrots, peeled and sliced (about 1½ cups)

Salt and pepper to taste

WASH the chiles well and pat dry. Roast the chiles according to the instructions on page 3, slit them along the side, and clean out according to the instructions on page 3. Slice them into ½-inch-wide strips and set aside.

HEAT the corn oil in a 10-inch skillet. Add the onion and carrots and sauté until the onion is transparent, about 5 minutes. Add the chiles and season with salt and pepper. Sauté for another 10 minutes, then serve immediately.

◆ **RAJAS DE CHILE** are delicious mixed with a melted white cheese, such as queso de Oaxaca, queso de Chihuahua, or Monterey jack. Just place an 8-ounce piece of cheese in a small cast-iron skillet and spoon the rajas over the top of the cheese. Bake in a 350°F oven until the cheese is melted and bubbling. Remove the pan from the oven and stir a bit to combine the melted cheese with the rajas. Serve the cheese with warm corn or flour tortillas, for either an appetizer or a casual dinner.

CHILES RELLENOS FILLED CHILES

SERVES 4-6

My in-laws always have family and guests for lunch on the weekends. In their
house at the ranch, they have a large, brightly lit dining room with a long mesquite dining
table that seats about 16 adults. The kids don't sit down; they scatter around the house, eating
in the breakfast room and kitchen. The conversation is always loud and lively, and the food
is plentiful. The extra-special visitors are always treated to these homemade chiles rellenos—
batter-coated and fried filled chiles that are highly prized here on the border.

Both cheese- and meat-filled chiles are on the menu, although family members tend to
casually yet intentionally serve themselves the cheese-filled chiles before the unsuspecting
guests notice. Cheese-filled chiles rellenos are sinfully rich, while the meat-filled ones have a
more complex flavor.

Platters of the chiles rellenos are passed around the enormous table somewhat franti-
cally at first (as we are starving and perhaps a little greedy). The golden fluff-jacketed chiles
disappear, and the platters are refilled for another round.

2 pounds fresh poblano chiles (8 to 10 medium chiles)	1 garlic clove
Salt and pepper to taste	¼ cup raisins
2 tablespoons corn oil	¼ cup slivered blanched almonds
1 cup chopped onion	5 large eggs, separated
1 pound lean ground beef	Vegetable oil, for frying
	1 cup all-purpose flour

WASH the chiles well. Roast them, slit along the side, and clean out according to
the instructions on page 3. Sprinkle lightly with salt and set aside.

HEAT the corn oil over medium heat in a 12-inch skillet. Add the onion and sauté
until transparent, about 5 minutes. Add the ground beef and cook until well
browned, about 10 minutes. Add the garlic, raisins, and almonds and simmer for

10 minutes. Season with salt and pepper. Remove the skillet from the heat and allow filling to cool slightly. (This can be made up to a day in advance and refrigerated.)

FILL each chile with 2 tablespoons filling and close the opening of the chile using 1 or 2 toothpicks. Place the egg whites in a large mixing bowl. Using an electric mixer, beat the whites until stiff peaks form. In a separate bowl, beat the egg yolks until they are lemon colored. Fold the yolks into the whites.

HEAT the vegetable oil in a 10-inch skillet over medium heat until it reaches 350°F. Pour the flour onto a plate. Preheat the oven to 200°F.

DIP a filled chile into the flour, then into the egg batter, coating well. One at a time, using tongs, place the coated chile into the hot oil and allow to brown on one side for 1 to 2 minutes. Carefully flip onto the other side, and brown for another 1 to 2 minutes. Remove the chile and place in a pan lined with paper toweling. Keep in a warm oven as you make the remaining chiles. Remove toothpicks before serving. Serve immediately.

❖ **TO MAKE CHEESE-FILLED CHILES RELLENOS**, substitute 8 ounces of queso Oaxaca or Monterey Jack cheese for the beef filling. Slice the cheese into 8 to 10 portions, and fill each chile, continuing as directed.

JALAPEÑOS EN ESCABECHE PICKLED JALAPEÑO CHILES

MAKES 2 QUARTS

I think one of the more telling signs of our mixed culture in the Wild Horse Desert is the presence of pickled jalapeños in every home and restaurant. In South Texas, we enthusiastically combine the pickled peppers of Mexico with most of our favorite American dishes. Fried chicken and hamburger stands in Texas serve lots of pickled jalapeños. We have added jalapeño flavor to cheese, gravy, biscuits, cornbread, even lollipops and beer. The rest of the United States is beginning to understand our passion for these hot little slices of pepper—I think we have all seen jalapeño cheese bagels.

You'll need two quart-size canning jars with lids for this recipe.

1½ pounds fresh whole jalapeños

2 carrots, peeled

4 ounces fresh pearl onions

2 bay leaves

2 sprigs fresh thyme

2 sprigs fresh oregano

2 garlic cloves

½ teaspoon black peppercorns

½ teaspoon whole cloves

4 teaspoons canning salt (see Notes)

2 cups olive oil

1½ cups apple cider vinegar

FILL a 3-quart saucepan with water and bring to a boil. Add the jalapeños and blanch for 2 minutes. Using a slotted spoon, remove jalapeños from the boiling water and divide equally between the 2 canning jars.

ADD the carrots to the boiling water and blanch for 2 minutes. Remove from water and divide between the canning jars. Place the pearl onions in the boiling water, blanch for 2 minutes, then remove from water and allow to cool. Cut the root ends from the onions and remove peel. Divide the onions between the jars. To each jar, add 1 bay leaf, 1 sprig each thyme and oregano, 1 garlic clove, ¼ teaspoon each peppercorns and cloves, and 2 teaspoons each canning salt. In a separate bowl, whisk together the oil and vinegar until emulsified. Pour an even amount of the mixture into each jar. Cap the jars and store in the refrigerator for at least one week.

THE JALAPEÑOS will keep indefinitely in the refrigerator, although for best flavor, I would recommend consuming them within 6 months.

◆ **PICKLED JALAPEÑOS AND MUSHROOMS**: Substitute 4 ounces fresh button or crimini mushrooms for an equivalent amount of jalapeños. Mushrooms can be added straight to the jar without blanching.

NOTES: Regular salt contains an anti-caking agent that turns cloudy in vinegar. Although this will not harm the flavor or quality of your jalapeños, the cloudiness could be a little unnerving to guests. Canning salt does not have the anti-caking agent and keeps the vinegar crystal clear.

This is a great recipe if you like to can vegetables. Be sure to follow the instructions from a reliable book on canning.

CHAPTER FOUR

SOUPS AND STEWS

SOUP IS MAGICAL. What other dish is made with water, bones, and odd pieces from the vegetable bin, and renders a rich, comforting meal so completely satisfying that it fills us to our very soul? I love to walk into a kitchen where soup is boiling. With the pot steamy and deeply perfumed with garlic and herbs, on cold days I sometimes think it would be nice to simmer myself as well. Hot and soothing, soup eases the aches and pains of daily life.

It takes time to make a truly glorious soup. I put my stockpot on the stove to boil in the morning, and won't take it off until our evening supper. The mixture simmers for hours. More than the ingredients, perhaps it is the time involved that we are savoring in our bowl as we slowly enjoy each spoonful.

Winter in the Wild Horse Desert is the perfect time for soup. Drizzly and windy, it is not particularly cold, but miserable nonetheless. Winter means hunting season, with crowds of people showing up for hot meals afterwards. The stamping of muddy boots on the back porch, felt cowboy hats damp from the mist, the musty smell of brown canvas jackets, and smiling friends—all come into a warm kitchen, where there usually is the aroma of my grandmother's *pozole* or perhaps my mother's *caldo de res*. Both friends and hot soup are well received.

BASIC SOUP STOCK

MAKES 4-6 QUARTS

To make a good soup, you must first start with a good stock, which is easy to make, provided you have a little time on your hands. Most of the flavor in stock comes from the marrow of the bones, and extracting their full measure of flavor takes several hours. This recipe offers the choice of making beef or chicken stock. The tomato and chile seranno give the stock a Mexican flavor.

FOR CHICKEN
2 pounds chicken necks or backs (see Notes)

FOR BEEF
2 pounds beef marrow bones (see Notes)

2 carrots, peeled and roughly chopped
2 celery stalks, with tops, roughly chopped

1 medium onion, roughly chopped
2 garlic cloves
2 bay leaves
½ teaspoon whole black peppercorns
Salt to taste
2 tablespoons chopped parsley
1 medium tomato, chopped (optional)
1 to 2 fresh serrano chiles (optional)

FILL an 8-quart stockpot with water. Add either the chicken or beef parts and all of the stock ingredients. Bring the pot to a boil and reduce to a gentle simmer. Cover the stockpot partially with a lid. Simmer the stock for at least 4 hours, adding more water as the liquid evaporates somewhat.

REMOVE the stockpot from the heat. Allow the stock to cool, then strain out the bones and vegetables. The stock is ready to use, or it can be stored in the refrigerator for up to one week. Soup stock can also be frozen in sealed freezer-proof containers for future use.

NOTES: There are times when I don't have chicken necks or backs on hand. A whole chicken will work well for this recipe, but once the chicken meat is cooked, after about 40 minutes, remove the chicken from the pot, allow to cool, then remove the meat from the bones. Otherwise, the chicken meat will become mushy and flavorless. Put the cooked chicken aside and return the chicken bones to the pot to simmer for the requisite 4 hours. Later, you can use both the stock and the cooked chicken meat for your soup recipe.

The same goes for beef. If you buy some meaty beef shanks, just boil them for 30 to 40 minutes, until tender, then remove the meat from the stockpot. Allow the beef shanks to cool, then remove the meat, set the meat aside for later use, and return the beef bones to the pot to simmer.

There are some chefs who prefer to first roast the chicken or beef bones in the oven to intensify the flavor of the soup. Using roasted bones to make stock is a classic French technique; however, this extra step is seldom done in the Wild Horse Desert.

TORTILLA SOUP

SERVES 8

Here, the deep red flavor of puréed chile, matched with the crunchy fried tortillas, renders this soup more interesting than your average bowl of chicken noodle. Guests can embellish the soup with the toppings themselves, which makes for a lively and delicious meal.

This soup tastes better when made in advance to give the flavors a chance to blend. Prepare the soup a day ahead and refrigerate it, but do not fry the tortilla strips until you're ready to use them.

2 dried pasilla chiles

2 dried ancho chiles

4 ripe medium tomatoes (or 6 plum tomatoes, about 1 pound), seeded and chopped

1 medium onion, chopped

4 garlic cloves

4 quarts Basic Soup Stock—chicken (see page 112)

Salt to taste

1 tablespoon chopped cilantro

Corn oil for frying

12 to 20 (8-inch) corn tortillas, cut into thin strips

1 (6-ounce) package queso fresco, queso cotija, or feta cheese, crumbled or cut into ½-inch cubes

3 to 4 avocados, peeled, pitted, and sliced

½ head iceberg lettuce, shredded

1 cup Mexican-style sour cream

1 medium onion, finely chopped

PREPARE the chiles for puréeing according to the instructions on page 5. Soften the chiles and remove the stems, seeds, and veins. Place the chiles in the container of a blender container along with tomatoes, onion, garlic, and about 1 cup of the chicken stock (enough to facilitate blending). Purée well.

HEAT the remaining chicken broth in a large stockpot and add the chile purée. Add salt and cilantro. Bring to a boil, then reduce the heat and simmer for about 30 minutes.

POUR about 2 cups of corn oil into a heavy 10-inch skillet and heat over medium heat until very hot, about 350°F on a deep-frying thermometer. Add as many of the tortilla strips as will fit into the skillet (you may have to do this in batches)

and fry until crisp, about 5 minutes. The strips should be slightly golden and not too brown. Drain on paper toweling.

SERVE the soup in individual bowls or in a large tureen. Present the hot tortilla strips, the cheese, avocados, lettuce, Mexican-style sour cream, and onion in separate dishes so that each person can garnish his or her soup as desired.

SOPA DE AJO GARLIC SOUP

SERVES 6

Although this recipe calls for an entire head of garlic, the flavor of Sopa de Ajo *is mild and rich, further enhanced with a fried egg atop the bread. This is an excellent comfort food, with all the curative benefits of chicken soup, garlic, and eggs combined.*

¼ cup olive oil

1 head of garlic, broken apart, cloves peeled and thinly sliced

6 slices dense, crusty French bread, 1 inch thick, preferably day old or stale

6 cups Basic Soup Stock—chicken (see page 112)

Salt to taste

6 eggs

HEAT the olive oil in a 10-inch skillet over medium heat. Add the sliced garlic and sauté for 2 minutes, until the garlic appears somewhat transparent but not browned. Using a slotted spoon, remove the garlic and set aside. Now place the French bread in the oil and toast well, about 2 minutes on each side. Remove from the pan and set aside.

PLACE the sautéed garlic in the container of a blender. Add 1 cup of stock and purée well.

BRING the remaining stock to a boil in a 4-quart saucepan. Lower the heat so that the stock continues to bubble gently. Add the puréed garlic and season with salt. As the stock is bubbling, carefully crack one of the eggs into a small dish and gently slip the egg from the dish into the stock so that the egg will poach, being very careful as to not break the yolk. Poach the egg for at least 1 minute, until the yolk has developed a white coating. (You may choose to cook them longer so that the yolk completely solidifes; however, don't cook them for longer than 3 minutes.) Remove the egg with a slotted spoon and place on top of one of the slices of fried French bread. Continue to poach the remaining eggs, one at a time, until each slice of fried bread has a poached egg on top.

REMOVE the stock from the heat. Ladle the hot soup into individual bowls. Top each bowl with a slice of toasted French bread and a poached egg.

SOPA DE AJO

ORIGINALLY FROM THE IBERIAN PENINSULA, sopa de ajo is found in some of the older family cookbooks from the Wild Horse Desert. The recipe must have been brought by settlers and missionaries from Spain, and handed down through the generations. It makes occasional appearances on local restaurant menus.

Sopa de ajo may have been a predecessor to tortilla soup. Leftover fried tortilla strips took the place of stale white bread fried in olive oil, and puréed chile was added to the mild-flavored chicken broth.

SOPA DE FIDEO STEWED VERMICELLI NOODLES

SERVES 4-6

At a wedding shower one of the guests, my friend Carmen Elvia, mentioned making sopa de fideo, *a type of chicken and noodle soup that we make here in the Wild Horse Desert. Fideo is serious comfort food: every household here has a specific combination of the traditional ingredients. People tend to cleave to their fideo recipes as if they were family members.*

There are two styles of fideo: sopa seca, *a "dry" version that uses less broth and produces more of a noodle dish; and* sopa aguada, *which has more broth and is more like a true soup. Carmen had learned to make a dry version, but her husband's family made it soupier; so when they got married, she had to learn to make it the way he liked it.*

Because there are so many delicious ways to make this dish, I have included several variations in the list of ingredients so you can develop your own household recipe. For example, the simplest, most humble version of this dish is chicken broth, fideo noodles, and potato cubes. For a fancier version, add all of the ingredients suggested below and top with crumbled queso cotija, *chopped fresh cilantro, and slices of ripe avocado. Personally, I like the drier version, with potatoes, as that is the way my grandmother made sopa de fideo.*

3 tablespoons corn oil

1 medium onion, chopped

1 (2-ounce) package fideo (vermicelli noodles; see Note)

About 4 cups Basic Soup Stock—chicken (see page 112)

1 ripe medium tomato, peeled, seeded, and chopped

1 garlic clove, minced

Salt and pepper to taste

1 waxy white potato, peeled and cut into ½-inch cubes (optional)

1 fresh serrano chile (optional)

Leftover cooked chicken or beef (optional)

HEAT the corn oil in a 4-quart saucepan over medium heat. Add the onion and fideo, and brown until the fideo is golden and the onion is translucent, about 5 minutes. Add the remaining ingredients. Allow the soup to simmer for about 30 minutes. (If adding potato, make sure it has cooked enough to easily be pierced with a fork.) Serve hot.

◆ **FOR A DRIER FIDEO**, simply reduce the amount of chicken stock to about 2½ cups, adding ½ cup more now and then to prevent the fideo from reducing to the point of scorching. For a soupier fideo, add more stock.

NOTE: Fideo, or vermicelli noodles, are sold in two forms: in short thin threads, or in long threads wrapped into bird's nest form. If you purchase the longer noodles, make sure you break them up into smaller threads while they are still dry and uncooked, for easier cooking and eating.

CHILE CON CARNE CHILI WITH MEAT

SERVES 12

A Texas classic, this is not found in Mexico. Hearty and spicy, chili is quintessential ranch fare. For best results, make it a day ahead to let the flavors blend. If you want a spicier chili, just add a few of the chile seeds to the mixture. You can also substitute ground venison for the beef, which is a winter favorite in our household.

4 ounces dried chipotle chiles (4 to 6)

4 ounces dried ancho chiles (about 4)

1 pound plum tomatoes, peeled and seeded (or a 15-ounce can peeled tomatoes, drained)

Salt

1 pound ground pork

4 pounds ground beef or ground venison

1 medium onion, chopped

Pepper

PREPARE the chiles for puréeing according to instructions on page 5. Place the prepared chiles in the container of a blender or food processor and add the tomatoes and 1 cup water. Purée well and add salt to taste.

BROWN the ground pork, ground beef, and onion in a Dutch oven or heavy pot over medium heat for about 20 minutes. Add the chile purée. Season with salt and pepper. Simmer for about 20 minutes over medium heat. Serve ladled into soup bowls.

NOTE: Although the chili can be served and eaten immediately, it reaches its fullest flavor when made a day in advance.

CHILE CON CARNE

CHILE CON CARNE, also known as chili, is a legendary dish from Texas that was developed along the hunting and cattle trails. *Carne seca,* or dried meat (see page 168), was prepared by the indigenous tribes and carried in saddlebags for sustenance during travels. The chile paste added to the dried meat serves two purposes: first, chile is a natural antiseptic and so it helped preserve the meat; second, the strong flavor of the chile masked any rotten or unpleasant flavors the meat might have acquired. Once the traveler made camp for the night, he would reconstitute some of the dried mixture in a little hot water, and *voilà*, a hot meal of chili.

Through the years, the technique for making chili transferred from the indigenous tribes to the European settlers, namely, cattle ranchers. Ranchers and cowboys adopted chili as their staple trail dish, as it was convenient to make on the long drives. As the cattle drives moved across Texas to their northern markets, the cowhands spread the popularity of this dish across the state.

During the turn of the century, San Antonio was the stage for chili appreciation. Every night around the Alamo, sawhorses topped with boards became makeshift dining tables. By the dim smoky light of kerosene lamps, hungry folks were served heaping bowls of steaming chili. Each family that ran a chili booth would dress its women in colorful, alluring costumes to attract customers. These women were known as the "Chili Queens." The competition was fierce. With the increase in urban life, a focus on health standards increased. The Alamo's chili stands met with opposition from city leaders, and they were eventually shut down.

Beans or no beans? There is much debate as to whether true chile con carne contains beans. My opinion is that the most authentic chili does not: beans would have been unavailable to the lone traveler carrying spiced dried meat in a saddle bag. I do think the Chili Queens would have used beans to reduce their costs and increase their profits, as beans are cheaper than meat.

However, I adore the sweet flavor and thick, silky body that the starch from beans adds to chile con carne, so I usually add them. If you wish, you can add 2 cups of cooked pinto beans to the recipe above, along with the tomatoes and chile purée.

CALDILLO DE CARNE SECA DRIED BEEF SOUP

SERVES 4-6

If my grandfather was sick, he would leave the ranch only to see Dr. Guerra, the family doctor. A trusted family friend, Dr. Guerra cared for patients all over South Texas. Folks traveled hours from their ranchitos to visit his clinic, and he never turned anyone away. Dr. Guerra always offered a grin, a joke, and deep concern for those he cared for. Over the years, he delivered 35,000 children into this world.

Dr. Guerra's wife Bertha shared this recipe for caldillo *with me. It is one of the older dishes from the Wild Horse Desert. The carne seca is pleasantly chewy and salty, and combined with the broth and vegetables, makes a hearty winter meal.*

2 cups carne seca (see page 168)

5 to 6 tablespoons corn oil

1 large potato, peeled and cubed

2 tablespoons white rice

¼ green bell pepper, chopped

½ medium onion, chopped

1 ripe medium tomato, diced

1 garlic clove, minced

Pinch ground cumin

Salt and pepper to taste

1 (16-ounce) can chickpeas, drained

SHRED the carne seca into fine threads. In a large skillet or Dutch oven, heat 3 tablespoons corn oil over medium heat, add the carne seca and brown, stirring and turning the meat to prevent it from burning. After about 3 minutes, the carne seca should be crisp. Remove from pan.

ADD 2 or 3 tablespoons corn oil to skillet, and add the potato, rice, green pepper, and onion. Continue to brown and stir the ingredients until the rice looks opaque, about 3 minutes. Return the carne seca to the skillet and add the tomato, garlic, cumin, salt, pepper, and 4 cups water. Bring to a simmer over medium heat, and cook until the potatoes are tender and the rice is cooked, about 25 minutes, adding more water if necessary (up to 4 cups). Right before serving, add the chickpeas. Serve hot.

CALDILLO

MAKING CALDILLO was a great way for early ranch settlers to break the monotony of a diet that depended on preserved beef. When a calf was slaughtered, the family could consume only a small portion of the hundreds of pounds of fresh meat. The rest would be dried and stored for future use. Texas-style chili began as a mere dried beef soup flavored with just a little chile.

POZOLE PORK AND HOMINY STEW

SERVES 12

Pozole *is a pork and chicken broth* that contains pieces of chicken and kernels of hominy (also known as pozole). It is served with a dazzling array of garnishes, so that each person can embellish the dish to his or her liking. Beer and hot corn tortillas are the requisite accompaniments.

Don't be shocked by the ingredients of chicken necks and pig's feet—they make superior stock. Chicken necks and pig's feet may not be on your regular weekly grocery list, but I assure you they are fairly common at your local butcher shop. Both contribute rich flavor and thick texture to the broth and are quite inexpensive. I don't recommend smoked ham hocks as a substitute for the fresh pig's feet, as their flavor is overpowering and nontraditional.

2 chicken breasts on the bone

1 pound chicken necks or backs

1 pound pig's feet

1 celery stalk

1 medium onion

2 carrots

1 head garlic

½ teaspoon whole black peppercorns

2 sprigs thyme

2 tablespoons chopped parsley

1 pound lean pork, cut into 1-inch cubes

1 (28-ounce) can hominy, drained

1 bunch radishes, washed and sliced

½ head lettuce, shredded

1 medium onion, finely chopped

Any salsa recipe (pages 94–103), or Tabasco

6 limes, cut into wedges

FILL a 6-quart stockpot with water and add the chicken breasts, necks or backs, pig's feet, celery, onion, carrots, garlic head, peppercorns, thyme, and parsley. Bring the pot to a boil, then lower the heat and cook at a gentle simmer, partially covered with a lid. After 45 minutes, remove the chicken breasts from the pot and reserve. Continue to simmer for 2 more hours. Remove pot from heat and allow to cool.

STRAIN the stock, removing and discarding all the bones and vegetables. Return the stock to the pot, skim off any unwanted fat, and bring to a gentle simmer again.

Add the pork and allow to cook in the stock for at least 30 minutes, until tender. Meanwhile, remove the meat from the chicken breasts and cut into bite-size pieces. Discard the bones and skin.

ADD the chicken and the drained hominy. Simmer for 5 more minutes. Serve the pozole in soup bowls, offering the radishes, lettuce, onion, salsa, and lime wedges on the side.

POZOLE

THE STATE OF JALISCO in Mexico is famous for its pozole, and this recipe is reminiscent of the style of pozole prepared in that state. And although we enjoy pozole in the Wild Horse Desert, the dish is actually more popular in New Mexico than in Texas, perhaps because people from Jalisco migrated to that state or perhaps because hot pozole hits the spot during cold New Mexico winters. Nevertheless, pozole is still the perfect dish to serve on misty, chilly winter nights in the Wild Horse Desert.

BLACK BEAN SOUP WITH EPAZOTE AND SHERRY

SERVES 12

The earthy flavor of black beans combines beautifully with the green, almost mint-like flavor of the epazote. *Pass the sherry at the table so each guest can add the perfect amount.*

You can substitute a leftover ham bone for the ham hocks. Holiday spiral sliced hams are quickly devoured in our household, leaving behind a flavor-packed meaty bone, which is perfect for this recipe.

1 pound smoked ham hocks

1 pound dried black beans, picked over and washed

2 carrots

2 ripe medium tomatoes, cored

1 head of garlic, cloves separated and peeled

1 medium onion

2 bay leaves

1 ounce epazote (about a handful)

Salt and pepper to taste

Mexican-style sour cream or crème fraîche

Dry sherry

FILL a 6-quart stockpot with water. Add the ham hocks, beans, carrots, tomatoes, garlic, onion, bay leaves, and epazote. Bring the soup to a boil, reduce the heat, and simmer for 2 to 3 hours, partially covered, until the beans are tender, adding up to 4 cups of water if the liquid in the pot ever appears less than half full. When the beans are well cooked and very tender, add salt and pepper (depending on the ham hocks' salt content, the soup may not need any more salt). Remove from heat and let cool.

REMOVE bay leaves and discard. Remove ham hocks. Chop and reserve the meat; discard the skin and bones.

PURÉE the soup until it is smooth using a blender, immersion blender, or food processor. Reheat the soup to serve, adding the reserved meat. Top each bowl with a drizzle of sour cream. Pass around a small pitcher of sherry so your guests can add a bit to their dishes.

CREMA DE CHILE POBLANO
CREAM OF POBLANO CHILE SOUP
SERVES 4-6

Elegant and easy, this is a great cream soup that can be enjoyed as a sauce as well. For example, it is superb over grilled chicken breast or with savory seafood crepes. Chile poblano is a common ingredient in the Wild Horse Desert, and its familiar flavor is well used in this elegant dish. Remember, though, that different crops of chiles have differing levels of heat. The soup may be spicy or not, depending on the quality of poblano you purchase. Make the soup a day in advance to give it time to develop full flavor.

1½ pounds fresh poblano chiles (about 6)

4 tablespoons unsalted butter

1 medium onion, chopped

2 cups heavy cream

2 cups Basic Soup Stock—chicken (see page 112)

Salt to taste

½ teaspoon white pepper

¼ cup tequila (optional)

PREPARE chiles for puréeing according to the instructions on page 5. Cut the chiles into strips.

MELT the butter in a 4-quart saucepan over medium heat. Add the onion and sauté until translucent. Add the chiles and continue to sauté for about 5 minutes, stirring occasionally, until the onion becomes translucent. Remove from the heat.

FILL the container of a blender with the sautéed chiles and onion. Add the cream and purée until very smooth. Return the purée to the saucepan, and add the chicken stock, salt, and white pepper. Bring the mixture to a simmer and then add the tequila, if using. Simmer for at least 15 minutes so that the flavors blend and the alcohol in the tequila evaporates, stirring occasionally so the soup does not scorch. Serve warm.

CILANTRO SOUP

SERVES 8

In South Texas, cilantro, with its piquant yet pleasing flavor, seems to be the favorite fresh herb, and people are constantly asking me for recipes that use it. My friend Diane told me of a creamy cilantro soup she enjoyed while in Fredericksburg, Texas, just north of San Antonio, so I decided I would try to create a recipe that captures cilantro's herbaceous allure.

My husband suggested that I use his recipe for squash soup as a base. Ridiculously easy, he developed this soup while cooking for hoards of hungry hunters at a camp. And it turned out to be a perfect pairing—the fresh peppery flavor of the cilantro with the buttery depth of the squash. And as an added bonus, the soup is incredibly low in calories. Diane loved it.

By adding the cilantro at the last minute, the bright green flavor is preserved. Once the cilantro is cooked, a bit of its herbal pungency is diminished. A flavorful chicken stock is a must for this recipe.

2 quarts Basic Soup Stock—chicken (see page 112)
2 pounds tatuma squash or zucchini, washed and cut into chunks
Salt and pepper to taste
4 ounces cilantro, chopped

BRING the chicken stock to a boil in a 4-quart saucepan. Add the squash and simmer for 10 minutes, until tender. Remove from the heat, and allow to cool.

PURÉE the squash with the stock using a food processor, blender, or immersion blender until it is very smooth. Return the purée to the saucepan.

HEAT the soup, stir in the cilantro, and serve at once.

TATUMA

TATUMA (OR TATUME) SQUASH, known locally in the Wild Horse Desert as *calabacita*, or "little squash," is an oval or egg-shaped squash similar to a zucchini. Its outer skin is light green and mottled, and there is sweet, cream-colored flesh and large soft seeds inside. Look for smaller squash, as they are more tender. Substitute any tender, green, globe-shaped summer squash or zucchini squash if you cannot find tatuma squash in your market.

CHAPTER FIVE

RICE AND BEANS

EVERY DAY when I returned from school, the aroma of *frijoles* cooking would greet me as I opened the door. Whether I went straight home or to one of my grandparents' houses, the gentle scent of pork and garlic would reach me even before anyone had a chance to say hello. Beans cooking on the stove were the unspoken signal that someone was home, waiting for me to arrive.

Later, as dinnertime approached, I would hear the rice frying in the pan amid the other kitchen noises. Then the bustle of the kitchen would suddenly cease the moment the broth was added—the roaring sizzle that made my heart jump, and even though I might be in another room, I would close my eyes until I heard the lid secured over the rice.

Rice and beans are so common in our lives on the Mexican border that we scarcely pay attention to them. But next to the availability of water, a supply of rice and beans in the pantry is what kept the early settlers alive. Before they had dried staples like rice and beans, the indigenous tribes subsisted mainly on game and the corn and beans that they grew or traded for. Spanish *conquistadores* and missionaries brought rice from Asia to be planted in the New World and also expanded the cultivation of beans. My great great grandfather wrote to his Irish cousins in 1903 that "We have beans, brown color, 6 pence a peck, they are substetud [*sic*] for potatoes, all over Mexico. When well cooked they are very fine. . . ."

Beverages and baby food were made with rice, and candy was made from beans during times when no other ingredients were available. Like an ever-present family member, they appear at every meal, on every plate.

Plentiful and inexpensive, rice and beans are still the foundation of Mexican border cuisine. Rice is usually prepared as a *sopa de arroz,* a fluffy, garlicky side dish of rice that accompanies almost every meal. Pinto beans, the regional bean of preference here in the borderlands of the Wild Horse Desert, are most commonly seen as a side dish, served in small bowls, heavily perfumed with garlic and onions, or served mashed and sautéed, known as *refritos,* or refried beans.

SOPA DE ARROZ TRADITIONAL MEXICAN RICE

SERVES 6-8

Rice was brought to the Americas by the Spanish conquistadores. However, the saffron that was used to color rice dishes in Spain was unavailable in the New World, so the readily available tomatoes were substituted to give the rice its familiar golden hue. Although tomato purée doesn't completely achieve the color or aroma of saffron, Mexican rice is a delicious side dish unto itself, served at almost every meal in Mexican homes.

2 tablespoons corn oil

½ medium onion, minced

2 cups white rice

1 garlic clove

1 medium tomato, peeled, seeded, and chopped

4 cups Basic Soup Stock—chicken (see page 112) or water

Salt and pepper to taste

Pinch ground cumin (optional)

HEAT the oil in a 12-inch skillet with a tight-fitting lid over medium heat. Add the onion and sauté for 2 to 3 minutes, then add the rice. Sauté the rice until it turns opaque and the onion is translucent, 5 to 7 minutes.

PLACE the garlic, tomato, and 1 cup of stock in the container of a blender and purée well. Add the tomato purée carefully to the rice (pan will steam and sizzle profusely). Season with salt and pepper; add cumin, if desired, and return the pan to a gentle simmer. Cover and simmer gently for 25 minutes. Turn off the heat, and leave the pan covered. When ready to serve, remove the lid, fluff the rice a bit with a spoon, then transfer to a covered serving dish.

COOKING MEXICAN RICE

ONE ANXIETY SHARED BY ALMOST ALL COOKS is a fear of their rice turning out poorly. Early in my cooking career, my rice was appalling. My husband, however, in his bachelor days, lived on oriental packaged noodle soups and *sopa de arroz,* so he was a rice expert. When we first got married, he taught me how to cook rice, and his method was quite simple. Here are the basic tenets of perfect rice:

- Use a shallow pan with a tight-fitting lid.

- Always use a 2:1 water to rice ratio; for 1 cup of rice, use 2 cups of water; for 2 cups of rice, use 4 cups of water; and so on.

- Simmer your rice over low heat for 25 minutes.

- Do not peek under the lid as the rice is cooking. Steam is needed to make fluffy rice, and releasing it will give you poor results. I can usually tell if the contents are gently simmering simply by touching the handle of the lid and feeling for a slight vibration.

You can make plain white rice with this method by omitting all the flavorings. Many of my students now use this method, with consistent results.

ARROZ ACILANTRADO CILANTRO RICE

SERVES 8

Guests love the color of this green-tinted rice and its fresh flavor. It's excellent with roasted chicken.

2 tablespoons corn oil

½ cup minced onion

2 cups white rice

1 bunch cilantro (about 2 ounces)

1 garlic clove

4 cups Basic Soup Stock—chicken (see page 112) or water

Salt and pepper to taste

HEAT the oil in a 12-inch sauté pan with a tight-fitting lid over medium heat. Add the onion, and sauté for 2 to 3 minutes, then add the rice. Sauté the rice until it turns opaque and the onion is translucent, 5 to 7 minutes.

PLACE the cilantro, garlic, and 1 cup of the stock in the container of a blender, and purée well. Add the cilantro purée carefully to the rice (pan will steam and sizzle profusely). Season with salt and pepper and return the pan to a gentle simmer. Cover and gently simmer for 25 minutes. Do not lift the lid while cooking. Turn off the heat, and leave the pan covered. When ready to serve, remove the lid, fluff the rice a bit with a spoon, then transfer to a covered serving dish.

FLAVORFUL FAT

I ALWAYS HAVE HOMEMADE CHICKEN STOCK on hand that I use for making rice. When I make the stock, I save the fat that congeals on the surface to use in my rice recipes, substituting it for the corn oil. It adds yet another dimension of flavor.

ARROZ CON AZAFRÁN Y CHICHAROS

RICE WITH TURMERIC ROOT AND PEAS

SERVES 8

In addition to using puréed tomatoes to add rich color and flavor to their rice dishes, Mexicans employ turmeric root as a substitute for saffron. In fact, saffron and turmeric share the same Mexican name, asafrán. *Turmeric gives the rice a gentle flavor and a pretty yellow color, which provides a sharp contrast when served next to a dark red Asado de Puerco (see page 184).*

2 tablespoons corn oil

1 small onion, chopped

2 cups white rice

1-inch piece of turmeric root, peeled, or 1 teaspoon ground turmeric

4 cups Basic Soup Stock—chicken (see page 112) or water

1 garlic clove, minced

Salt and pepper to taste

½ cup frozen green peas

HEAT the oil in a 4-quart saucepan or Dutch oven over medium heat. Add the onion and sauté for 2 to 3 minutes. Add the rice and sauté until the rice becomes opaque and the onion is translucent, about 5 minutes.

COMBINE the turmeric with 1 cup of the stock in a blender and purée. Pass through a mesh strainer to strain out the fibrous remains of the turmeric and reserve the liquid. Add the remaining turmeric liquid to the rice along with the remaining stock. Add the garlic, and season with salt and pepper. Once the rice begins to simmer, add the peas and cover. Turn down to a low heat and simmer for 25 minutes. Do not lift the lid while cooking. Turn off the heat, and leave the pan covered. When ready to serve, remove the lid, fluff the rice a bit with a spoon, then transfer to a covered serving dish.

FRIJOLES CON MANITAS DE PUERCO
BEANS WITH PIG'S FEET
SERVES 12

I always have cooked beans on hand and can't imagine a meal without them. These beans are great as a side dish or as the base for tostadas, chalupas, or enfrijoladas. And while they're wonderful on their own—velvety and rich in pork flavor—I especially like frijoles con manitas de puerco when converted to refritos, or refried beans (see following recipe). This infusion of pork flavor into the beans makes a hearty filling for tacos or a sauce for enfrijoladas. After traveling, my father-in-law always says he is glad to return to his frijolitos normalitos, or the regular beans served at his table.

This recipe works well with any type of dried bean. Try black beans, flor de mayo beans, or frijoles peruanos (Peruvian beans) for a change. Once cooled, any extra beans can be frozen for future use, which is a huge time-saver.

1 pound dried pinto beans, picked over and washed

1 medium onion, chopped

1 large tomato, diced

2 garlic cloves

1 bunch cilantro, chopped (about 1 ounce)

4 ounces fresh or frozen pig's feet

Salt and pepper to taste

2 serrano chiles (optional)

FILL a 6-quart stockpot with water and add all of the ingredients, seasoning with salt and pepper. Bring to a boil, then reduce the heat and simmer, partially covered, for approximately 3 hours, until the beans are tender.

◆ **FRIJOLES CON CUERITOS (BEANS WITH FRESH PORK RINDS):** If you are doubtful, try fresh pork rinds just once. Their nutty, rich flavor is delicious. Follow the above recipe, however, and substitute 4 ounces of fresh or frozen (they will thaw as they cook) pork belly skin for the pig's feet. Cut the pork skin into 2-inch squares before adding them to the beans. (Scissors are an excellent way to cut the pork bellies, as they can be a bit leathery when uncooked.)

(continued)

FRIJOLES CON MANITAS DE PUERCO, CON'T.

- **FRIJOLES A LA CHARRA (COWBOY BEANS):** Substitute salt pork, ham, bacon, or sausage for the pork skin or pig's feet. Salt pork was always on hand in the cow camps, and they prepared plenty of beans, thus the recipe and name.

- **VEGETARIAN BEANS:** Just skip the meat for a beautiful and authentic batch of vegetarian beans.

TEQUESQUITE

TO MAKE the skin of the beans tender, old ranch cooks would add to their pots a bit of *tequesquite* (*saleratus,* in English), an effervescent clay found in local lake beds, that was exposed as the water receded during the dry seasons. The chunks of tequesquite were either dissolved in water or ground into a fine powder. The result looks a lot like ashen gray dirt, with the same flavor. However, tequesquite was indispensable in early border kitchens, used as a leavener (see Gaznates, page 238) and as a poor man's salt substitute. Tequesquite was also used when boiling cactus to reduce the gooey liquid that exudes. And vegetables retained their brilliant color when a pinch of tequesquite was added to the water, similar to the effect of bicarbonate of soda. In fact, tequesquite is a mineral salt containing bicarbonate of soda, sodium chloride, and sodium nitrate, the proportions of which vary depending on the lake bed where the tequesquite is excavated.

FREEZING BEANS

BECAUSE BEANS TAKE A LONG TIME to cook, they are traditionally made in large batches. Well-cooled leftover beans can be frozen in small portions. A caution: Don't ever put warm or hot beans directly into your freezer. The outer layer of beans will freeze before the cen-ter portion can cool, and so the temperature in the middle will be conducive to spoilage. I usu-ally cool the beans for an hour, then store them in the refrigerator overnight before dividing them into smaller containers for freezing.

REFRITOS REFRIED BEANS

THE TERM REFRIED BEANS is a misnomer be-cause these beans are fried only once. The pre-fix re in Spanish implies that something has been done well or completely, so refrito actually means "completely fried." Refritos are made with any type of beans that have been cooked until soft. Frijoles con Manitas de Puerco (see page 137), Frijoles Borrachos (see page 140), and any of the other bean recipes in this chapter are perfectly suited for a tasty batch of refritos.

You will need cooked frijoles in order to make refritos, about ½ cup per person. Heat a couple of tablespoons of corn oil in a medium skillet over medium heat. Once it is hot, add the beans. As they simmer, use a potato masher to mash the beans, adding some bean cooking liquid or water if they seem dry. Simmer the refritos for about 10 minutes, stirring and scrap-ing the bottom of the pan so they do not scorch.

"A soupbone was used not once but many times, and was even passed from one poor family to another to boil with beans."

PAUL HORGAN, *GREAT RIVER*

FRIJOLES BORRACHOS DRUNKEN BEANS

SERVES 12

Beer and beans may sound like an unlikely combination, but the yeasty aroma released as the beer boils with the bacon, chiles, and onions will convince you. Of course, the folks who live in northern Mexico and South Texas are very fond of their beer, an ingredient that marks this bean recipe as a signature norteño dish. A restaurant standard, these beans pair perfectly with Enchiladas Norteñas (see page 65) to make the quintessential Tex-Mex meal.

1 pound dried pinto beans, picked over and washed

1 medium onion, chopped

1 pound bacon or salt pork, chopped

2 serrano chiles, chopped

1 bunch cilantro, chopped (about 1 ounce)

1 large tomato, diced

3 garlic cloves

Salt and pepper to taste

1 (12-ounce) can beer

FILL a 6-quart stockpot with water and add all ingredients. Bring to a boil, cover with the lid slightly ajar to allow for steam to escape, and simmer for 3 hours, until the beans are tender.

◆ **FOR EXTRA FLAVORFUL REFRITOS**, sauté 2 to 3 tablespoons of leftover pico de gallo (see page 104) in the oil for a minute or two before adding the beans. Once the beans are added and heated through, mash as you would regular refritos.

NOTE: I have found that *borracho* beans do not keep in the refrigerator as well as other beans, which I attribute to the yeast in the beer. That's all the more reason to save this bean recipe for when you invite a hungry crowd to dinner. Or, as this is a large recipe, freeze the leftovers within 48 hours of cooking the beans.

DRUNKEN FOOD

AROUND MEXICO CITY, many taco stands serve *salsa borracha,* or "drunken sauce." These sauces are flavored with *pulque,* a fermented alcoholic beverage made from the agave plant. As "drunken" dishes crawled north toward the border and away from the source of pulque, beer became the ingredient of necessity.

I don't know for sure where *frijoles borrachos* originated, I believe the dish drew inspiration from the "drunken sauces" of Mexico City. Possibly, the beans were invented in the same taco stands as the salsas. Nonetheless, frijoles borrachos are hugely popular on the border.

CHAPTER SIX

BEEF

THE HISTORY OF BEEF in Texas is the history of Texas itself. Christopher Columbus is credited with bringing the first horses and cattle to the New World. Canvas slings, suspended from either the riggings or the rafters, were used to support the animals as they were transported. The sling fit under the animal's belly like a wide belt and prevented it from moving or falling overboard during the rough trip across the Atlantic.

The Spanish monarchy wished to claim as much territory in the New World as possible, so missions were established to bring Christianity to the natives and to maintain a physical presence in the land. The few cattle that were brought by ship to the New World multiplied under the care of missionary priests, initiating the cattle industry in Texas. In this way, Spanish priests were the original "cowboys" of Texas, with the local Native American tribesmen drafted as assistant herdsmen. The herds grew tremendously, though the exact number of head is not known, as the priests were often reluctant to confess to the accumulation of wealth.

The presence of cattle and horses changed the appearance of the land. What had formerly been large stretches of empty desert plains now developed clumps of cactus and motts of mesquite trees. Livestock relish the sugary seed pods of the mesquite and will eat succulent cactus as well if the thorns are removed. As live-stock herds wandered the plains, they "distributed" seeds along the trail.

The territory north of the Rio Grande became known as the Wild Horse Desert because of the thousands of wild horses and cattle that roamed that area. There are three basic reasons for the formation of the wild herds of cattle and horses:

1. **NO FENCES**. For centuries, there were no fences, and animals escaped from their vast established herds and banded together.

2. **NATIVE ATTACKS**. Many of the native tribes that lived along the banks of the Rio Grande were fierce warriors. Missionaries and settlers who pushed toward the river were seen as intruders, and the tribes defended their territory by killing them. The livestock that the settlers brought with them were abandoned and scattered.

3. **THE BATTLE FOR TEXAS INDEPENDENCE FROM MEXICO**. Before Texas became one of the United States, it was considered to be part of Mexico. The present-day boundaries of Mexico and Texas were established through a declaration of independence and war. After Texas's southern boundary was declared to be the Rio Grande, the Mexican government commanded all of its citizens living north of the river to abandon their homesteads. In doing so, herds of live-stock were abandoned as well. Later, the independent Republic of Texas was annexed by the United States as its twenty-eighth state.

Many perceived the great herds of wild, unclaimed livestock as an untapped source of wealth. Horses were rounded up and sold to the army. The cattle were driven to Midwestern markets, fetching higher prices. In some instances, the animals' only value was perceived to be their hide and, as there was no refrigerated transportation, herds were rounded up, slaughtered, and the meat left behind.

As more settlers from the United States came to the area, fencing property became necessary. As the dominance of the Spanish missions faded, cattle raising shifted to private ranching companies. Landowners began to fence the borders of their ranches, surreptitiously including the land of adjacent landowners at times. Wild cattle and mustang herds were contained within the boundaries of the fenced ranches. The vast open desert ceased to exist, and the wild herds vanished.

"In the country between Laredo and Corpus Christi we encountered countless droves of mustangs. . . . In many places cattle were numerous. These were the increase of the animals abandoned by Mexicans when they were ordered (by the Mexican Government) to evacuate the country between the Nueces and Rio Grande. . . ."
RIP FORD, MEMOIRS CIRCA 1849 (PUBLISHED AS *RIP FORD'S TEXAS*, 1963)

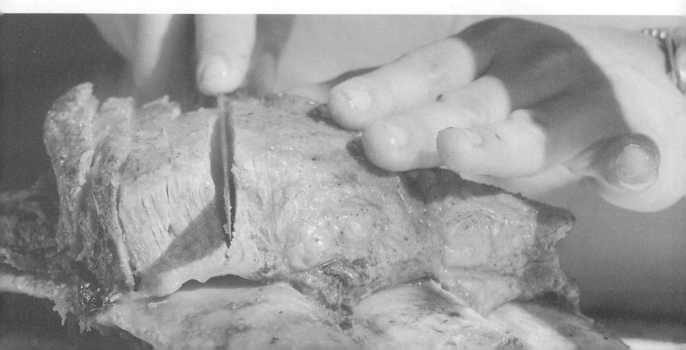

PICADILLO SIMPLE GROUND BEEF HASH
SERVES 8

Early in my marriage, my husband and I agreed that we both passionately hated pica-dillo, *a traditional ground beef hash. It was an unexplainable prejudice that we had both felt since childhood. I promised him I would never make it, and for a long time, I didn't. Then we had children, and dinners had to be assembled quickly. A package of hamburger meat appeared from the depths of the freezer, and grudgingly I made a batch of picadillo, mainly because I knew the baby could easily eat the ground meat. My husband and I were surprised how good it was, and that it was even more delicious the next day. Why did we change our minds about picadillo, after a lifetime of refusing to eat it?*

After a bit of talking, it turns out that in both of our households, picadillo was what was left with the babysitter when our parents went out for a night on the town. It was easy to cook, not too spicy, and as a package of ground meat was always on hand, it could be made at the last minute. So, we finally enjoy picadillo, especially on those nights when we sneak out to the movies.

2 pounds lean ground beef (see Note)	2 medium tomatoes, quartered
1 onion, finely chopped (about 1 cup)	1 cup diced carrots
1 garlic clove, peeled and minced	1 potato, diced (about 1 cup)
Salt and pepper to taste	¾ cup fresh or frozen peas

BROWN the beef and onion in a 12-inch covered skillet over medium heat until meat is cooked through, about 10 minutes. Add the garlic, salt and pepper. The meat should release a good amount of liquid—if your meat is extremely lean and gives off no liquid, add 1 cup of water.

MAKE a fresh tomato purée by blending the tomatoes with 2 cups of water in a blender. Add the tomato purée to the pan, cover, and simmer over low heat for

20 minutes. Add the carrots and potato. Cover and simmer until the potato is cooked, about 15 minutes. Add the peas during the last 5 minutes of cooking. Transfer the picadillo to a serving bowl and serve immediately.

NOTE: You can start browning the meat even if it is frozen. Place the frozen block straight into the covered skillet. Check the meat every 5 minutes, and scrape up the meat that has browned, exposing the frozen parts. It should take about 15 minutes to thaw. Add the onion when the majority of the meat is thawed.

PICADILLO

PICADILLO IS NOT REALLY a recipe unto itself, but a variation of a *guisado,* a traditional Mexican stew. *Picar* means "to mince," so this is a minced guisado. Similarly, as *cortar* means "to cut or slice," so *cortadillo* (see page 163) is a sliced guisado.

FAJITAS GRILLED SKIRT STEAK

SERVES 4

Even though there are quite a few fancy recipes for fajita *marinades and sauces, the classic (and my favorite) way to prepare this meat is simply to grill it over a mesquite fire (see "Mesquite Smoke and Fire," page 150), as a mesquite fire imparts a truly noble flavor to this humble cut. I like to serve fajita steaks unadorned, accompanied by a flavorful homemade salsa and warm, handmade corn tortillas.*

I am quite spoiled by the abundance of mesquite trees here in the Wild Horse Desert, but of course most people do not have a mesquite forest in their backyard. Gas and charcoal grills also work very well, or in a pinch you could broil or pan-fry them. However, in my neck of the woods, fajitas are the classic outdoor barbecue choice.

Two pounds of meat should be enough to feed four people. Serve with warm tortillas and salsa.

One 2-pound skirt or hanger steak
Salt and pepper
Pico de gallo (page 104) or any salsa recipe
8 to 12 corn tortillas

PREHEAT a gas grill on low or start a charcoal or mesquite fire (see "Mesquite Smoke and Fire," page 150) until you achieve a low, steady heat, 20 to 25 minutes. If you are broiling, preheat the broiler. If you are pan-grilling, add a little corn oil to a cast-iron skillet or ridged stovetop griddle and preheat over medium heat.

SEASON the steak on both sides with salt and pepper. If you are pan-grilling, you may have to cut the steak in half or into quarters (across the grain) to make it fit in the pan, and cook these smaller portions in batches.

GRILL, broil, or pan-grill the steak for 5 to 10 minutes on each side. The cooking time will depend on the thickness of the meat. Cook to your desired degree of doneness, checking the temperature with a meat thermometer (see "Meat

Doneness," page 153) and remember that the meat will continue to cook after it is removed from heat.

ALLOW the fajitas to rest for 10 to 20 minutes. While the fajitas are resting, warm the tortillas on the grill or in a 200°F oven. Slice the fajitas across the grain into ½-inch strips and serve immediately with pico de gallo or salsa, and warm tortillas.

TRUE FAJITAS

THE TERM "FAJITA" does not refer to a cooking style but rather to a cut of meat. The word *faja* means "a sash," or "girdle-like band," and thus *fajita* means a "little girdle." The name has come to apply to the band of muscle located on the belly of the cow, as it looks and acts like a girdle. Chicken and fish do not have the anatomy that necessitates a fajita; therefore, chicken, shrimp, and fish fajitas are misnomers.

There are two types of fajitas, the outside and the inside fajita. The outside fajita is the diaphragm muscle, and is located outside of the cow's rib. Known in English as a skirt steak, it has a thick outer membrane on both sides. This membrane, called the skin, is usually peeled off before serving. Removing the skin can be a bit messy and inconvenient, so most butchers trim this membrane. The meat is then sold as skinless fajitas. When you buy skirt steak, this is the cut of meat you'll generally receive.

The inside fajita is located inside the cow's ribs. The membrane is usually removed before it is sold. In my opinion, the inside fajita has a better flavor than the outside fajita, and some grillers consider it to be the true fajita.

Outside fajitas are positioned vertically on the outer belly of a carcass, while the inside fajita is positioned horizontally inside the ribs. When a carcass is divided, there will be two outside fajita portions, but the inside fajita, as it stretches across the belly, is kept intact at the time of slaughter. It hangs in a long strip from the carcass, and for that reason it is also known as the hanger steak. As each animal has only one true inside fajita, this variety is a little more difficult to find in the supermarket meat case—you may have more luck asking a good butcher for hanger steak.

Fajitas initially became popular because they were cheap. Working-class people who couldn't afford more expensive cuts of beef like ribeye and T-bone could afford this cut to feed their large families. Now the foodies have discovered the flavorful fajitas, and the price has risen.

MESQUITE SMOKE AND FIRE

MESQUITE SMOKE IS CRUCIAL TO the authenticity of any *norteño*-style *carne asada,* or barbecue. Most families in the Wild Horse Desert have a wood-burning barbecue pit, or at least an area of their yard that has been cleared away and is used for lighting a fire, over which they place an iron grill for cooking. If you prefer to use a more conventional gas or charcoal grill, usingmesquite chips allows you to infuse your grilled meats and vegetables with real mesquite flavor.

SELECTING A BARBECUE PIT OR GRILL: There are numerous types of barbecue pits and grills on the market, of all shapes, sizes, and price ranges. Mesquite wood is dense and oily, and generates enormous heat, so select a barbecue pit that is well constructed of steel or iron. The traditional barbecue pit in South Texas is made of salvaged iron pipe 24 to 36 inches in diameter. The ends are welded with sheet metal to make a sealed cylinder, and a hinged lid is usually cut in the center. The ¼-inch-thick metal withstands high heat for prolonged cooking time. Smaller bombe-shaped barbecue pits made of aluminum alloys are not adequate for mesquite wood fires. In a pinch, I have an iron grid with legs that I simply place on the ground and shovel coals underneath. It is great for traveling demonstrations of grilling techniques.

TO START A HARDWOOD MESQUITE FIRE: Setting a hardwood mesquite fire is the traditional way to have a mesquite barbecue. You will need about five or six 5-inch-wide mesquite logs, cut into 2-foot lengths, for a fire that will last you about 2 hours, from starting to dying embers. A shovel is very handy as well.

Select a location for your fire that is away from buildings and dried grass. Mesquite wood takes time to ignite, as it is quite hard and dense. My tried-and-true method to start a good mesquite fire (or any hardwood fire, for that matter) is to soak three or four paper towels or newspapers in about 1 cup vegetable oil and place them underneath the kindling and logs. Once ignited, the oil burns for a long time, giving the wood time to ignite as well. Petroleum products (such as lighter fluid) are volatile, rapidly dying off after being lit. The vegetable oil method is safer, does not die off, and leaves no petroleum residue on your food.

Once you are sure the fire has ignited the center of the wood, place the grill over the fire in order to preheat. While the grill is heating, use a metal grill brush to scrape and clean the grill. When first lit, the flames will appear high and orange, fueled by the bark of the wood and any paper or fire starter you may have added, which burns up quickly. Once the wood ignites, after about 10 minutes, the fire becomes hotter and embers form. The orange flames should burn close to the glowing embers; no high, roaring flames, please. A low but steady heat can be achieved after about 20 to 25 minutes of burning—you should be able to hold your bare hand over the grill for only 1 to 2 seconds.

My husband is a fire master. He prefers to build a large fire off to the side, and then, using a shovel, transfer the hot coals to his barbecue pit as they are needed. This gives him better control of the heat levels, and he can add or remove coals as he deems necessary.

TO GIVE A MESQUITE FLAVOR TO GAS GRILLS: Small bags of mesquite chips are sold at most hardware and outdoor specialty stores. Some grills have small smoke boxes where you can add water-soaked wood chips for a good smoky flavor. Check the grill directions to see what your options are.

TO GIVE A MESQUITE FLAVOR TO CHARCOAL GRILLS: Just add a couple of handfuls of water-soaked mesquite chips to your charcoal fire to get a good smoky aroma. However, this is my least favorite method of grilling larger cuts. Briquettes have a very short cooking time and burn out after about 30 minutes. Chickens can take up to 1 hour to grill, so at some point during the grilling process you have to remove the grill and add more charcoal. Also, because of the short grilling time, many people opt to put the lid on the grill while they are cooking in order to capture more heat. I think this gives inferior grilling results. The food is no longer grilled, but baked and steamed.

Some charcoal briquettes are laced with petroleum-based additives for easier starting. I would avoid these brands, and use the vegetable oil method described above.

Small charcoal grills are excellent for when you head to the beach and need a few quick hot dogs and hamburgers. Mesquite-grilled hamburgers are simply delicious, so take your bag of mesquite chips with you.

PEPITOS GRILLED STEAK SANDWICHES

SERVES 4

This great sandwich is traditionally served on the crusty white dinner rolls known throughout Mexico as bolillos. *The soft bread inside the roll absorbs all of the succulent beef juices, while the outer crust crunches in concert with the crisp onions, showering your plate and your lap with golden flaky crumbs. Delicious!*

I usually pan-grill this on a cast iron skillet, but you can also grill the meat outdoors on a conventional grill or in a barbecue pit (see "Mesquite Smoke and Fire," page 150).

4 crusty dinner rolls (bolillos), cut in half lengthwise

1 pound flank, skirt, or hanger steak, about ½ inch thick (or butterflied to make ½ inch thick, see Note), cut into 4 equal pieces

2 tablespoons corn oil

1 medium onion, sliced into rings

8 fresh serrano chiles

1 avocado, peeled, pitted, and mashed with a fork

1 ripe medium tomato, sliced

Mexican-style sour cream or crème fraîche

4 ounces crumbled queso cotija or feta cheese

Pickled Jalapeños and Mushrooms (see page 109)

KEEP the dinner rolls warm in a 200°F oven while you prepare the meat. Heat a cast-iron griddle or skillet over medium heat and add the corn oil. After the oil is hot, about 2 minutes, add the steak and sear for 5 to 10 minutes on each side (5 for rare, 10 for well done). Cook to your desired degree of doneness, checking the temperature with a meat thermometer (see "Meat Doneness" below) and remember that the meat will continue to cook after it is removed from heat. You can grill the sliced onion and chiles along with the meat, if you wish, to give them added flavor.

SPREAD the avocado on the inside of each of the rolls. Place one piece of grilled steak on each roll and pile on the onion slices and tomato. Drizzle over a bit of the sour cream, and top with crumbled queso cotija. Serve the chiles on the side, along with the pickled jalapeños and mushrooms.

NOTE: Most of these steaks come thicker than ½ inch. Butterflying them will not only reduce cooking time but also make the sandwich more tender, as well as easier to bite into. But it is all a matter of personal preference.

MEAT DONENESS

THERE ARE SO MANY VARIABLES when grilling meats that it is difficult to give concise cooking times that will result in a specific degree of doneness. The best method is to use a meat thermometer and test the internal temperature of the meat. Below are the USDA guidelines for meat doneness.

Remember: Any meat removed from its cooking environment (grill, broiler, etc.) will retain heat and continue to cook. Remove the meat once the internal temperature on the thermometer measures 10 degrees less than the desired degree of doneness indicated above. As the meat rests, the internal temperature will continue to rise. Also, the meat becomes easier to carve if it rests. However, in our household, we are never able to curb our enthusiasm (or appetite) well enough to wait 25 minutes, until the meat has reached the perfect internal temperature.

	TEMPERATURE (°F) WHEN DONE	TEMPERATURE (°F) WHEN YOU SHOULD REMOVE FROM HEAT
Rare	140	130
Medium Rare	145	135
Medium	160	150
Well Done	170	160

FALDILLA A LA TAMPIQUEÑA
PAN-SEARED FLANK STEAK WITH POBLANO CHILES AND ONIONS
SERVES 4-6

One of my favorite things to order in a restaurant is carne a la tampiqueña, *a grand creation that is not so much a single recipe but a presentation of several dishes all on one plate. Along with the steak, there are the requisite refried beans, topped with a little* queso cotija *and a triangular* tostada, *a side of* guacamole, *an* enchilada, *some* rajas de chile *(sliced seasoned* chile poblano *strips, see page 105), and maybe some rice. The dish was developed in the 1940s by José Inés Loredo at his famous restaurant Tampico Club (which gives the dish its name), in Mexico City, but has since become a favorite throughout Mexico and into South Texas. Almost every Mexican restaurant has its version of carne a la tampiqueña, and I have enjoyed my fair share.*

*The traditional tampiqueña is made with a butterflied beef filet, thin and quickly seared. However, as beef filets are rather pricey, most restaurants opt to serve less expensive cuts in their place. The usual substitutes are flank or skirt steak (*faldilla *or* fajitas*). So I am presenting a modified, more humble version of carne a la tampiqueña.*

You can recreate the famed tampiqueña plate in your home, if you so choose. Granted, restaurants usually have enchiladas, guacamole, and refried beans on hand, and it is no trouble for them to quickly compile all of the standard side dishes. At home, you can add all the traditional side dishes you desire, or simply serve the steak by itself with a salad.

2 pounds flank, skirt, or hanger steak, cut into 4 to 6 individual servings

2 cups sour orange juice (see Note) or apple cider vinegar

Salt and freshly cracked black peppercorns

3 poblano chiles

2 tablespoons olive oil

1 medium red onion, sliced into rounds

1 white onion, sliced into rounds

2 carrots, sliced into rounds

PLACE the flank steak in a large nonreactive dish. Pour the sour orange juice over the steaks and season with salt and cracked peppercorns. Cover and place the dish in the refrigerator. Let the meat marinate for about 20 minutes.

ROAST the chiles according to the instructions on page 3. When cool, peel and seed the chiles, and set aside.

COAT a large cast-iron skillet with olive oil and heat over medium-high heat until the oil is almost smoking. Add the flank steak and sear it for 5 to 10 minutes on each side. The cooking time will depend on the thickness of the meat. Cook to your desired degree of doneness, checking the temperature with a meat thermometer (see "Meat Doneness," page 153) and remember that the meat will continue to cook after it is removed from heat. Remove from pan.

ADD the onions, carrots, and chiles to the pan. Over medium heat, cook the vegetables until the onions are caramelized, about 10 minutes. Pour the mixture over the steak and serve.

NOTE: Sour orange juice can be found in bottles at most Latin American food stores. If you know of an ornamental sour orange tree in your neighborhood, you can use the juice from the fruit for this recipe.

FILETE NORTEÑO NORTHERN-STYLE FILET OF BEEF

SERVES 4

This dish is also called a **sombrero,** *or a "hat." The filet of beef crowns a crispy* tostada, *which looks like a brim circling the steak. Northern Mexican dishes are sometimes characterized by the combination of meat and cheese, therefore this is a northern-style steak.*

Corn or vegetable oil for frying

4 corn tortillas

Olive oil

4 beef tenderloin filets, 6 ounces each, about 1 inch thick

2 ripe medium tomatoes, cored

½ medium onion, chopped

2 garlic cloves

4 piquín chiles

Salt and pepper to taste

½ cup shredded Monterey Jack cheese (optional)

POUR the corn oil, at least 1 inch deep, into a 12-inch skillet, and heat over medium heat. Once the oil is hot, about 350°F, place a tortilla into the skillet and fry on each side for 1 minute, until crispy. Remove the tortilla from the oil and drain on a baking sheet lined with paper toweling. Continue to fry all the tortillas in this fashion. This fried tortilla is now called a tostada.

HEAT a stainless steel or other nonreactive skillet until very hot (see Note). Add a few tablespoons oil. After the oil has become hot, 1 to 2 minutes, grill the steaks for about 5 minutes on each side, for medium-rare doneness. Remove the steaks and set aside. In the same skillet, combine the tomatoes and onion, and allow them to roast in the meat juices over medium-high heat until they develop brown roasted spots, about 5 minutes.

GRIND the garlic, chiles, salt, and pepper into a coarse paste using a molcajete or a stone mortar and pestle. When the tomatoes and onion are done, remove them from the skillet and remove and discard the tomato skins. Add them to the molcajete and grind with the spices to form a chunky sauce. Return the sauce to the skillet and simmer for about 10 minutes, adding a tablespoon or two of water if the sauce seems too dry.

PLACE each steak in the center of a tostada. Pour the warm sauce over the steaks. Top each with a bit of cheese, if using. Serve immediately.

NOTE: Usually, one would sear meat in a cast-iron skillet, but simmering a tomato-based sauce in an iron pan would cause the sauce to taste metallic.

LONGHORN CATTLE

THE BLOODLINE OF CATTLE most associated with Texas is the Longhorn. Texans are famous for their propensity to exaggerate; everything in Texas is bigger. It seems fitting that the exaggerated image of the Longhorn represents Texas cattle. These incredibly lanky beeves could grow horns seven feet from tip to tip.

However, the true value of the Longhorn was its ability to withstand harsh climates. These qualities made it possible to conduct large cattle drives from Texas to the Midwestern United States. Cattle prices in Texas after the Civil War were around $5 a head, whereas the price at the end of the trail in Kansas or St. Louis could be five times that amount.

CHICKEN-FRIED STEAK WITH CREAM GRAVY

SERVES 6-8

The term "chicken-fried" refers to the fact that the steak is battered and fried like traditional Southern fried chicken. *Chicken-fried steak was invented to cover the flaws of poorer cuts of meat and turn unpalatable protein into a decent meal. Considering the sources of meat in the early years of the Wild Horse Desert (old cattle, jackrabbits, horses, etc.), I imagine that much of the meat benefited from being tenderized with a hammer, battered, and deep-fried. Gravy not only embellished the meal but also utilized the precious flavors and calories left in the pan, so nothing went to waste.*

STEAK

2 pounds beef round steak, trimmed of fat

About 2 cups vegetable shortening or vegetable oil for frying

1 to 2 eggs

¾ cup milk

1 cup all-purpose flour

Salt and pepper

GRAVY

¼ cup all-purpose flour

3 cups milk

Salt to taste

Freshly cracked black peppercorns

CUT the steaks into 4 or 6 portions, about 3 x 4 inches each. Using a meat-tenderizing hammer, pound the steaks well on both sides.

HEAT the shortening to a depth of 1 inch in a large skillet until about 325°F. In a glass pie plate, whisk the eggs together with the milk, and set aside. Place the flour in another glass pie plate and season with salt and pepper. Dip a steak in the egg mixture, and then dredge in the seasoned flour. Continue with remaining steaks.

PLACE the coated steaks in the heated skillet. Add as many steaks as will fit into the pan (you may have to fry the steaks in batches). When the accumulated juices on the top of each steak turn dark red, turn the steaks over to brown on the other side; they'll cook about 5 minutes on each side. Make sure the coating is well browned. When steaks are cooked, remove from the pan and drain on paper toweling. Continue to cook remaining steaks. The cooked steaks can be held on a plate in a warm oven, about 200°F, until you are ready to serve your meal.

MAKE THE GRAVY: Drain all but 3 tablespoons of drippings from the frying pan. Leave any browned bits of coating that may have accumulated, scraping the bottom of the pan gently to loosen them. Return the pan to medium heat. Add the flour, utilizing any of the dredging flour that may be left over. Mix the flour with the drippings, continuing to scrape up brown bits with spoon. Once the drippings and browned bits are well combined, add the milk (I usually include any leftover egg-milk mixture in addition to the 3 cups of milk). Using a mixing spoon, stir the gravy, continually scraping up the bottom of the pan. Simmer the gravy until it starts to thicken, 10 to 15 minutes. Salt and pepper to taste. Serve the steaks with the warm gravy.

COMFORT FOOD, TEXAS STYLE

IN MY MOTHER'S HOUSE, chicken-fried steak was our "soul food." On Thursdays on the ranch, a calf would be slaughtered. The cowhands would divide up the meat, with the tenderloin going to my grandparents and parents. Mom would receive the meat, neatly wrapped in a brown grocery bag, and would store it in the refrigerator for a few days so it would age and tenderize. On Sunday, she would slice the tenderloin into steaks, and I would help pound the steaks with the tenderizing hammer. (This was not the delicate, buttery beef tenderloin from the country club, but grass-fed ranch beef, with plenty of texture.) The floured steaks were then placed in the hot oil, where they sizzled away as we set the table. Once the steaks were fried, Mom would put them in a baking pan to stay warm in the oven while she made the gravy. Flecked with toasted bits of dredging flour and rich with milk, the gravy thickened and bubbled in the pan, as she called everyone for dinner.

Our chicken-fried steak was always served with plenty of mashed potatoes, green peas, and iced tea. I am not ashamed to say I still love it with lots of ketchup on top. Sometimes Mom made biscuits, too, which gave us a better opportunity to enjoy the cream gravy. Warmed and split in half, biscuits with gravy is still my dad's favorite breakfast.

I believe this is the first main dish that I learned to cook. I remember Dad had brought home some cattle buyers, and my mother was in town running errands, so I volunteered to cook lunch. The chicken fried steak turned out beautifully, just like Mom's, but I can still remember those men trying to pry the gravy out of the ladle. It was rather thick.

MOLLEJAS CON CHILES TOREADOS
SWEETBREAD TAQUITOS WITH GRILLED CHILES
SERVES 8

One of my earliest memories of family barbecues was my affinity for sweetbreads. *Crunchy and delicate, they have always been a favorite. Sweetbreads can be either the thymus gland or the pancreas of a calf, and are quite rich. I like serving them as* taquitos, *or "little tacos," with a mixture of finely chopped onion and cilantro, a nice salsa, and the grilled chiles in this recipe.*

The chiles should be served on the side, and your guests can choose whether they will chop it to add to their sweetbread taquito or eat it whole between bites of taco, as we do in our family.

2 pounds fresh sweetbreads

1 medium onion, finely chopped

1 bunch cilantro (about 2 ounces), finely chopped

Salt to taste

1 dozen (8-inch) corn tortillas

3 tablespoons corn oil

12 fresh serrano chiles

Any salsa recipe (pages 94–103)

PLACE the sweetbreads in a 4- or 5-quart saucepan and cover with water. Lightly salt, bring to a gentle boil, and cook the sweetbreads for 30 minutes. Remove the sweetbreads from the boiling water and peel off and discard any outer membrane. Cool the sweetbreads, then chop into bite-size pieces.

TOSS the onion and cilantro together in a small bowl, and add salt. (This can be prepared in advance. Cover and store in the refrigerator until you are ready to serve your meal.)

WARM the tortillas either by wrapping them in aluminum foil and warming in a 300°F oven or placing them individually on a hot griddle (about 1 minute per tortilla) and wrapping the bunch in a clean kitchen towel to keep warm.

HEAT the oil in a 10-inch skillet over medium heat. Add the sweetbreads and fresh chiles. Cook the sweetbreads, stirring occasionally, until the sweetbreads are golden and crispy, 15 to 20 minutes. The chiles should be slightly browned and shriveled. Remove the skillet from the heat, salt to taste, and transfer the sweetbreads and chiles to a serving platter. Serve immediately with the warm tortillas, passing the onion and cilantro mixture, and salsa.

◆ **GRILLED SWEETBREADS**: Sweetbreads are fantastic grilled over an open flame. After you boil the sweetbreads, leave them whole instead of chopping them, and grill directly over hot coals for 15 to 20 minutes, until they are golden and crispy. For the fresh chiles, thread them on bamboo skewers, lightly coat them with oil, and grill alongside the sweetbreads until they are slightly charred, about 10 minutes. Salt as desired. Both the chiles and sweetbreads are especially memorable when grilled over mesquite coals (see "Mesquite Smoke and Fire," page 150).

CHILES TOREADOS

THE TERM "TOREAR" means "to bullfight." *Chiles toreados* are turned and passed through the flames, just as the bull turns and passes underneath the cape of the *matador*. Some people prefer to roll the chiles a bit on a hard surface before grilling to loosen the interior seeds and render the chiles more piquant.

ALBONDIGAS MEATBALLS IN TOMATO SAUCE

SERVES 8

As my mother had five children, she usually had someone helping her with the enormous amount of housework. There was one woman that worked in our house, and she was an excellent cook. Her name was Amada ("Beloved"), but everyone called her Mayo, as that was the month when she was born. I spent a good many years following her around the house, helping with the chores, putting away the laundry, and watching her cook. Sometimes, she would ask me what I wanted for dinner. "Pelotas" (the term for a toy rubber ball) was always my response. She would laugh and make a skillet of albondigas for me. There was something about meatballs with rice in them that I found magical, as if it were some incredible trick. How did the rice get in there? I wondered between bites.

I still think of Mayo every time I make this dish for my family. Leftover meatballs are incredibly good when made into an impromptu taco with fresh corn tortillas.

3 pounds ground beef

2 eggs

1 cup minced onion

½ cup white rice

Salt and pepper

1½ pounds ripe tomatoes, seeded (about 6)

3 garlic cloves

KNEAD together the ground beef, eggs, onion, rice, salt, and pepper in a large bowl. Form bite-size (1-inch) meatballs with the ground meat, and arrange them in one layer in a large 14-inch skillet or Dutch oven (or use 2 smaller skillets, or brown in batches). Once the skillet is filled, place it over medium heat. Brown the meatballs on both sides, about 15 minutes total.

COMBINE the tomatoes and garlic in the container of a blender or food processor. Add 2 cups of water and purée well. Add the purée to the skillet, cover, reduce the heat, and simmer for 30 minutes. To prevent the meatballs from scorching, occasionally lift with a spatula—do not stir or they might break apart. Meatballs are done when the rice is cooked.

CORTADILLO SLICED MEAT STEW

SERVES 6

Cortadillo, *which means "that which is cut,"* comes from the northern
*Mexican state of Coahuila, just south of the Wild Horse Desert. I believe that the meat was
cut into thin strips against the grain in order to make a tender stew out of a tough piece of
beef.* Fajitas, *although grilled instead of stewed, are popular in this northern Mexican state as
well, and are cut the same way to remedy their sometimes-tough texture.*

2 tablespoons corn oil

1 small onion, chopped

2 pounds boneless beef, cut into ¼ x 2-inch
slices (round steak works well)

1 pound ripe tomatoes, peeled and seeded
(about 4)

2 whole serrano chiles

2 garlic cloves, minced

Salt and pepper to taste

HEAT the oil in a 10-inch lidded skillet over medium heat. Add the onion and sauté
until the onion is transparent, about 5 minutes. Add the beef and cook until the
meat is well browned, about 5 minutes.

PURÉE the tomatoes in a food processor or a blender. Add the tomato purée,
chiles, garlic, salt, and pepper to the meat. Stir to combine well. Cover, reduce
the heat, and simmer for 45 to 60 minutes, stirring occasionally, until tender.
Uncover for the last 10 minutes of cooking in order for the stewing liquid to
reduce and thicken.

BEEF RIBS AND VEGETABLES BRAISED IN DARK BEER

SERVES 4-6

This recipe is a variation of my grandmother's pot roast. We ate dinner with her often, as she lived in town, and we would stay at her house while my mother finished her errands. Grandmother cooked her famous chuck roast at least once a week.

My version is a little naughtier than my grandmother's. I love stewing the beef in beer, especially dark beer, which gets its color from toasted grain. The yeasty essence of the beer is absorbed by the beef, potatoes, and carrots and fills the air with complete distraction. I also prefer using short ribs, as they are more flavorful than chuck roast, for the simple fact that they have more bones. My husband absolutely loves this dish, as do my boys.

2 to 3 tablespoons corn oil

4 pounds English-style beef short ribs

1 medium onion

4 to 5 bay leaves (fresh, if possible)

1 whole head of garlic

1 ripe medium tomato, chopped

2 celery stalks, chopped, with leaves

2 carrots

½ cup fresh parsley, chopped

1 bottle beer, preferably dark

Salt and freshly cracked black peppercorns

1 pound small new potatoes (about 2 inches in diameter), well scrubbed

PREHEAT the oven to 375°F. Adjust the oven racks to accommodate a 6-quart casserole (see Note).

HEAT the oil in a 12-inch skillet over medium-high heat, add the ribs, and brown on all sides, about 10 minutes. (You may need to brown them in batches, depending on how many fit in your skillet.) Meanwhile, assemble the remaining ingredients except for the potatoes in a 6-quart Dutch oven or other heavy lidded casserole. Add the browned ribs, cover, and place in the oven. Bake 2 to 3 hours, until meat is tender. Add the potatoes during the last 30 minutes of cooking.

REMOVE the ribs and potatoes, and place on a serving plate. Remove the garlic, squeeze the cloves to express the roasted pulp inside, and add the pulp to the sauce. Remove and discard the bay leaves. Skim off any unwanted fat. Now make a sauce by puréeing the leftover cooking liquid with the vegetables using a hand-held blender, blender, or food processor. Serve sauce on the side.

NOTE: To cook this, you will need a heavy lidded 6-quart pot at least 6 inches deep. I use a large clay baking dish, but a ceramic casserole or enamel-coated cast-iron Dutch oven works just as well. Clay is an insulator of heat, as opposed to metal, which is a conductor of heat. My clay pot retains the heat of the oven longer and keeps the ribs warm and aromatic throughout the meal (see "Olla Cookery," page 187).

CARNE GUISADA CON NOPALITOS
BEEF STEW WITH CACTUS
SERVES 6-8

Nopalitos, or chopped prickly pear cactus pads, *are delicious, with a flavor reminiscent of green beans. Added to this spicy beef stew, nopalitos provide a pleasing texture. I prefer to add precooked nopalitos to this dish, as the cactus pieces exude a gooey juice when cooked, which would ruin the lovely sauce that the puréed ancho chile forms. You can also use jarred nopalitos for this dish, which are already cooked and ready for use.*

Serve this stew with a batch of homemade frijoles *and warmed corn tortillas.*

3 dried ancho chiles	Salt and pepper to taste
2 tablespoons corn oil	1 to 2 garlic cloves, minced
1 medium onion, chopped	1 large ripe tomato, cored and diced
2 pounds boneless beef stew meat, cut into 2-inch cubes	1 cup cubed cooked nopalitos, in ½-inch dice (see page 25)

FILL a small saucepan with water and bring to a boil. Add the dried chiles, and boil for 10 minutes, until the chiles are soft. Drain the chiles and remove the stems. Using a food processor or a blender, purée the chiles with 1 cup of fresh water. Strain the purée through a mesh strainer to remove the seeds and set aside.

HEAT the oil in a 10-inch lidded skillet over medium heat. Add the onion and sauté until transparent, about 5 minutes. Add the meat, season with salt and pepper, and brown well for about 15 minutes. Add the chile purée, garlic, tomato, and 1 cup of water. Cover the carne guisada with a lid and simmer over medium-low heat for another 30 to 40 minutes. If the stew looks like it is drying out, add more water, 1 cup at a time. Test the beef to see if it is tender by cutting a piece with a fork. If the beef is still tough, continue to stew for another 15 minutes, or until tender. Once the beef is tender, add the nopalitos and stir well to combine.

CARNE SECA DRIED MEAT

CATTLE AND HORSES that roamed the Wild Horse Desert at the turn of the twentieth century numbered in the hundreds of thousands. So it is no surprise that many people made their living at the time by rounding up the animals and selling them. Livestock went to ranchers and the military, but much of the cattle was slaughtered and sent to tanneries as hides. Leather was in great demand and was worth more than the meat. More important, the hides were easier to transport.

Because there was no refrigeration at the time, abandoning the meat of an animal and taking only the hide was commonplace. However, some of the meat could be preserved by making *carne seca,* or dried meat. Processing carne seca for transportation was almost identical to processing hides for leather: a thin slice of meat (or an animal hide) would be covered in salt, hung on a line, and dried in the sun. The meat then could be stored for the journey ahead.

There are different forms and definitions for carne seca. The general term can refer to any dried, jerky-style meat. Although cooking is not necessary, many recipes call for it to be pan-fried before other ingredients are added, mainly to enhance the flavor and give it a crispier texture. In addition to beef, venison and pork can be made into carne seca. When food sources were less than plentiful, other meat sources, including horse, donkey, buffalo, turtle, snake, or even coyote, were processed and dried for consumption as carne seca. The resulting carne seca of any of these animals would be prepared and consumed the same way as dried beef.

Cecina is a particular form of carne seca, which is sometimes marinated in vinegar or sour orange juice, salted, and sometimes seasoned with other spices, then dried. Cecina is usually presented in thin filets and browned in oil before eating. Cecina is extremely popular throughout the northern Mexican region known as the Huasteca, in the state of Tamaulipas, south of the Wild Horse Desert. In Oaxaca, Mexico, cecina is known as *tasajo,* and known in the United States and Canada as *pemmican.* Cecina has a bit tangier, spicier flavor than regular carne seca, owing to the marinades used.

Machacado is shredded carne seca; its name means "to pound or mash," and refers to the shredding process used to make carne seca. The meat is first salted and dried in thin filets (like *cecina*), then is pounded with the blunt end of a hatchet blade in order to separate the muscle fibers. Machacado is then browned in oil and added to eggs or tacos. In South Texas and northern Mexico, machacado (also called *machaca*) is sold on its own as a snack at the register of any truck stop or gas station, along with a small packet of lemon juice for flavoring. Machacado is the most popular form of carne seca in the Wild Horse Desert.

The technique for making dried meat can be traced to the Incan empire, which occupied present-day Ecuador, Bolivia, and Peru. The ancient Incan word for dried meat, *charqui,* is still part of our lexicon, known more commonly in English as jerky. The technique for drying meat was passed from tribe to tribe, as they traveled and traded across the continent.

SALT IN THE WILD HORSE DESERT

WHEN THE SPANISH ARRIVED in the New World, one of the first orders of business was to dominate all sources of salt. From a modern perspective, it may seem that the Spanish were going to extreme lengths for a mere flavor enhancer. But salt was key to unlocking the riches found in this new land:

SILVER. Silver metal was extracted from silver ore by crushing the ore with large amounts of salt, in a process known as the "patio method." Donkeys were tethered to a central post and walked inside a circular, low-walled "patio," crushing the ore and salt under their feet. The salt caused the silver to be released from the ore; it was then collected, purified, and smelted into bars. Saltworks were usually set up around silver mines.

LEATHER. The herds of wild cattle and horses that roamed the Wild Horse Desert became an important source of leather, which quickly became a major and lucrative export to Spain. Salt was necessary to preserve the hides until they could be treated. Horses and cattle became, in fact, the first source of wealth for the Spanish in the New World.

FOOD PRESERVATION. When cattle were slaughtered, the meat would be thinly sliced and preserved by coating with salt or soaking in brine before being air-dried to create a nonperishable dried beef. Such readily available food sources were the key to survival for both natives and Spanish colonists in the New World.

Upon their discovery, natural salt lakes such as La Sal del Rey and La Sal Vieja, located in the center of the Wild Horse Desert (near present-day Raymondville, Texas), were immediately claimed for the Spanish Crown. Salt was also mined by the indigenous tribesmen drafted into labor. As technological advances in salt production evolved, the labor-intensive production of salt from the lakes decreased until the American Civil War, when demand for salt skyrocketed. The need became so great that camels, which could carry 600-pound loads, were brought to the area from North Africa to deliver salt to Confederate troops. Eventually, the camel experiment was abandoned. Some believe that the decline in camel use was due to increased freight theft, while others believe the camels were simply too much trouble, as they tended to spit, kick, disobey, and inspire hysteria among the other livestock.

The original lawmakers of Texas grappled with ownership lawsuits of subsurface salt rights. Today, Texas is famous for its oil and gas production. Although oil and gas aren't minerals, today's oil and gas ownership laws are derived from earlier salt ownership questions, thus the name "mineral rights" is carried over to refer to petroleum.

Salt was commercially mined and shipped as late as 1920 from La Sal Vieja. Even today, Texas ranks second in salt production in the United States, after Louisiana.

HOMEMADE MACHACADO HOMEMADE DRIED MEAT

MAKES 1½ POUNDS

My neighbor Fred has been making carne seca *for years in his home oven, so I called him for a recipe. He said he usually made carne seca with venison, and that his kids grew up on this stuff. One liked it so much that she would always ask her dad to make more, which he did until he found out she was taking it to her school to sell to her classmates.*

Like Fred, many folks use their oven to dry meat for carne seca, but I have not had good results. The required low, constant temperature of 140°F is below what my oven thermostat can control. However, I have an electric home food dehydrator that works extremely well for making carne seca. (My dad bought it for me after watching a late-night infomercial.) It keeps a constant temperature, and I don't feel as nervous leaving it on all night as the meat dries. The dehydrator has several layers of food trays, which stack over a central heating element. The trays must be rearranged midway through the drying process so that everything dries evenly.

Rump roast is a good choice for making machacado *(or any carne seca). Have your butcher slice the roast into ¼-inch-thick slices, with the grain. Regular jerky is more tender if the meat is sliced across the grain, but for machacado you want to preserve the muscle fibers so that, when the meat is pounded, the fibers separate into strands, giving machacado its traditional thread-like texture.*

To pound the machacado, I use a large wooden cutting board with a couple of kitchen towels under it to protect the surface of my countertop. The towels also help reduce the noise of the pounding.

3 pounds lean beef or venison, trimmed of fat and sliced ¼ inch thick, cut with the grain (in the direction of the muscle fiber; if you have difficulty judging the direction of the muscle fiber, ask your butcher)

Fine sea salt

COAT the beef slices lightly and evenly with sea salt. Arrange the slices in a food dehydrator and dry according to the manufacturer's instructions. Check the carne seca after 4 hours to see if it is drying evenly. Rearrange the slices or the food trays if necessary. Dry for another 4 hours. Remove the carne seca from the dehydrator and allow to cool completely.

POUND a slice of the carne seca on a sturdy surface with a meat tenderizer until the muscle fibers separate. Shred the carne seca by pulling it into strands. It should look like thin brown twigs, or straw. Enjoy carne seca as the natives did, as a snack on the run. Store in an airtight container, where it will keep for six months at room temperature or indefinitely in the refrigerator.

MACHACADO CON HUEVO DRIED BEEF WITH EGGS
SERVES 2

Of all the places to enjoy a meal, I had this version of machacado con huevo *in a hospital cafeteria in Reynosa, Tamaulipas, Mexico. I was wholly impressed and have made it this way ever since. It's excellent for breakfast or an easy dinner. Look for machacado at your local Mexican or Latin American market, or make it yourself (see "Homemade Machacado," page 170).*

1 tablespoon corn oil

1 ounce machacado

2 tablespoons chopped onion

2 tablespoons chopped green bell pepper

1 small plum tomato, seeded and chopped

4 large eggs

4 corn tortillas

HEAT the oil in a small skillet over medium heat and add the machacado. Brown the meat for 1 minute, then add the onion, bell pepper, and tomato. Sauté the mixture for another 2 minutes, then crack the eggs directly into the pan. Stir the eggs and the sautéed mixture well. The strands of machacado, tomato, pepper, and onion should be evenly distributed among the eggs. When the eggs are cooked, remove from heat and serve immediately with warm tortillas.

MENUDO SPICY TRIPE SOUP

SERVES 15

There is only one way to acquire a hangover, but there is much debate on how to rid oneself of this affliction. Menudo, *a spicy tripe soup, is known throughout Mexico as* the traditional *cure. After a night of wedding festivities, the bride, groom, and the rest of the wedding party congregate at midnight or in early morning at a family member's house for the* torna boda, *an after-party where everyone is served huge steaming basins of menudo topped with chopped oregano and fresh corn tortillas, all washed down with a Coke or beer. Menudo is not something that you eat by yourself. This is a large recipe, intended for parties. You can cut the recipe in half very easily, if you like, or freeze any leftovers.*

Tripe is available in most supermarkets, and is mostly sold in frozen blocks. Latin American supermarkets always have a supply on hand.

10 pounds beef honeycomb tripe, rinsed and cut into 2- to 2½-inch squares

12 ounces fresh or frozen pig's feet

4 ounces tequila

4 ounces ancho chiles

1 head garlic, peeled

2 teaspoons cumin seeds

2 teaspoons whole black peppercorns

2 teaspoons salt or to taste

1 pound fresh hominy (pozole) or 1 (30-ounce) can white hominy, drained

Fresh or dried oregano

1 medium onion, chopped

Limes, cut in quarters

PLACE the tripe and pig's feet in a large pot or an electric turkey roaster. Fill the pot or roaster with water, barely covering the tripe. Add the tequila. Bring the pot to a boil, and cook over medium-high heat for about 1½ hours. The menudo should cook at a rate between a simmer and a full rolling boil.

SOFTEN the chiles, and remove the stems and seeds, following the instructions on page 50. Add the softened chiles to the container of a blender, along with just enough water to facilitate blending. Blend the chiles until you have a smooth paste. You will need 1 quart of chile purée. Set aside.

(continued)

MENUDO, CON'T.

GRIND the garlic and spices in a molcajete or spice grinder until you have a fine paste. When the menudo has cooked for about an hour, add the spice paste and the chile purée to the pot.

REMOVE the menudo from the heat when the tripe is fork tender but slightly firm. Add the fresh or canned hominy and allow it to simmer for another 5 to 10 minutes. Add 1 or 2 tablespoons oregano, if desired, or serve the oregano on the side. Serve with chopped onion and wedges of limes.

To say one has a hangover in Spanish is to say they are *crudo*, which means "under cooked." I couldn't resist including the poem below:

O Menudo sabroso, te saludo
En esta alegre y refrescante aurora
En que reclamo alimento, pues es
Hora
En que tú estás cocido y yo estoy crudo

Here's the translation:

"O delicious Menudo, I greet you on this festive and refreshing morning as I require nourishment, since now is the hour in which you are well cooked, and I am feeling rather raw . . . "

COOKING MENUDO OUTSIDE

EVERYONE I KNOW cooks menudo outside the house on the porch, using an electric turkey roaster. Just remove the inner roasting pan and boil the tripe in the water basin portion.

The aroma of cooking tripe can be overwhelming inside your home. I very much recommend this method.

BARBACOA ROASTED BEEF CHEEKS
SERVES 8

Early in the morning, fog clings to the thorny brushland of the Wild Horse Desert. The weak, salmon-colored sun filters through the dove-blue haze. You can barely make out the forms of a few cowboys dressed in brown canvas jackets, laughing and joking in the distance. They have been there since the night before, tending a hole in the ground, making barbacoa.

This is the velvety succulent meat taken from the roasted head of a calf. When a calf is slaughtered on the ranch, every part is used. What modern consumers would throw away, we find ways of cooking—which often turns up a delicious delicacy. The entire calf's head (minus the hide and horns) is traditionally roasted in a pit that has been dug into the ground and lined with hot mesquite coals and maguey (century plant) leaves, which results in what we call barbacoa. Every bit of the head, from the tongue to the brains, is consumed. Barbacoa is sold all over South Texas and Mexico for a special Sunday morning breakfast treat. Purchased by the pound, it is whisked home while still hot and made into delicious taquitos with fresh warm corn tortillas and a good salsa. I like serving plenty of crisp onion, cilantro, acidic lime juice, and spicy, tangy salsa on the side, as they cut through the rich flavor of the meat and provide a perfect balance of flavor and texture.

As most people don't have the real estate (or the desire) to bake a calf's head in a hole in the ground, I have put together an abbreviated version using just the jowl meat of a calf. This part is tender, unctuous, and delicious in every way—many consider this the best part of a good barbacoa.

2 pounds beef cheek (jowl; see Notes)

Salt

24 to 32 fresh corn tortillas (see Notes)

½ cup finely chopped cilantro

1 cup finely chopped onion

Any recipe salsa (optional; see pages 94–103)

4 limes, sliced into wedges

PREHEAT the oven to 300°F. Sprinkle the meat lightly with salt and wrap in a double layer of aluminum foil so as to not allow any steam to escape. Place the foil packet in a baking pan and bake for at least 6 hours, until tender.

REMOVE the meat from the foil and finely chop it. Serve immediately, making tacos with the meat, cilantro, onion, and salsa, adding just a few drops of lime juice on top.

NOTES: Beef cheek meat, as well as whole cow's heads, are available in most Latin American supermarkets, or you can ask your butcher if he or she can get it for you. You can make barbacoa in the oven a day in advance; it reheats wonderfully the next day for a traditional breakfast.

If your corn tortillas are not freshly made, or if you don't have time to heat the tortillas on a comal (griddle) on the stove, wrap the tortillas in foil, and place in the oven for 20 minutes to heat as the barbacoa finishes its cooking time.

COOKING UNDER THE GROUND

INDIGENOUS TRIBES throughout the Americas dug pits in the earth to cook meals, filling the pits with hot stones. Peruvians still use this method for their *pachamanca,* a complete meal cooked in an earthen hole heated with hot stones. However, some believe that it was the Spanish explorers who disseminated the technique of cooking in holes, having learned it from their African slaves. The former African natives, meanwhile, are said to have done this to cook elephant legs. The holes would be filled with hot stones, the legs would be placed in the hole and covered with earth, and the meat would emerge tender and ready to serve several days later.

CHAPTER SEVEN

CHICKEN, PORK, AND SEAFOOD

OUT ON THE RANCHES of the Wild Horse Desert, the daily bread was the tortilla and the daily meat, if any, was beef or game, either fresh or dried. Any deviance from this diet of beef and tortillas meant that company was coming.

Chickens were needed for the eggs they laid, therefore only lame or non-producing birds were plucked for Sunday dinner. A pig was fattened all year long for slaughter in December. Pork was a Christmas treat, unless you happened across a *javelina*, a wild boar, on a hunting sojourn. And even though the

Wild Horse Desert stretches to the Gulf of Mexico, seafood was most commonly available in its dried form, as fresh fish spoiled quickly on the hot overland journey to local markets. Nowadays, motor-driven boats and refrigerated trucks bring in the catch from the Gulf and safely distribute fish and shrimp, even in our 104°F weather.

So these are special-occasion dishes, made on Sundays or holidays when we have the time to truly savor them and the company to enjoy them with us.

ARROZ CON POLLO CHICKEN WITH RICE

SERVES 6-8

Everyone in Latin America makes arroz con pollo, *and all claim it as an authentic regional dish. The rice soaks up every last bit of flavor from the chicken and tomatoes as it stews. Its garlicky aroma is a delicious greeting when you walk into the kitchen.*

You can add other vegetables for more flavor, such as peas, chopped carrots, celery, corn—whatever you like. Add them after you have added the puréed tomatoes. Every family has its secret key ingredient, so once you master this recipe, be creative.

2 tablespoons corn oil

1 chicken (3 to 4 pounds), cut into pieces

1 garlic clove

1 pound ripe tomatoes, seeded and chopped

3 cups Basic Soup Stock—chicken (see page 112) or water

1 medium onion, chopped

1½ cups white rice

Salt and pepper to taste

HEAT the oil in a 6-quart Dutch oven or skillet over medium heat. Add the chicken pieces and brown evenly, turning pieces as necessary, for about 25 minutes.

COMBINE the garlic, tomatoes, and stock in the container of a blender and purée until smooth. Set aside.

REMOVE the chicken from the pan and place in another dish. Drain excess fat from the pan, leaving 2 or 3 tablespoons. Return the pan to medium heat. Add the onion and rice, and sauté until the onion is translucent and the rice is opaque, about 10 minutes. Add the tomato purée carefully, as the mixture will steam and sizzle. Return the chicken pieces to the pan. Add salt and pepper. When the liquid begins to simmer, cover the pan with a tight-fitting lid and simmer over medium-low heat for 25 minutes.

CALABACITA CON POLLO SQUASH WITH CHICKEN

SERVES 6-8

This is another of my mom's recipes. She plants a garden every summer, with several different varieties of squash (banana, zucchini, patty pan, etc.), but the traditional local—and my family's—favorite is calabacita, *called tatuma squash in the rest of the United States. They are small green globes, with nutty seeds and creamy white flesh. In the hot Wild Horse Desert sun, and with my Mom's care, her garden virtually explodes with calabacita, which we enjoy the summer long.*

2 tablespoons corn oil

4- to 5-pound chicken, cut into pieces

1 medium onion, chopped

3 pounds young tatuma squash (2 to 3), cut into ½-inch cubes (do not peel)

4 ears of corn, kernels removed and reserved

2 garlic cloves, minced

Salt and pepper to taste

HEAT the oil in a large lidded skillet or Dutch oven over medium heat, turning the pan to coat evenly with the oil. When the oil is hot, add the chicken pieces and onion, reduce the heat to low, and brown for about 25 minutes, until the chicken is cooked through.

ADD the squash and corn. Add the garlic, and season with salt and pepper. Cover the chicken, reduce the heat, and simmer for 15 to 20 minutes.

PECHUGAS DE POLLO CON CHILE POBLANO

CHICKEN BREASTS SMOTHERED IN POBLANO CHILES

SERVES 6

In this health-conscious era, cream is relegated to desserts and other "sinful" eating. However, I much prefer the flavor and consistency of fresh, real cream over any jarred, shelf-stable, artificially thickened cream soup or sauce preparation. I would rather add one delicious ingredient to a dish than a host of artificial ingredients that I cannot pronounce.

This recipe is my own concoction, as I was desperate for a special dish for when company popped by. The sweet carrots and onions and the piquant chiles marry beautifully with the rich cream in this recipe. White rice or noodles are an excellent accompaniment.

2 tablespoons corn oil

4 to 6 whole chicken breasts, with ribs and skin (4 to 5 pounds)

1 medium onion, sliced into rings

1 pint heavy cream

1 pound poblano chiles, roasted, peeled, and sliced into ½-inch strips (see page 3)

1 pound carrots, sliced

Salt and pepper to taste

HEAT the oil in a 10-inch skillet. Season the chicken breasts with salt and pepper, and place them rib side up in the hot oil. Add the onion, and brown over medium heat until the skin is golden, about 20 minutes. Turn the chicken breasts over, and continue to brown for 10 minutes more. Add the cream, chiles, and carrots. Add salt and pepper as desired. Simmer over low heat, uncovered, for 20 minutes, until the cream has reduced and thickened and chicken is cooked through.

CARNITAS PORK PIECES PREPARED CAULDRON STYLE

SERVES 6-8

This is a great dish to pair with an excellent salsa; I prefer a tomato-less salsa, such as *Salsa de Chile Chipotle Ahumado (page 103) or Salsa de Chile de Arbol (page 100).* Carnitas beg to be served with a bracingly cold Mexican beer.

3 pounds lean boneless pork (boneless ribs work well), cut into 2-inch cubes
¼ cup lard or vegetable shortening
1 unpeeled orange, cut in half
1 cup whole milk
Any salsa recipe (pages 94–103)
12 to 15 corn tortillas

PLACE the pork in a 6-quart Dutch oven or heavy pot, and add 1 cup water. Bring to a boil, cover, and simmer for 20 to 25 minutes, until the pork is cooked through. Uncover the pork and continue to simmer until the water has evaporated, about 15 minutes. (Turn the pork with a spatula so it does not stick to the bottom of the pot.)

ADD the lard and orange halves, and continue to cook for about 20 minutes, stirring occasionally so that the pork browns evenly. Add the milk and continue to simmer for another 20 minutes, until the pork pieces are golden. Using a slotted spoon, remove the carnitas from the liquid remaining in the pot and drain on paper towels. Discard the cooking liquid. Serve the carnitas warm with corn tortillas and salsa.

ASADO DE PUERCO PORK ROASTED IN CHILES

SERVES 8

I love old photos of ranch life, especially family gatherings. Men in stiff collars and copious mustaches, women in starched white linen, children with lop-eared bows and dirty knee breeches, all gathered on a porch or around a banquet table made of planks and saw horses. I imagine these were Sunday visits, or Saturday weddings. Before the cousins arrived from another ranch, or from town, there was washing, ironing, sweeping, beans to boil, cactus to gather and clean for cooking, and a pig to slaughter. Making Asado de Puerco *always transports me to the era of these photos. I know this is what they served.*

Asado de Puerco appears frequently at ranch weddings in Northern Mexico—in fact some call this Asado de Bodas, *or "Wedding Roast." The pork simmers until all the water in the cooking liquid is gone, a technique that preserves the pork. This enables the host to cook the meal ahead of the ceremony, and continue to rely on the leftovers to serve straggling guests over the next few days. A recipe from the early nineteenth century indicated the meat would keep for up to four months, making it an obvious menu choice for the overwhelmed turn-of-the-century hostess. (Remember, she didn't have the luxury of a refrigerator.) However, by today's standards, I would either consume or freeze it within a week.*

Rice is the perfect side dish for Asado de Puerco, especially Arroz con Azafrán y Chicharos (see page 136). The vibrant yellow color and mild onion aroma complement the rich, red pork. Most important, the rice picks up every last drop of sauce on your plate.

½ pound dried ancho chiles (about 20 chiles)

4 pounds bone-in country style pork ribs

1 medium onion, chopped

½ teaspoon pepper

Pinch ground cloves

2 tablespoons salt

1 head garlic, unpeeled

2 sprigs fresh oregano or 1 teaspoon dried

2 sprigs fresh thyme or 1 teaspoon dried

1 stick cinnamon (Mexican if possible, see page 29)

2 tablespoons cider vinegar

PREPARE the chiles for puréeing according to the instructions on page 5. Drain and purée in batches in the container of a blender, filling half of the blender container with the cooked chiles and using 1 to 2 cups of fresh water per batch to facilitate blending. Strain the purée though a mesh colander or chinois to remove seeds and skins. (The purée may be made in advance and refrigerated for a few days or frozen for future use.)

PREHEAT the oven to 350°F, and position a rack in the lower third of the oven to accommodate a large casserole. Heat a 6-quart lidded Dutch oven or other oven-proof casserole over medium heat. (I have an enamel-coated cast-iron pot that goes from stove to oven to table, which works beautifully.) Add the pork in 2 batches and brown each batch on both sides, about 10 minutes per batch. As the pork begins to render its fat, add the onion to brown as well.

ADD the chile purée, pepper, cloves, salt, whole head of garlic, oregano, thyme, cinnamon, vinegar, and ½ cup water. Stir to distribute the seasonings. Cover, place in the oven, and roast for 2 to 2½ hours. The asado is ready when the meat is tender, pulling away from the bones, and permeated with the flavor and color of the thickened ancho chile sauce.

◆ **STOVETOP ASADO DE PUERCO**: While I love slow oven roasting my asado de puerco to extract all the flavor from the bones, the dish can also be prepared on the stovetop, which is how the dish was traditionally made (see "Asado," page 186). Make as you would any stew. You can still get that great flavor, but watch the level of liquid in your asado. The direct flame of the stove may cause scorching. Peek under the lid every 30 minutes and add ½ cup of water, as needed.

ASADO

THE NAME "ASADO DE PUERCO" is based on the word *azar,* which means "to roast," as in dry roasting over a fire. I found this tremendously confusing, as I had always seen this dish cooked on the stove, like a *guisado,* or a stew. It was being stewed, not roasted.

Then, I found that *asar* can also mean "to braise." The *Nuevo Cocinero Mexicano,* a cookbook published in 1845, states: "There are different classes of *asados* (roasts): over coals or *del pastor* (shepherd-style, on a spit), on a grill, in the oven or fried in lard, butter or oil. " Further research showed that the same term applies to both cooking techniques of high-temperature fire roasting and slow fire braising. After much pondering, it dawned on me: It's pot roast.

Before the arrival of oven-equipped modern kitchens, the pot of meat would have been surrounded by heat: placed on live coals, with more live coals heaped on the lid. As the use of live fire in the kitchen waned, the asado was no longer enveloped in live coals, but was placed on top of the stove. Initially, I made mine on the stovetop, but after research, trial, error, and success, I now make Asado de Puerco in the oven to get the succulent, slow-roasted flavor.

OLLA COOKERY

MODERN COOKWARE produces excellent asado de puerco, but I love to use my traditional clay *olla* (pot) for this dish, as well as the Beef Ribs and Vegetables Braised in Dark Beer (page 164). During Lent I use it for making a whopping great *Capirotada* for my family (see page 261). My olla was made by hand and was engraved with flowers when the clay was still wet, before it was kiln-fired. It barely fits in my oven. Once the asado is cooked, I simply place the clay vessel on the table and serve. The clay retains the oven heat for hours and keeps the dish warm throughout the meal.

Few ollas make it to American markets, as their size prevents tourists from carrying them onto airplanes. Also, many of them have glazes on the inside that contain lead and so they cannot be imported into the United States or sold commercially for food use. I fully admit to using my olla, whether it contains lead or not, and this passage is certainly not meant to promote the idea of including more lead in your diet. But I have used this traditional cookware all my life, with no ill effect.

If you would like to use a Mexican clay pot, it must be cured with pickling lime (calcium hydroxide) before used for the first time. Once cured, the clay pot never has to be cured again.

TO SEASON AN OLLA. Using rubber gloves, make a paste with 1 cup pickling lime and 2 cups water, and rub over every inch of the *outside* of your pot. Once it is covered, fill with water 3 inches below the edge of the pot's rim. Add 2 to 3 tablespoons of pickling lime powder and stir to dissolve. Heat the olla over medium heat. Slowly bring the water to a boil, boil for 10 minutes, turn off the heat, and allow the pot and water to cool completely. If possible, remove the pot with water to an outdoor area and allow it to cure in a sunny area for 2 or 3 days. This helps the lime to completely penetrate all the pores of the clay. After 2 or 3 days, discard the water and wash the pot, inside and out. It is now ready for use.

CHORIZO SPANISH-STYLE SAUSAGE
MAKES 6 POUNDS

The one dish my grandfather would make for us was chorizo con huevo. *If you behaved, and agreed to get up at 5:00 A.M. before he went to tend the cattle, you could watch him putter around the kitchen, chopping onion and toasting bread as he prepared his very special breakfast. I can still see him is his khaki work clothes, leaning up against the green Formica counter of his kitchen, in front of the still-dark window. The house was quiet except for the sizzle of chorizo in the pan. The aroma of coffee, chiles, garlic, and vinegar still takes me back to that moment in time, slumped at the kitchen table, sleepy-eyed, dazed, and wondering why I agreed to get up so early. Later, I could hear my grandmother's slippers scuffing down the hallway. By this time, the chorizo was gone, and Granddad was picking up his hat, heading out the screen door.*

I think there are lots of us norteños *who have early morning memories of chorizo, as breakfast tacos filled with chorizo and eggs are our regional comfort food. I receive many requests for this recipe.*

I want to emphasize that this recipe is very easy to make. Many people are intimidated by the thought of making sausages because they envision grinding the meat and stuffing it into casings. However, ground pork is now available in most meat markets. And, while our local fresh chorizos are stuffed into natural casings, the meat is then usually removed before it is cooked—the casing serves only as packaging. (In Mexico, where chorizo is dried, the casing keeps the sausage intact during the drying process, but it still might be removed before the meat is cooked.) This recipe is really no harder to make than meat loaf.

6 ancho chiles (about 4 ounces)
2 to 3 garlic cloves
1 cup white vinegar
1 tablespoon salt
1 tablespoon ground pepper
½ teaspoon ground cumin
5 pounds ground pork

RENDER a purée from the chiles according the instructions on page 5, puréeing them with the garlic and 1½ cups fresh water. Pour the chile purée into an extra-large mixing bowl. Add the vinegar, salt, pepper, and cumin, and mix well. Using your hands, add the ground pork and mix well, making sure that the chile purée is evenly distributed throughout the meat. Cover and chill in the refrigerator at least 24 hours before using, or pack into 1-pound portions to store tightly wrapped in the freezer.

LITTLE MEATS

LOTS OF LITTLE MOM AND POP TACO STANDS serve tacos made with *carnitas* on the weekends. In Mexico, many of these stands have a large copper pot positioned at the front of their establishment. The carnitas are prepared in this cauldron on Sunday, and the pot, along with its mesquite fire, is tended carefully by young men wielding large batons. Carefully, they nudge and push the pieces of meat around in the copper cauldron, cooking these precious bits as their customers gather around to place their orders.

Here on the border, many folks recreate the carnitas of Mexico on the stovetops in their home kitchens. The name *carnitas* simply means "little meats," and they are considered an affordable indulgence. Chunks of savory pork are first simmered slowly in water, then further cooked in lard until they are tender and flavorful. The sugars in the orange half and milk added in the last stage of cooking give each piece of meat a scrumptiously crisp crust. Carnitas can be enjoyed at breakfast, lunch, and dinner or eaten as a snack.

CHORIZO CON HUEVO SAUSAGE WITH EGGS

SERVES 4-6

Even though this is a breakfast dish, we often have it for a quick light supper, as we always have all the ingredients on hand.

8 ounces Chorizo (see page 188), casing removed, if necessary

6 eggs

8 corn or flour tortillas, warmed

HEAT a small skillet over medium heat and add the chorizo. Break up the chorizo meat with the back of a spoon until it is finely crumbled. Continue to cook the chorizo until it is well browned, about 5 minutes. Crack the eggs directly into the pan and stir to scramble the mixture well. Stir the mixture so that it cooks evenly. Once the eggs are cooked and no longer seem watery, spoon equal amounts of the chorizo mixture into the warmed tortillas. Serve immediately.

NOPALITOS CON CAMARÓN CACTUS WITH DRIED SHRIMP

SERVES 4-6

Nopalitos *("little cactus")* are traditionally served for Lent in South Texas. The tender new cactus shoots are harvested and used in seasonal meatless dishes.

As refrigeration is a relatively recent development in the history of food, dried shrimp was the only local seafood available on the ranches of the Wild Horse Desert. Shrimp caught in the surf were dried in the hot South Texas sun on the sandy shore and transported to market. Salty, with a concentrated shrimp aroma and flavor, this recipe is very old and yet is still incredibly popular.

3 cups chopped cleaned nopalitos (about 20 pads; see page 24)

1 ounce dried shrimp

1 tablespoon corn oil

1 small onion, chopped

2 teaspoons chili powder

1 garlic clove

½ teaspoon fresh oregano (optional)

Salt and pepper to taste

BOIL the nopalitos according to the instructions on page 25, but add the dried shrimp to boil along with them. Drain and rinse briefly under running water.

HEAT the oil in a 10-inch skillet over medium heat. Add the onion and sauté until translucent, about 2 minutes. Add the nopalitos and the chili powder, garlic, oregano, salt, and pepper. Sauté for 5 to 10 minutes, then serve.

CRISP RED SNAPPER FILLETS WITH TOMATOES AND CILANTRO DRESSING

SERVES 8

Lent is a joyful time in South Texas. *Bluebonnets burst open in the clear spring light, and dainty pink primroses wave and nod in a grassy sea. In the evening, the melon-colored sunsets are perfumed with confederate jasmine and mountain laurel. The gray of the winter brushland is gone. From church to fields, the feeling of rebirth surrounds me.*

On Fridays during Lent, fish is always on the menu. Local Gulf-caught red snapper is a local favorite. When freshly caught, they are mild in flavor and meaty.

DRESSING

½ cup olive oil

1 garlic clove

½ cup chopped cilantro

Salt to taste

2 to 3 tablespoons vinegar

FISH

Peanut oil for frying (2 to 3 cups)

¾ cup dry bread crumbs

Salt pepper

2 pounds red snapper fillets

2 ripe medium tomatoes, cut in half

MAKE THE DRESSING: Combine the olive oil, garlic, cilantro, and salt in a blender or food processor, and purée well. Add the vinegar through the feed hole. Blend for 5 seconds, then remove. Set aside. Preheat the oven to 200°F.

HEAT the peanut oil in a medium skillet over medium heat. Pour the bread crumbs onto a pie plate, and season with salt and pepper. Dip the fillets into the bread crumbs to coat. Place as many of the fillets as will fit into the pan flesh side down. (If you add the fillets skin side down, the skin may shrink and the fillet will curl up and cook unevenly.) Fry gently for 5 minutes on each side. Place fillets on a heatpoof serving platter, and set aside in warm oven.

DIP the cut faces of the tomato halves in the bread crumbs and place them, crumb side down, into the hot pan. Fry gently for 2 minutes, then remove from the pan. To serve, place the tomatoes on the platter with the fish and drizzle the cilantro dressing on top or serve separately.

PESCADO AL MOJO DE AJO FISH IN GARLIC SAUCE

SERVES 4

The term mojo, *which means "sauce," comes from the word* mojar, *which means "to wet." Flavorful mojos are used in the cuisines of Puerto Rico, Cuba, Haiti, and Mexico—all countries with Caribbean coastlines. The best-known mojo is* mojo de ajo, *which is a garlic-infused oil usually served with seafood, such as fish and shrimp. Quick, light, healthful, and flavorful, pescado al mojo de ajo is a restaurant favorite, especially during the meatless days of Lent.*

1 cup whole milk

2 pounds thin fish fillets, such as flounder, red snapper, or trout

1 cup olive oil

1 head of garlic, cloves separated and thinly sliced

1 cup all-purpose flour

Salt and pepper to taste

Lime wedges

POUR the milk into a medium bowl and add the fish fillets. Soak the fillets in the refrigerator for at least 30 minutes.

HEAT the oil in a 12-inch skillet over medium heat. Add the garlic and gently sauté for 2 minutes. Using a slotted spoon, remove the garlic and set aside. Keep pan with oil hot.

POUR the flour into a shallow plate. Remove a fish fillet from the milk, dredge well in the flour, and place in the hot oil. Fry the fish for approximately 3 minutes on each side, seasoning them with salt and pepper as they cook, then remove and place on a serving platter. Prepare all the fillets in this fashion. Spoon a small amount of the cooking oil over the hot fillets and garnish with a few slices of the sautéed garlic. Serve with lime wedges.

❖ **CAMARONES AL MOJO DE AJO (SHRIMP IN GARLIC BROTH)**: Substitute 2 pounds of jumbo shrimp for the fish. Peel the shrimp, but add the shells to the frying pan when frying the garlic to extract all of the shrimp flavor, removing them along with the garlic. (Shrimp shells adhere to the meat as they cook, making them difficult to shell afterward, but you lose a lot of shrimp flavor by not cooking them in their shells. Frying the shells first in the oil is a good solution.)

CAMARONES EN SALSA VERDE

SHRIMP WITH GREEN SAUCE

SERVES 4-6

My husband and I are fascinated with the shrimp boats that sail in and out of Port Isabel on the southernmost tip of the Texas Gulf Coast. The Gulf of Mexico is famous for its shrimp, and every day fresh loads arrive, brought in by crews that may have been at sea for three, maybe four weeks. The 15-foot boats chug along the jetties, followed by gulls and led by porpoises. Their hoisted nets dry in the salt air and sunshine, and their engines drum low and steady beneath the crashing of the waves. I often wonder, when I look out across the Gulf, how many shrimpers are out there, away from their families, bobbing along in a rusty shrimp boat, waiting for the shrimp.

The heavy cream here gives the shrimp a golden, crisp crust, which is nicely complemented by the slightly sour, herbaceous flavor of the sauce.

2 pounds jumbo shrimp, peeled and deveined (see Note), reserving the shells

1 pint heavy cream

SAUCE

1 pound fresh tomatillos, husked and washed, or two 8-ounce cans, drained

1 garlic clove

Salt and pepper to taste

1 cup olive oil

1 cup all-purpose flour

½ cup chopped cilantro

PLACE the shrimp in a medium bowl and add the cream. Let the shrimp soak in the cream for at least 30 minutes in the refrigerator.

PLACE the shrimp shells in a small saucepan, cover with water, and bring to a boil; boil for about 5 minutes, then strain and discard the shells; reserve 1 cup of the liquid and set aside to cool.

FILL a 2- quart saucepan with water and add the tomatillos. Bring to a boil, reduce heat, and simmer for 10 minutes, until the tomatillos change from bright to dull green. Drain and add the tomatillos to the container of a blender or a food processor. Add the garlic, salt and pepper, and reserved shrimp broth. Purée the sauce until it is smooth. Set aside.

HEAT the olive oil in a 10-inch skillet. Remove the shrimp from the cream and season the shrimp with salt and pepper. Pour the flour into a shallow pie plate. Dredge the shrimp in the flour and place in the hot pan in batches, frying them on one side for 60 seconds, then flipping to the other side for another 60 seconds. Remove from the oil and serve immediately, topped with the sauce and garnished with the cilantro.

NOTE: Deveining the shrimp involves removing the gritty, sand-filled intestine that runs along its back. After shelling the shrimp, slide the blade of a knife vertically along the back of the shrimp, just a bit to the right of center. The "vein" runs directly in the center, so you want to cut to the side of it. Push the cut flap open with the tip of the knife. The long vein should pull out easily.

TRADITIONAL BACALAO PREPARED SALTED COD

SERVES 6-8

A local historian, Bertha Young Ibaldi, was born on the Santa Anita ranch, in the heart of the Wild Horse Desert. She was a descendant of a family that received the ranch through a land grant from the Spanish crown in the mid-1700s. Below is an excerpt from her manuscript "A Childhood History of Santa Anita," which contains recipes and memoirs of ranch life at the turn of the century. I think it is particularly telling of how Spanish food traditions were established and continued in the isolated Texas ranch communities through the generations.

1 pound bacalao (dried salt cod)	½ cup finely chopped red bell pepper
¼ cup olive oil	1 tablespoon minced parsley
2 tablespoons minced onion	2 tablespoons capers
1 pound ripe tomatoes, peeled, seeded, and finely chopped	½ cup chopped green olives

REMOVE the bacalao from its package and rinse in a colander under running water for 15 minutes to remove excess salt. Place the bacalao in a large bowl, cover with fresh water, and soak overnight. Cover the bowl with plastic wrap, if desired.

DRAIN and discard the water from the bowl. Place the bacalao in a 10-inch skillet and cover with fresh water. Turn the heat on low and cook the bacalao gently for 15 or 20 minutes, without letting the water boil. Taste the bacalao to make sure the flavor is not too salty or strong. Simmer 10 minutes longer if it is still too salty. Remove the bacalao from the skillet and drain and discard the water.

HEAT the olive oil in a clean 12-inch skillet over medium heat. Add the onion, tomatoes, red pepper, and parsley, and sauté until the tomatoes have dissolved into a pulp, about 10 minutes. Add 1 cup of water when the mixture gets dry, but do not add more. Add the bacalao, capers, and olives. Cover the skillet and simmer the bacalao for 30 minutes. Occasionally remove the cover from the skillet to check on the progress of the bacalao, and break the fish into flakes with the back of a spoon as it is cooking. After 30 minutes, uncover the skillet and continue to simmer until the stewing liquid is reduced, about 10 minutes. Serve immediately.

"It so happened that mother was preparing Spanish cod fish, bacalao *. . . . We sat down to eat, one of the guests, a Spaniard and his brother, remarked to my mother 'Nora, I have had* bacalao *in Spain and in Mexico but will you tell me how you know how to prepare such a delicious dish when you have been born and reared in South Texas,' . . . . My mother said 'you, I hope, have not forgotten that my own mother's people came from Valladolid, Castilla de Vieja, and my own mother used to prepare fish this way,' which was true. Most of the cuisine was handed down from generation to generation. . . ."*

SALT COD

BACALAO, dried salt cod, is yet another food item brought to the New World by the *conquistadores*. Bacalao has always been popular in Europe, and was introduced to the Americas by the Spanish. But, as codfish are native to the North Atlantic, not the Gulf of Mexico, bacalao has always been considered by the people of the Wild Horse Desert to be an imported delicacy.

The origin of salted dried cod can be traced to both the Vikings and the Basque people, around the ninth century. The Vikings were excellent shipbuilders and sailed the cold North Atlantic, where the cod is plentiful. The cod was filleted and "freeze-dried" in the cold Atlantic air, thus preserving the catch for future use.

Meanwhile, the Basque fishermen hunted whale in their region of the Bay of Biscay. The Lenten fasts mandated by the Catholic Church made fish an extremely profitable commodity. (The whale was considered a fish in those days.) The whale meat and blubber was sliced and salted for preservation, and sold in distant markets across Europe. But whale meat is fatty and tends to go rancid quickly. Fat does not absorb salt as efficiently as lean meat, making the salting process for whale meat difficult and costly.

In time, the intrepid Vikings and the tenacious Basque whalers crossed paths. The Basques admired the craftsmanship of the Viking boats and quickly learned the Viking techniques of boatbuilding. Also, the Basque fishermen discovered the virtually fat-free codfish that the Vikings consumed. The lean codfish absorbed salt easily and were better preserved and tastier than whale meat. With better boats, the Basque could reach the codfish of the North Atlantic. The salted cod could be distributed throughout Europe, even in warmer climates. An industry was born.

EMPANADAS DE BACALAO SALT COD TURNOVERS

MAKES 45 EMPANADAS

Empanadas are a great way to introduce the strong flavor of bacalao to the unen-lightened. The mellow, buttery puff pastry is the perfect foil for the intense, salty flavor of the dried cod, tomatoes, and olives.

2½ pounds frozen puff pastry sheets, thawed
Traditional Bacalao (see page 198)

PREHEAT the oven to 375°F. Cut the puff pastry into 3 x 3-inch squares (45 squares total). Fill each square with 2 teaspoons of the bacalao. Fold over each filled square to form a triangle and pinch the edges together. Place the empanadas on an ungreased cookie sheet and bake for 20 to 25 minutes, until golden brown. Remove from cookie sheet and allow to cool briefly before serving.

POINT ISABEL STUFFED CRAB

SERVES 6

As a girl, *I loved to order stuffed crab when I went with my grandparents to South Padre Island, the long sandy barrier island that stretches along the eastern shore of Texas. We always went to eat at The Jetties, a turquoise and pink restaurant that faced the channel. As we waited for our meal, we would watch the shrimp boats as they headed off into the Gulf of Mexico. The sunbathers on the public beach were right outside the panoramic windows of the restaurant, and someone was always flying a kite or throwing a boomerang into the gusty winds that swirled above the surf. My stuffed crab eventually arrived, bready, devoid of any actual crab meat, and deeply fried—I ordered this dish every time we went to The Jetties.*

I still love stuffed crab, but now that I am grown up I prefer my homemade version, which has plenty of real crab meat. The crunchy vegetables and the high notes of sherry complement the luxurious seafood flavor.

6 tablespoons butter

¾ cup chopped green onions

¼ cup chopped red bell pepper

¼ cup chopped celery

1 pound crab meat, picked over to remove the bits of shell (do not rinse)

1 cup bread crumbs

½ cup white wine or dry sherry

Juice of 1 lime

Pinch cayenne

Salt and pepper to taste

MELT the butter in a 10-inch skillet over medium heat. Add the green onions, red pepper, and celery, and sauté for 3 minutes. Stir in the crab meat and mix well. Add the bread crumbs and combine well. Add the wine, lime juice, cayenne, and salt and pepper. Remove the skillet from the heat.

PREHEAT the oven to 350°F. Divide the crab mixture among 6 half-cup ramekins. Bake the crab for 30 minutes, until the outer crust is golden brown.

❖ **IF YOU CAN FIND THEM**, using the original crab shells in lieu of ramekins will impart a tad more crab flavor. You can also use the large scallop shells traditionally used for coquilles St. Jacques for a nice presentation.

ALBONDIGAS DE CAMARON SHRIMP MEATBALLS

SERVES 4

Recipes for this traditional Lenten dish can be found in both the Wild Horse Desert and the coastal state of Veracruz, Mexico. The shrimp is quite delicate in texture and flavor, and the fresh tomato sauce dappled with cilantro demands a side dish of mellow *frijoles, fluffy* arroz a la mexicana, *and a basket of hot, fresh corn tortillas.*

SAUCE

1 pound ripe tomatoes
2 to 3 serrano chiles
1 garlic clove
Salt and pepper to taste

ALBONDIGAS

1 pound shrimp, peeled and deveined
1 egg
½ cup dry bread crumbs
¼ cup chopped cilantro
Salt and pepper to taste
Corn oil for frying

HEAT a cast-iron or other heavy skillet over high heat with oil. Add the tomatoes and chiles, and roast until they have blackened in a few places (10 minutes). Remove from the heat, peel and core the tomatoes, cut in half, and remove the seeds. Remove the stems of the chiles. Place the tomatoes and chiles in a food processor and add the garlic. Process until the sauce is smooth. Pour the sauce into a small skillet, season with salt and pepper, bring to a simmer, and reduce the liquid to thicken the sauce about 10 minutes. Set aside.

PLACE the shrimp in a food processor and pulse just until they become a chunky paste. Transfer to a medium bowl. Add the egg, bread crumbs, cilantro, salt, and pepper. Stir to combine well. The mixture will thicken slightly once the bread crumbs have absorbed some moisture, so let the mixture stand for 2 or 3 minutes.

ADD approximately 1 inch of oil to a 10-inch skillet and heat over medium heat until hot. Form walnut-size balls with the shrimp mixture and carefully place in the hot oil, cooking a few at a time, in batches. Fry one side until the shrimp turns pink, about 3 minutes, and then flip to the other side and fry for another 3 minutes. Remove the cooked albondigas to drain on paper towels. Serve hot with the sauce.

SPECKLED TROUT CEVICHE

SERVES 8

While researching for this book I stopped at South Padre Island to visit my friend Rod Bates. He is involved with the local museum, and is an expert on South Texas military history. He told me of a speckled trout ceviche that the Union soldiers concocted during their stay on the island. The troops fished in the surf, and would put together a hasty meal that required no cooking.

I am guessing that the original version of this dish used vinegar instead of lime juice, and that the troops did not have the luxury of fresh avocados, tomatoes, or cilantro. However, I am sure the soldiers' spartan version of ceviche was far tastier than the generous amounts of hardtack that constituted their daily rations.

1 pound speckled trout fillets or any other white fish fillets

1 cup fresh lime juice

1 pound ripe tomatoes, seeded, and finely chopped

2 avocados, seeded and cut into small cubes

1 red onion, minced

1 ounce cilantro (about a handful), minced

Salt and pepper to taste

CUT the trout into ½-inch chunks and place in a medium bowl. Add the lime juice and toss so that it completely coats each piece of fish. Allow the fish to soak in the lime juice for 45 minutes in the refrigerator. The fish will turn opaque as it soaks and will be ready when no longer translucent.

ADD the remaining ingredients and combine well. Serve immediately.

❖ **YOU CAN SUBSTITUTE RAW OYSTERS** for the speckled trout in this dish, which the troops enjoyed as well.

SEARED TUNA WITH GRILLED SALSA

SERVES 4

Gilbert Vela, a legendary fishing guide from Port Isabel, Texas, knows every-thing about the fish of the Texas Gulf Coast. Yellowfin tuna is common and has a lovely tex-ture and flavor, while blackfin is slightly more common, although not as flavorful. However, the best tuna, according to Gilbert, is the bluefin, which is a rare catch in these waters. It has an exquisite, meaty flavor that is best appreciated when minimally prepared, such as in this recipe.

½ cup minced onion

1 cup seeded and finely chopped ripe tomato

2 serrano chiles, seeded and minced

½ cup minced cilantro

1 avocado, peeled, pitted, and cubed

Salt and pepper to taste

¼ cup olive oil

2 pounds fresh tuna steaks, 1 to 1½ inches thick

Fresh lime wedges

COMBINE the onion, tomato, chiles, cilantro, and avocado in a mixing bowl. Sea-son with salt and pepper (this can be prepared in advance and refrigerated). Heat the olive oil in a 12-inch cast-iron skillet over medium-high heat. Season the tuna steaks with salt and pepper. Gently place the steaks in the pan, searing the tuna for 3 to 4 minutes on each side. The steaks are best eaten rare, though you can sear them longer for medium doneness. Remove from skillet and set aside.

ADD the vegetable mixture to the skillet, stirring occasionally. When the onion has caramelized, remove the skillet from the heat. Pour the grilled sauce over the tuna. Serve immediately with fresh lime wedges.

NOTE: Tuna steaks have natural striations in the muscle that pull apart easily into ¼-inch slices after the steak is cooked. To serve as an appetizer, simply separate the steak into slices using a fork. Serve the warm slices arranged around the grilled salsa on a platter. Serves 12 as an appetizer.

CHAPTER EIGHT

GAME AND GOAT

FIRE AND MEAT kept people alive in this arid country. The existence of animals that could survive with little water and sparse edible vegetation meant survival for indigenous tribes and settlers alike. And as we have ample supply of mesquite wood, there was always fuel for a fire.

I am combining game and goat dishes because they make a natural pair in my frame of reference. These are wily creatures who survive on their wits. They thrive in the harsh desert climate with little or no water. Whether wild or domesticated, they live on vast tracks of what is essentially wilderness, foraging for the tiniest amounts of edible greenery, managing to fatten themselves where other animals would perish.

Yes, goats are domesticated, but anyone who has been around goats knows that they meet only the barest of requirements for this designation. Like game, they have no predictable habits (other than being unpredictable). They travel far and wide, and without a goatherd, would probably never return home. However, more than pigs or cattle, goats proved convenient for slaughtering on the region's many small ranches, as the meat could be used in one meal. When a cow was slaughtered (producing hundreds of pounds of meat), the meat that was not immediately consumed needed to be salted and dried for preservation, which was time-consuming and dependant on good weather.

My grandfather told me that when he moved to his family's ranch in the early 1930s, not a trace of wildlife could be found. Game was often the only protein available to the small homesteads, and over time it was virtually hunted out. As with other ranchers in Texas, fencing the family ranch became his priority, as it kept his cattle from roaming the plains of Wild Horse Desert and kept hunters from trespassing. In his lifetime he saw the resurgence of white-tailed deer, bobcat, quail, dove, *javelina* (wild boar), rabbit, and even wild turkey.

These are the historic, rustic, and treasured family recipes that have been with us since people first settled in the Wild Horse Desert. These are the dishes that kept us here.

BUYING KID GOAT

FINDING KID GOAT IN YOUR AREA may not be as hard as you think. First, try the Latin American supermarkets; ask in the meat department because they may be able to special-order one for you. Kid goat is also very popular in Middle Eastern cuisine, as well as Greek and Indian cuisines, so there is definitely a demand within certain cultures. Ask at local restaurants if they have a supplier.

Kid goat can be a bit expensive, owing to the hand labor involved in butchering. There are no industrialized processing plants for goat meat, so make sure your supplier delivers the meat cleaned and fully dressed. The kidneys should be intact and attached to the spine. If you ask, a butcher should be able to supply you with the blood, cleaned offal, and head. Make sure you select a small *cabrito*. The best cabritos are milk fed and not more than 45 days old. Don't buy any goat over 12 pounds, as that indicates a more mature animal with a stronger flavor and tougher meat.

ROASTED CABRITO KID GOAT

SERVES 4-6

Goat is very popular in northern Mexico and South Texas. Even so, cabrito is not easy to come by. It can be expensive, even more so if you plan to feed a crowd. When you are served cabrito in someone's home, then you know they have pulled out all the stops for your visit. Do we serve cabrito for a celebration, or is it the serving of cabrito that we are celebrating? Who knows? We enjoy it thoroughly when we have it.

To me, cabrito has a flavor and texture similar to dark turkey meat. It does not make the world's best cold leftovers—this is a dish you want to dig in and enjoy while it is hot and fresh! Make sure you have plenty of salsa, like Salsa de Chile Chipotle Ahumado (see page 103) and hot corn tortillas on hand. There is nothing as delicious as a hot morsel of cabrito made into a taquito with a fresh corn tortilla and a fiery salsa!

1 small cabrito (kid goat), 10 to 12 pounds (see "Buying Kid Goat," page 208)
Salt and pepper

ROASTING a cabrito is quite simple. You'll need a large baking pan in which to place the cabrito. Seventeen by eleven inches is a good size. Place the cabrito in the pan, rib side down. You may have to cut the cabrito in half or in quarters in order to make it fit in your oven; as long as the pieces are laid out flat and not stacked on top of each other, it will be fine.

PREHEAT the oven to 350°F. Generously season the outside of the cabrito with salt and pepper. In order to retain the moisture in the meat, place a sheet of aluminum foil over the cabrito, but don't seal the edges—you don't want the meat to steam. Roast for 1 to 1½ hours, until it is tender. Remove the foil during the last 30 minutes of roasting so that the skin crisps a bit.

TO SERVE CABRITO

JUST LIKE A CHICKEN, a roast *cabrito* is divided into specific parts, with nothing wasted. First, the carcass is split vertically down the spine, then it is spilt into the following cuts:

- *La paleta*—The front shoulder, which includes the scapula and foreleg.

- *La riñonada*—The saddle along the lower spine with the kidney attached, which includes a few ribs, and half of the tenderloin.

- *La pierna*—The back leg.

- *Las costillas*—The ribs and the other half of the tenderloin.

- *El pezcuezo*—The neck (not served in restaurants—too bony).

- *La cabeza*—The head (roasted along with the cabrito).

- *Los machitos*—A crude version of a liver sausage in which the liver, heart, and lungs are roughly chopped into 1/2-inch pieces, wrapped in the caul fat of the goat, and then bound together with the cleaned intestines. The machito is boiled for 1 hour and then roasted with the cabrito. It is served along with the cabrito, and can be sliced and made into *taquitos*.

GUISADO DE CABRITO STEWED KID GOAT

SERVE 4-6

This dish has a beautiful balance of flavors: rich meat, salty broth, and sour tomatillos. *It is classic northern Mexico and South Texas home cooking, hearty and simple. Although we use kid goat, you can substitute a young lamb in this recipe.*

My husband usually volunteers to chop the cabrito *with a cleaver, but you can ask your butcher to do the job; request it chopped into 2- to 3-inch pieces, bones and all (the bones add a lot of flavor). Make sure to include the kidneys, leaving them whole, as they are a delicacy. If your butcher is not as patient as my husband, you can have it cut into two dozen larger pieces. You will still have a glorious* guisado, *and the cooking time won't change.*

2 tablespoons corn oil

1 small kid goat (cabrito) with kidneys, about 8 to 10 pounds (see "Buying Kid Goat," page 208), cut into 2- to 3-inch pieces, kidneys left whole

1 tablespoon salt

2 teaspoons pepper

2 serrano chiles

1 (28-ounce) can tomatillos, drained, or 1 pound fresh tomatillos, husks removed, washed, and boiled (see page 27)

1 to 2 garlic cloves

8 to 12 corn tortillas

HEAT the oil in a 12-inch lidded sauté pan or a Dutch oven over medium heat. Add the meat and cook for about 15 minutes, turning the pieces so that they brown evenly. Once the meat is browned, add 1 cup water, the salt, pepper, and chiles. Cover and simmer over medium heat for about 30 minutes.

PURÉE the tomatillos and garlic in a blender or food processor. After the kid goat has simmered for 30 minutes, add the tomatillo purée, cover again, and simmer for another 30 minutes. Once the goat has simmered for 60 minutes, test a piece for tenderness. If it cuts easily with a fork, it is ready. If not, stew for another 15 to 20 minutes and test again. Serve immediately with hot corn tortillas.

❖ **CABRITO EN SU SANGRE (KID GOAT IN BLOOD SAUCE):** I've included a variation on the above recipe, which is basically the same dish using the goat's blood in place of the tomatillos. On the isolated, humble ranches of yesteryear, no source of protein was wasted. The flavor is earthy and rich, and very traditional. This is probably one of the oldest dishes in this book. If you can get the goat's blood from your kid goat purveyor, you can make this dish. Substitute 2 cups of blood for the tomatillos, making a purée with the garlic and blood in a blender or food processor as the recipe indicates above. (Blood will coagulate—it will probably be coagulated when you buy it—blending will make it liquid again.) Add the purée to the stew as indicated above, but after 45 minutes of stewing rather than 30, then stew for 15 minutes more before checking for doneness.

GOATS IN THE NORTEÑO

GOAT'S MILK AND MEAT are particularly favored in northern Mexico, where goats thrive and proliferate in the region's dry desert climate. The *conquistadores* originally brought domesticated goats to the New World from Spain; however, many attribute the local popularity of cabrito to the influx of Middle Eastern immigrants in the mid-1600s. The use of cumin in Mexican cooking and the development of the flour tortilla are also attributed to a Middle Eastern influence.

CABRITO AL ATAÚD KID GOAT IN A TOMB

An *ataúd* is a coffin or casket. In parts of northern Mexico, rectangular casket-like boxes are constructed in which to roast cabritos. My brothers-in-law Memo and Cuco are fanatics for cabrito al ataúd. They participate in cook-offs, swearing that their ataúd keeps the kid goat moist and tender.

The ataúd uses a similar cooking concept as *barbacoa*, that is, a pit in the ground (see page 176). In this case, the box functions as a large, insulated oven. In Michoacan, a southern state in Mexico, they use a similar cooking method to make their popular *birria*, a lamb stew. The stew is traditionally cooked in a hole in the ground, but for convenience, roadside restaurants there often use an aboveground roaster, sometimes made out of a 55-gallon drum. It is possible that the ataúd took its inspiration from the roadside birria roaster.

Finding information on the origin of the ataúd is sketchy at best. However, cooking meat in an insulated environment is an old tradition, and one that is being revived. It may be that the ataúd was constructed to ensure cooking success with meats that are difficult to roast. Our favorite celebration meat, cabrito has the potential to become dry and stringy when roasted improperly. The ataúd might have been developed to remedy this problem. Not only do the cabritos stay moist, but the ataúd works very well when roasting suckling pigs and chickens.

The ataúd is built entirely of wood, then the interior is lined with metal, as is the top of the exterior lid. Ours is about 4 feet long, 4 feet tall, and 3 feet wide. There is a grill inside, on which the cabrito (or chicken or small pig) is placed. There is a pan underneath the grill to catch the meat juices. Once the meat is in the box and the cover is placed on top, the live coals are shoveled on top of the lid. The sole source of heat is the coals on top. Once the meat is roasted, some enthusiasts prefer to finish the cooking over live coals to crisp the skin and infuse the meat with smoke flavor. They simply lift the entire grill with the meat on it from the steamy ataúd chamber and place it on top of the lid loaded with live coals for about 10 minutes.

Mystery and anticipation surround the ataúd during the long cooking process: Is it ready? Is it undercooked? Overcooked? Removing the heavy, coal-filled lid requires two men: sweating and swearing, they wrestle off the lid, releasing the aroma of roast meat. The children look on in bewildered, hungry anticipation. Someone smiles—it's ready.

FRIED RABBIT

SERVES 4-6

There are vast legions of rabbits hopping across the Wild Horse Desert. We had plenty around my house when I was growing up, and occasionally we would hunt them and fry them, as in this recipe. For a completely authentic South Texas meal, serve the fried rabbit warm with Salsa Cruda de Chile Piquín (see page 94).

2 cups corn oil

2 cups milk

2 eggs

1½ cups all-purpose flour

Salt and pepper to taste

5-pound rabbit, cleaned and dressed, cut into pieces

ADD the corn oil to a 12-inch skillet, and heat over medium heat until it registers about 350°F on a deep-frying thermometer.

WHISK the milk and eggs in a bowl, combining well. Pour the flour into a shallow dish and season with salt and pepper. In batches, dip the pieces of rabbit in the milk mixture and then dredge in the flour mixture. Place the pieces of rabbit in the skillet, and fry slowly, about 10 minutes, until golden brown. Flip the pieces over, then fry for another 10 minutes. Remove the rabbit from the oil and drain on paper towels. Serve immediately.

"When mama prepared a sack lunch, it was—in season—often of fried rabbit. We were introduced to Conejo Frito *early in life and relished it. Daddy enjoyed hunting cottontail and jackrabbit which were plentiful in our area. Daddy would take his gun and in his pickup drive to check on his fields and pastures late in the afternoons. As the sun set and it grew darker, rabbits would come from cover of the brush to forage in the grassy open spaces. There they fell prey to his gun. . . . The cottontail were usually fried and the jackrabbits were used for chili meat. Jackrabbit meat is dark, tough, stringy and has a gamier flavor than cottontail. For this reason it is preferred for chili meat. Rabbit is best in spring and early summer and at school I could hardly wait for lunch hour to eat our fried rabbit. Our lunch was communal. I shared with my brothers and the school principal, Simon Gomez. Invariably Principal Gomez on his rounds at lunch would come to our table and ask what we were having. I would always reply, 'fried chicken.' He knew it was mama's best fried rabbit, and never refused a sample."*

LUCY M. GARZA, *SOUTH TEXAS MEXICAN COOKBOOK*

BUTTERED QUAIL
SERVES 4

We have an abundance of scaled quail in the Wild Horse Desert, as well as our famous bobwhite quail. The flavor is similar to free-range chicken, the meat white and firm. Domestic quail differ from wild quail in that they are fatter but have less quail flavor, and are usually marinated with a vinegar-based preparation that breaks down the muscle fiber, making the meat mushy. Nonmarinated domestic quail are a better choice if you can find them. Ask your butcher. Whether domestic or wild, serving quail always indicates a special meal.

8 quail, cut in half down the spine
½ cup unsalted butter
Salt and pepper to taste
1 tablespoon minced fresh thyme

PREHEAT the broiler. Adjust the oven racks so that the quail will be about 8 inches from the flame or heating element.

PLACE the quail halves rib side down on a broiler rack. In a small saucepan, melt the butter. Season the butter with salt and pepper, and add the thyme. Stir and remove from the heat. Using a pastry brush, coat the quail well with the herbed butter.

BROIL the quail for 10 minutes, until they are golden and toasted. Serve immediately.

NOTE: Because the quail halves are so thin, they completely cook through without needing to be flipped. Even though they are not flipped, watch them carefully so they don't overcook, which would make them dry.

❖ **SUBSTITUTE OTHER HERBS** for a different flavor: parsley, cilantro, and tarragon all work well.

QUAIL HUNTING

QUAIL HUNTING is our sport of kings in the Wild Horse Desert. Bing Crosby, Phil Harris, Sam Walton, President Dwight Eisenhower, and President George Bush (both father and son) have all been to South Texas to hunt quail. The sport is expensive, and unlike the solitary task of deer hunting, quail hunting requires a fair-sized group of hunters to bring home a meal. Quail hunting provides an excellent opportunity to invite your friends and family out for a weekend adventure.

And the hunting dogs! Everyone brings two or three dogs, and maybe a pup, to tag along and train with the big dogs. Few things are as exciting as watching a perfectly trained bird dog point out a covey of quail. The dogs sniff and smell the air, as they listen to some internal instinct telling them where the birds are. Once the quail are spotted, the dogs creep toward the covey, wholly focused, seeing nothing but the birds. Their masters notice their gaze and tenuously stalk nearer to the point of focus. Together, the dogs hold their pose, a foreleg angled toward the quail. No one moves, then a whir and whistle of wings— They're off!

I am not the hunter in the family; I am the cook. I enjoy listening to the stories at the end of the afternoon's hunt, as we clean the birds and ready them for the grill. Some of our best family times have involved quail hunts, and the evening meals afterward. The delight of quail hunting goes beyond mere shooting.

CODORNIZ EN ESCABECHE PICKLED QUAIL

MAKES APPETIZERS FOR 12

I prefer lean appetizers to mayonnaise-based dips and cheese boards—I figure you should save the heavier dishes for the main meal and not fill up before you get to the table. I first had Codorniz en Escabeche, which are pickled quail, at a family wedding in Saltillo, Coahuila, in northern Mexico. This escabeche fits perfectly with any menu, either casual or elegant. It has certainly become a favorite among my friends for its flavor and because quail is a true regional Texas delicacy.

You can have a lot of fun with this escabeche. Below are suggested vegetables, but you should select the freshest vegetables that are in season to combine with your quail. Having a mix of colors is extremely important in composing an appetizing platter like this one. Use a mixture of onions in different colors for good effect; like red and white pearl onions mixed with cippolini onions. Occasionally, I add boiled new potatoes; the blue ones are my favorite!

2 tablespoons olive oil

8 quail, cut into quarters (see "To Quarter Quail," page 223)

2 pounds mixed small onions (red and white pearl, cippolini)

1 pound carrots, cut into sticks

1 pound fresh asparagus or green beans, trimmed

1 pound mushrooms (I prefer crimini)

1 pound zucchini, cut into sticks

DRESSING

1½ cups olive oil

3 garlic cloves, minced

1 sprig fresh oregano

Salt and pepper to taste

¾ cup red wine vinegar

HEAT the olive oil in a 10-inch skillet over medium heat. Brown the quail in the skillet until they are golden, about 5 minutes on each side. Remove the quail from the skillet, and cool.

FILL a large bowl with ice water and keep handy. Fill a medium skillet with about 2 inches of water and bring to a boil. Add the pearl onions and boil (blanch) for

(continued)

CODORNIZ EN ESCABECHE, CON'T.

1 minute. Using a slotted spoon, remove the onions from the water and plunge into the ice water to stop the cooking. When cool, remove from water, cut the root ends of the onions off, then peel the onions by slitting the skins with the tip of a knife and sliding it off.

DISCARD the cooking water and refill the pan with water and bring to a boil. Add the carrot sticks and blanch for 3 minutes. Remove the carrots from the water using a slotted spoon and cool in the ice water (keep adding ice to keep the water cold). One at a time, blanch the asparagus, mushrooms, and zucchini each for 1 minute, using fresh water each time (this helps preserve each vegetable's vivid color). Remove the vegetables from the boiling water and cool in the ice water. Place the cooled quail, pearl onions, and vegetables in a large ziplock bag.

WHISK together the dressing ingredients, and add the dressing to the ziplock bag. Seal the bag and store for 24 hours in the refrigerator. (Alternatively, you can use a bowl covered in plastic wrap, but the vegetables are more likely to break when you toss them with marinade.) Turn the bag over occasionally so that the dressing evenly coats the quail and vegetables.

WHEN ready to serve, remove the quail and vegetables from the bag using a slotted spoon. Arrange the pearl onions and vegetables on a large platter and place the pickled quail in the middle.

◆ **SPICY PICKLED QUAIL**: For a hotter pickled quail, add a 7-ounce can of sliced pickled jalapeños to the marinating bag.

TO QUARTER QUAIL

QUARTERING THE QUAIL is easy if you have poultry shears or a large chef's knife. Usually when the quail are dressed (internal organs removed), the body is cut along one side of the spine. Using poultry shears, I usually snip along the other side of the spine as well, removing the spinal column. Then I separate the leg quarters from the whole breast by cutting through the connective flesh that joins the breasts to the thighs. All that is left is to separate the breast into two halves as you would a chicken breast. Simply cut vertically between the breasts, parting the bones.

ESCABECHE

THE TERM "ESCABECHE" comes from the ancient Arabic word *sikbaj,* which basically means "meat stew in vinegar." The Moors, who invaded Spain in A.D. 711 and brought with them the food, culture, architecture, and language influences of the Middle East and North Africa, must have introduced the term and possibly the recipe. Jamaican *escovitch* and Italian *scapece* are both vinegar-laced meat dishes that indicate the widespread popularity of this techinique. The Spanish *conquistadores* would have brought the recipe with them when they arrived in the Americas. It is theorized that the term *ceviche,* the marinated fish and onion cocktail described on page 204, came from the marriage of the words *cebolla* ("onion") and *escabeche.*

LOMITO DE VENADO CON JALAPEÑO

JALAPEÑO VENISON BACKSTRAP

SERVES 8

My sister Elizabeth insists that she is a terrible cook, but it is simply not true. Her husband Barry is an avid hunter, and he comes home with ducks, quail, dove, venison, and fish almost on a weekly basis. Elizabeth has come up with some superb yet simple recipes for these many different types of game. Her jalapeño venison is fabulous and easy to make, even when one is out at a remote deer camp in the brush.

I will say that Elizabeth has a tendency to add lots of chiles to whatever she cooks, and so I was dubious when I first tried this recipe. Lo and behold, the jalapeño flavor does not overpower the meat. In fact, the vinegar in which the chiles have been pickled tenderizes the venison perfectly and reduces the gamey flavor.

Elizabeth usually serves the venison with a homemade salsa and a side of Red Cabbage with Mustang Grape Glaze (recipe follows), another easy dish that uses our local mustang grapes from the ranch.

1 (28-ounce) can sliced jalapeños, packed in vinegar
1 venison backstrap (1½ to 2 pounds)
Salt and pepper to taste

POUR the contents of the can of jalapeños into a large ziplock bag. Add the venison backstrap and seal. Turn the bag a few times to coat the venison well with the jalapeños. Place the bag in the refrigerator and marinate overnight.

PREHEAT the oven to 400°F. Remove the venison from the plastic bag and discard the bag with the jalapeños. Place the venison in a large baking dish and season with salt and pepper. Roast for about 25 minutes, until the internal temperature reaches 140°F. This should give you a medium-rare venison backstrap. Roast 10 minutes longer for medium doneness.

◆ **VENISON BACKSTRAP SALAD:** Venison backstrap is very similar to beef tenderloin. Therefore the chilled leftovers are especially nice when thinly sliced and served with a pungent sauce, such as a good mustard. Although it's not South Texan, I am particularly enthusiastic about a good arugula salad topped with sliced cold rare venison, garlicky dressing, and a few thick curls of Parmigiano-Reggiano.

RED CABBAGE WITH MUSTANG GRAPE GLAZE

MAKES 8 SERVINGS

Elizabeth serves a lovely side dish of sweet-and-sour red cabbage when she cooks game. I substituted our familiar mustang grape jelly for the more European red currant jelly she was using, and voilà, *a new family tradition was born. Mustang grape jelly is available at many Texas tourist stands and museum shops, as well on many Texas food delicacy Web sites.*

2 cups Basic Soup Stock–chicken (see page 112)

1 medium to large head red cabbage, shredded finely

2 garlic cloves, minced

1 cup grated Parmigiano-Reggiano cheese

3 tablespoons mustang grape jelly (substitute red currant jelly)

½ cup pecans, finely chopped

POUR the chicken stock in a 4-quart saucepan and bring to a boil. Add the shredded cabbage, cover, and simmer for 10 minutes. Remove from the heat and drain and discard the liquid. Return cabbage to saucepan and add the garlic, cheese, and jelly; cover again and heat gently for 7 to 10 minutes. Toss with pecans before serving.

MUSTANG GRAPES

MY GRANDMOTHER had a grape arbor behind her house, and on it grew mustang grapes (*Vitaceae Vitis* subsp. *mustangensis*), which grows wild throughout Texas. Sour and unpleasant to eat straight from the vine, mustang grapes yield a decent wine and a distinctively flavored jelly.

We would make jelly with the grapes we harvested, and we sealed the tops of the jars with hot paraffin. The jelly was enjoyed on toast during the remainder of the year, as we sat and drank tea with our grandmother.

CHAPTER NINE

SWEETS

I HAD A PONY when I was young. I don't quite remember her name—in fact I believe I changed the name many times, depending on the last book I read or television show I watched. Dad said she did the Teaberry Shuffle as she trotted. She was a palomino paint, and she could be feisty when she felt like it, as well as greedy. She threw me only once, when she heard the horn of the ranch truck honking, signaling feeding time. I couldn't rope, so I would catch her attention by gathering mesquite beans for her. She would follow me wherever I wanted to go, as long as she got another mouthful of the sweet, caramel-flavored pods.

Growing up on the ranch, I found it was child's play to locate the trees and shrubs that produced edible sweets and feast on their fruits. *Capules* from the Brazil tree, mustang grapes, *chapote, coma, duraznillo, manzanita,* and *granjeno* berries were fun to gather when they were in season. *Palo Blanco* trees offered a tiny fruit, enjoyed mostly by pesky grackles and worthy of only an occasional chew by someone who wanted to show off for a city friend. My grandmother collected the thorned strawberry *pitayas* that grew on stumpy cacti clusters on the limestone and red dirt hills, in the dappled shade of mesquite motts. Paper wasp nests, shaped like large gray footballs, were occasionally retrieved by the cowboys. The honey from the nests was light colored and profoundly sweet, although the only way to enjoy it was by putting a paper-textured, honey-loaded wad of the nest in your mouth and chewing it.

It wasn't until I began this chapter that I realized that the natives and early settlers of the Wild Horse Desert had no sweets to choose from other than the sparse offerings from the brush. Bringing home fresh game was easier than finding something sweet to share with your family. As more settlers moved to the area, *piloncillo* (raw sugar loaves) and refined sugar were bought from the town merchants and country peddlers, and sweets were enjoyed more often. What was gleaned from the brushland eventually lost favor as a dessert course and became a curiosity.

Even though sweets have become more common the world over, we are most enthusiastic about what is offered at the end of a meal. We have to have our dessert. And like my greedy little nameless pony, we would do just about anything for another mouthful.

PAN DE POLVO SUGAR COOKIES

MAKES 12 DOZEN

This is the most popular cookie at Christmastime in South Texas. Thousands of *dozens are baked and given to neighbors and friends. The cookies melt in your mouth, filling your senses with the warm, sweet flavor of cinnamon.*

TEA

2 sticks cinnamon (Mexican if possible; see page 29)

DOUGH

5 cups all-purpose flour

2¾ cups vegetable shortening

1¼ cups sugar

1½ teaspoons baking powder

1 tablespoon ground cinnamon

SUGAR TOPPING

1 cup sugar

1 tablespoon ground cinnamon

BRING 2 cups of water and the cinnamon sticks to a boil in a small saucepan, reduce the heat, and simmer for about 5 minutes. Remove the cinnamon sticks and allow the liquid to cool.

COMBINE the flour, shortening, sugar, baking powder, and cinnamon in a large bowl. Knead the ingredients together with your hands (the warmth from your hands softens the shortening and helps to combine the dough more easily). Add ¾ cup of the cooled cinnamon tea liquid to the mixture and continue to knead gently with your hands. Do not overwork the dough—it should be tender and flaky; overkneading will develop the gluten in the flour, making it tough. When the dough is well combined, allow to rest covered with a clean towel for 15 minutes. Preheat the oven to 350°F.

COMBINE the sugar and cinnamon for the topping in a shallow dish.

ROLL OUT the cookie dough on a floured surface to a ¼-inch thickness. Cut into 2-inch circles with a cookie cutter or a small glass. (Try not to re-roll any dough, which makes for tougher cookies.) Arrange on an ungreased cookie sheet and bake for 12 to 15 minutes, until pale golden in color and firm to the touch. Roll cookies in the sugar topping while hot, and let cool completely on a rack.

PEMOLES TRADITIONAL CORN FLOUR CINNAMON RINGS

MAKES 48 PEMOLES

Pemoles *are an old ranch-style cookie.* If *an oven were not available, they would have been baked on a warm griddle, although I have never tried it. The corn tortilla mix is crunchy and nutty, and the cookie is only slightly sweet.*

4 cups corn tortilla mix

1 cup sugar

1 cup shortening

2 teaspoon baking powder

1 tablespoon ground cinnamon (Mexican if possible; see page 29)

1 cup strongly brewed coffee, cooled

POUR the corn tortilla mix into a large mixing bowl and add the sugar, shortening, baking powder, and cinnamon. Knead the mixture with your hands until it resembles coarse meal. Add the coffee and continue to knead the dough until it is smooth. Remove the dough from the bowl and knead it for a minute or two on a smooth countertop. Preheat the oven to 350°F.

DIVIDE the dough into 4 pieces, then divide each piece into 12 smaller equal portions (48 total). Roll 1 portion into a ball, then place it on an ungreased cookie sheet. Pat the dough into a 2-inch circle, being careful not to allow the edges of the dough to crack. Using your index finger, push a hole all the way through the center of the dough circle. You can make the hole larger by moving your finger in a circular motion. Form and shape each pemol in this fashion.

BAKE the pemoles for 20 to 25 minutes, until they are firm to the touch and brown on their edges.

HOJARASCAS TRADITIONAL FLAKY SHORTBREAD
MAKES ABOUT 15 DOZEN COOKIES

These cookies are flaky, tender, and ever so fragile. In this version, the cookies utilize the yeast in the beer as a leavener. There are many variations of this recipe; other renditions of hojarascas *use milk, eggs, and some even use Coca-Cola as a leavener instead of beer. Each family that makes them has its own formula. The following recipe is my version, which is a fair representation of what is most traditional, and most delicious.*

I very much recommend using real lard for these cookies, as the flavor is superior to vegetable shortening.

1 cup sugar

1 tablespoon freshly ground cinnamon (Mexican if possible; see page 29)

2 cups all-purpose flour

2 cups instant tortilla mix

1 pound lard or vegetable shortening

8 ounces (1 cup) beer

COMBINE the sugar and cinnamon in a plate and set aside.

PREHEAT the oven to 350°F. In a large bowl, combine the flour and corn tortilla mix. Set aside. In a separate bowl, using an electric mixer, beat the lard until it is fluffy. Alternately add small amounts of the flour mixture and the beer to the lard, beating each time just until fully incorporated (do not overbeat; you want a tender, flaky cookie).

DIVIDE the dough into 4 smaller portions. Roll out each portion on a floured surface to ¼-inch thickness and cut with a 2-inch round cookie cutter. Place the cookies on an ungreased cookie sheet and bake until they are golden brown, about 10 minutes. Remove the hot cookies from the pan and roll them immediately in the cinnamon sugar. Cool completely on wire racks before serving.

GORDITAS DE AZUCAR SWEET FAT TORTILLAS

MAKES 24 GORDITAS

How many paper bags full of gorditas de azucar *did I carry as a child? I would clutch the warm bag to my chest as I walked home from my grandmother's house. The bags were spotted with grease and smelled of toasted wheat and hot brown paper. However many gorditas my grandmother had packed into them, it was never enough. The bag was always empty by the time I reached my house.*

4 cups all-purpose flour

½ cup sugar

1 cup vegetable shortening or lard

2 teaspoons baking powder

1 teaspoon salt

½ cup milk

1 egg

COMBINE all the ingredients in a large mixing bowl. Knead the dough together with your hands. Once it is well combined, divide the dough into 16 equal portions and cover with a clean kitchen towel. Allow the dough to rest for at least 20 minutes.

PREHEAT a griddle on the stove over medium-low heat. With floured hands, pinch the dough into a rough circle about ¼ inch thick and 3 to 4 inches in diameter. (You can also roll them out on a floured surface, but using your hands makes the edges rounder and gives the dough a pleasant texture.) As you make them, place the gorditas one at a time onto a heated griddle, and grill at a moderate heat for 10 minutes on each side, or until golden brown.

◆ **VARIATION:**You can also bake the gorditas in a 400°F oven for 7 minutes. Remove the gorditas from the oven, then flip over and bake for another 7 minutes. However, the griddle method is infinitely more authentic, and gives the gordita a toastier crust.

MARRANITOS LITTLE GINGER PIGS

MAKES 30 COOKIES

My boys grew up on these, a childhood favorite of mine as well. As we made the rounds in the supermarket, we would pass by the bakery first for one of these traditional pastries. I liked them because they have no frosting or artificial colors. My boys would bury their faces in the warm spicy cookie, covering themselves in moist, brown crumbs.

If you don't have a pig-shaped cookie cutter, use a round biscuit cutter or a 3-inch diameter drinking glass to press out round cookies.

10 ounces piloncillo (unrefined sugar; see page 26)	4 cups all-purpose flour
2 pieces star anise	2 teaspooons baking powder
1 stick cinnamon (Mexican preferred; see page 29)	1 teaspoon salt
½ teaspoon ground cloves	4 ounces vegetable shortening or lard
1 tablespoon ground ginger	¼ cup sugar
	1 egg whisked with 1 tablespoon water for brushing onto cookies

PLACE the piloncillo in a small saucepan. Add 1 cup water, the star anise, cinnamon, and cloves. Bring the saucepan to a boil, reduce the heat, and simmer for 2 minutes. Remove from the heat and allow to cool completely. Make sure that you continue to stir the mixture so that the piloncillo completely dissolves. Once the syrup is cooled, remove the whole spices and add the ginger. Preheat the oven to 400°F.

COMBINE the flour, baking powder, salt, shortening, sugar, and the piloncillo syrup in a large mixing bowl. Stir the mixture until it is smooth. Divide the dough in half. Turn one half of the dough onto a floured surface and roll to a ½-inch thickness (about 3 inches in diameter). Cut with a pig-shaped cookie cutter. Using a pastry brush, brush the surface of the marranitos with the egg wash. Bake on an ungreased cookie sheet for 12 to 15 minutes. Remove the marranitos from the pan and place on wire racks to cool completely.

CHURROS SPANISH DOUGH FRITTERS

MAKES 4 DOZEN CHURROS

Originally from Spain, churros *have found a second home on the fairgrounds of northern Mexico and southern Texas. Usually paired with a cup of Mexican hot chocolate, they are terrific for dunking.*

3 cups all-purpose flour

1 teaspoon baking powder

1 teaspoon salt

2 tablespoons plus 1 cup sugar

¼ cup cornstarch

1 egg

2 cups milk

Corn oil for frying

1 tablespoon ground cinnamon (Mexican if possible; see page 29)

COMBINE the flour, baking powder, salt, 2 tablespoons sugar, and cornstarch in a large bowl. Add the egg and gradually add the milk while stirring. (Your batter should be thick.) Spoon the batter into a cloth or vinyl pastry bag, using either a large star tip, or no tip at all.

HEAT a 10-inch skillet over medium heat and add oil to a depth of at least 1½ inches. Heat the oil to 350°F on a deep-frying thermometer. Meanwhile, combine the remaining 1 cup sugar and the cinnamon in a clean pie plate and line a separate pan with paper toweling.

PIPE the batter in 6-inch-long stick shapes directly into the hot oil, piping only 3 or 4 churros into the oil at a time. Allow the churros to fry until golden brown, 2 to 3 minutes on each side. Using tongs, remove the churros from the hot oil and drain briefly on the paper toweling. While the churros are still warm, roll in the cinnamon-sugar mixture. (As you fry your churros, use the thermometer to keep an eye on your oil temperature; raise or lower the heat slightly if the oil is too hot or too cold.) Serve warm.

BUÑUELOS TORTILLA FRITTERS

MAKES 40

Every Christmas my grandmother would make piles and piles of buñuelos, *our traditional crispy tortilla-style fritter, and sprinkle them twice with sugar and freshly ground cinnamon. Over the next two weeks, they would be doled out on foil-covered paper plates to family and neighbors.*

There was no "sneak eating" with buñuelos; everyone knew you had indulged. Flaky and crispy, they left you smiling, with a dusting of sugar at the corner of your mouth. Even the floor tattled on you, crunching with sugar granules as you slowly backed away.

Now, it is my floor that crunches at Christmastime. I make them for my kids, but I can be found with a fair amount of sugar at corner of my mouth, too. Serve with hot chocolate.

7 cups all-purpose flour

1 tablespoon salt

1⅓ cups vegetable shortening

2 cups hot water

Corn oil for frying

2 cups sugar

1 tablespoon freshly ground cinnamon (Mexican if possible; see page 29)

COMBINE the flour, salt, and shortening in a large bowl. Knead well with your hands. Add the water a little at a time until you have a smooth dough. Knead the dough for a minute or two until elastic. Form the dough into 40 small equal patties by dividing the dough into equal halves and then each half into 2 equal portions, then each portion into 5 equal patties. Return the patties to the mixing bowl and allow to rest covered with a damp towel for 20 minutes.

ROLL out the patties into large 8-inch circles, as thin as possible. When all are rolled out, heat the oil in a large skillet about 2 inches deep. Fry each dough circle one at a time in the hot oil, about 30 seconds on each side, until golden and crisp. Remove from hot oil and drain on paper towels. Continue until all the buñuelos are fried.

COMBINE the sugar and cinnamon in a large baking pan. Pass the buñuelos though the cinnamon sugar mixture one at a time until each is well coated. Buñuelos will stay crisp for several days if stored in airtight containers or ziplock bags.

EMPANADAS DE CAMOTE SWEET POTATO TURNOVERS

MAKES 30 EMPANADAS

This is another recipe of my grandmother's, who got it from Maxine Guerra, her good friend and neighbor. I imagine these empanadas have been passed around every table in South Texas. The crust turns out tender and flaky every time, making this a popular recipe at many of our local social functions.

DOUGH

4 cups all-purpose flour

¼ cup sugar

1 teaspoon salt

1¾ cups vegetable shortening

1 egg

1 tablespoon vinegar

FILLING

2 pounds sweet potatoes

2 sticks cinnamon (Mexican if possible; see page 29)

½ to 1 cup sugar, or to taste

MIX the flour, sugar, and salt. Knead in the shortening briefly with your hands, about 30 seconds. Add the egg, ½ cup water, and the vinegar, mixing well to form a soft dough. Form the dough into a ball, wrap in plastic, and chill for 1 hour.

WASH the sweet potatoes well and cut into large chunks. Fill a 4-quart saucepan with water, add the sweet potatoes and cinnamon sticks, and bring to a boil. Cook the sweet potatoes until they are easily pierced with a fork, about 20 minutes. Remove the saucepan from the heat and drain the water. Remove the cinnamon sticks. After the sweet potatoes have cooled, peel them and return them to the saucepan. Using a potato masher, mash the sweet potatoes until they are a smooth purée. Add the sugar to sweeten them, as desired.

PREHEAT the oven to 350°F. Divide the dough into 30 portions by first dividing the dough into equal halves, then each half into 3 pieces, then each piece into 5 equal portions. Using a tortilla press or a rolling pin, flatten the dough into circles about 3 inches in diameter. Fill each circle with 1 tablespoon of the mashed sweet pota-toes. Do not overfill. Fold the dough over the filling to form a half-circle. Pinch the edges together. Place on an ungreased cookie sheet. When all empanadas are formed, take a fork and press the sealed edges to make a crimped pattern along the outer edge. Bake for 20 to 25 minutes, until browned.

NOTE: In order to achieve a beautifully tender crust, be careful to not overknead your dough.

❖ **VARIATIONS:** Substitute pineapple jam for the filling to make Empanadas de Piña. You can also use strawberry, peach, mango, or guava jam. Or use Mexican goat's milk caramel, called cajeta, as a filling, which is especially nice when you add a few chopped pecans.

GAZNATES TRADITIONAL MEXICAN FRITTER
MAKES 24-30 GAZNATES

Gaznate *means "windpipe" or "trachea,"* which refers to the tubular shape of *these traditional sweet fritters. The creamy meringue filling pushes them to the outer limits of sinful.*

DOUGH

6 egg yolks

1 cup all-purpose flour, plus extra as needed

½ teaspoon baking powder

2 tablespoons (1 ounce) whiskey

1 cup sugar

1 tablespoon freshly ground cinnamon (Mexican if possible; see page 29)

4 cups corn oil for deep frying

FILLING

2 egg whites

1½ cups sugar

¼ teaspoon cream of tartar

1 teaspoon vanilla extract

Red food coloring (optional)

WHIP the egg yolks in a large bowl until lemon colored. Add the flour, baking powder, and whiskey, and stir until you have a cohesive dough. (You can add a bit more flour if your dough is sticky.)

ROLL out the dough on a floured surface to about an ⅛-inch thickness. Use as much flour as you need on your rolling pin and on the surface of the dough so that the dough will not stick. Cut the dough into 3 x 3-inch squares.

COMBINE the sugar and cinnamon in a separate bowl. Set aside.

HEAT the oil in a heavy 4-quart saucepan until it registers 350°F on a deep-frying thermometer. Once the oil is hot, you can begin to shape and fry your gaznates. Wrap a dough square around your index finger to form a tube, pinching the seam together well. (You should end up with a 3-inch tube of dough.) Carefully place the tube in the hot oil and fry until golden, about 1 minute. Remove from the oil and drain on paper toweling. Fry all of the tubes, one at a time, in this fashion. When they are cool, roll in the sugar and cinnamon mixture.

ADD the egg whites, sugar, $\frac{1}{3}$ cup water, and the cream of tartar to the top portion of a double boiler. Heat the ingredients over boiling water while whipping for 5 to 7 minutes with either a hand whisk or an electric mixture. Once the mixture begins to form stiff peaks, remove from the heat and add the vanilla. Add a drop or two of red food coloring, if you want a pink colored filling, and stir until combined well.

PLACE the filling in a pastry bag (don't use a tip) and fill the gaznates by piping a little filling into either end of the tube.

CLAY BAKING POWDER

IN MY GRANDMOTHER'S crammed pantry, next to a turquoise ice bucket and her box of lobster picks, was an old mayonnaise jar that contained some strange gritty stones. Ever mysterious, her house was filled with odds and ends such as these, which I occasionally questioned but rarely understood. It wasn't until she died and my sister lovingly recorded all my grandmother's family recipes that I understood what was in that jar. They were *tequesquite*, a leavener commonly used before baking powder was commercially available (see "Tequesquite," page 138). Its bitter aftertaste was reason enough for it to lose favor as a leavening ingredient. Even though she could have used baking powder (as I have above), my grandmother kept her jar, as it was the traditional ingredient in gaznates.

TURCOS

MAKES 2 DOZEN

Turcos is one of the oldest recipes in the Wild Horse Desert. I imagine that, as a fattened hog was usually slaughtered on the ranchitos at Christmastime for tamales, some of the meat trimmings and fat would be reserved for these sweet and savory pies. This old Christmas recipe is becoming less common every year. I found the recipe in a regional cookbook from 1845.

You can make the filling a day in advance, which will give the meat mixture time to absorb all of the spice flavor, resulting in a more flavorful turco.

FILLING

1 pound bone-in country style ribs

2 large sticks cinnamon (Mexican if possible; see page 29)

½ teaspoon whole cloves

½ orange

1 pound 8 ounces piloncillo (unrefined sugar; see page 26) or brown sugar

½ cup chopped pecans

½ cup chopped almonds

½ cup raisins

DOUGH

4 cups all-purpose flour

½ cup granulated sugar

½ teaspoon salt

1½ cups vegetable shortening

FILL a 4-quart saucepan with water; add the pork, 1 stick of cinnamon, cloves, and half orange. Bring to a boil, reduce the heat, and simmer, covered, for 45 minutes, until the pork is cooked. Remove pork from the broth and allow to cool. Reserve the broth.

REMOVE the bones from the pork and chop the meat finely. In a 3-quart saucepan, combine 1 cup of the reserved broth with the piloncillo and remaining stick of cinnamon; bring to a boil and simmer over medium heat until you have a thin syrup, about 10 minutes. Add the chopped pork, the pecans, almonds, and raisins.

Continue to simmer, stirring occasionally so the mixture doesn't burn, until the liquid is reduced by one-third, then remove from the heat. Preheat the oven to 400°F.

SIFT the flour, sugar, and salt together into a large bowl. Knead in the shortening with your hands. Add enough of the reserved broth to make a sturdy, yet tender dough (approximately ½ cup). Do not overwork the dough, or the crust will be tough. Divide dough into 4 equal parts, then divide each part into 12 pieces (48 total). Roll each piece into a ball about 2 inches in diameter.

USING a tortilla press lined with 2 round sheets of plastic (see page 7), press each piece into a thin circle about ¼ inch thick. Fill the circle with 1 to 2 tablespoons of the filling. Press out another circle of dough with the tortilla press. Wet the edge of the first circle with water, place the second circle on top (making a sandwich), and pinch the edges together to seal well. Place the turco on an ungreased baking sheet and continue to shape all the turcos in this fashion. Slash a cross in the top of each turco. Bake for 20 to 25 minutes, until golden brown. Serve at once or store in the refrigerator.

TURCOS

THE RECIPE FOR TURCOS, which has endured for centuries here in the Wild Horse Desert, is based on the original recipe the Spanish *conquistadores* brought with them. The word *turco* or "turks," is a reference to the pastry's filling, known in English as mincemeat. In Europe, mincemeat has been a holiday pie and pastry filling since medieval times; however, the origin of mincemeat can be traced to Egypt. The term *turk* throughout the ages has been a common catch-all description for anything bearing Middle Eastern influence, thus the name for this dessert. Because most modern recipes for mincemeat no longer include meat of any kind (they're commonly composed of dried currants, apples, nuts, and figs), I think it is fascinating that our version still uses pork. It may well be the same recipe that arrived with the Spanish explorers 400 years ago.

PASTEL TRES LECHES THREE-MILKS CAKE

SERVES 16

This popular cake shows up at nearly every social function in South Texas, and is becoming a favorite in restaurants around the United States. The three milks are evaporated milk, condensed milk, and heavy cream, which are combined and completely absorbed by a tender sponge cake. I receive many requests for this recipe.

CAKE

7 eggs, separated

½ cup butter, softened

1 cup sugar

2½ cups all-purpose flour

1 teaspoon baking powder

½ teaspoon salt

1 cup milk

1 teaspoon vanilla extract

MILKS

1 (5-ounce) can evaporated milk

1 (14-ounce) can sweetened condensed milk

½ cup heavy cream

FROSTING

6 egg whites

1 cup sugar

1 cup corn syrup

Juice of ½ lemon

Lemon or lime zest for garnish

PREHEAT the oven to 350°F. Grease and flour a 9 x 13-inch baking pan.

CREAM together the egg yolks, butter, and sugar in a large bowl. In a separate bowl, combine the flour, baking powder, and salt. Add the flour mixture alternately with the milk to the egg mixture. Add the vanilla. Beat the egg whites until stiff peaks form when the beater is raised. Fold the egg whites into the cake batter and then pour batter into prepared pan. Bake for 25 to 30 minutes, until a toothpick comes out clean from the center. Cool cake in the pan on a cake rack.

COMBINE the evaporated milk, condensed milk, and cream. Pour over the cake while it is still in the pan. Allow the cake to absorb the milk for about 2 hours.

FILL the bottom of a double boiler with water and bring to a boil. In the top of the double boiler, combine the egg whites and sugar. Beat the egg whites until stiff with a handheld electric mixer. In a very thin stream, beating constantly, pour in the corn syrup. Add the lemon juice. The frosting should be thick and shiny.

SPREAD frosting over the top of the cake. Garnish with lemon or lime zest.

SOAKED CAKES

CAKES SOAKED IN FLAVORFUL CREAM and liqueur were very popular with the European gentry during the seventeenth and eighteenth centuries. *Sopa dourada,* or "golden soup," which consists of a sponge cake soaked in custard, is a dessert that originated in Portugal and remains popular on the Iberian Peninsula even today. *Zuppa inglese* or "English soup," also a sponge cake soaked in custard, was a similar dessert popular in Italy. In England, the same dish is called a trifle. It is believed that the recipe for Pastel Tres Leches was a reinvention of this European favorite, and was repopularized in the 1940s as it circulated throughout Latin America on the labels of canned sweetened condensed and evaporated milk.

GRAPEFRUIT BLOSSOM CAKE WITH BROWNED BUTTER FROSTING

SERVES 12

Here's a tribute to the spectacular citrus fruit that is grown in South Texas.

FILLING

1 cup granulated sugar

3 eggs

½ cup grapefruit juice (see Note)

½ cup unsalted butter, cut into pieces

1 teaspoon grapefruit zest

CAKE

2¼ cups sifted cake flour

2 teaspoons baking powder

1 teaspoon salt

½ cup unsalted butter, softened

½ cup vegetable shortening

1½ cups granulated sugar

2 eggs

2 teaspoons vanilla extract

1 cup milk

FROSTING

¾ cup (1½ sticks) unsalted butter

6 cups confectioners' sugar

8 to 10 tablespoons grapefruit juice

WHISK together the sugar and eggs in a 4-quart nonreactive saucepan until they are light in color. Whisk in the juice and butter, and heat over medium heat until the butter is melted. Continue to whisk until the mixture thickens, about 3 to 5 minutes. Remove from heat, whisk in the grapefruit zest, and let cool.

PREHEAT the oven to 350°F. Grease and flour two 8-inch round cake pans.

SIFT together the flour, baking powder, and salt in a large bowl. Set aside. Using an electric mixer, cream the butter, shortening, and sugar in a large mixing bowl for 3 minutes, or until light and fluffy. Add the eggs, one at a time and mixing well after each addition. Add the vanilla. Alternately add to this the flour mixture and the milk, stirring after each addition to incorporate without overmixing.

POUR the batter into the prepared cake pans, and bake for 25 to 30 minutes, until an inserted toothpick comes out clean. Cool in the pans for 10 minutes, then remove and place on wire racks to finish cooling.

GENTLY heat the butter in a small saucepan over low heat. The butter will foam, and as foam subsides, it will begin to show signs of browning almost immediately. As soon as this happens, remove it from heat and cool thoroughly.

COMBINE the melted browned butter and sugar in a medium bowl and beat until well combined. Add 1 tablespoon of grapefruit juice at a time, and mix well with a hand mixer. Add grapefruit juice as needed to reach the desired spreading consistency.

SLICE each in half horizontally once the layers have cooled. Spread each bottom half with 1 cup of the grapefruit filling. Replace tops. Place one filled cake on a serving plate, frost the top, and place second cake on top. Frost the top and sides of the entire cake.

NOTE: Use the juice of Ruby Red grapefruit, which will give the filling a delicate rose-colored hue. The border town of Mission, Texas, is considered the birthplace of the Ruby Red grapefruit, making the addition even more appropriate. If you can find them, grapefruit blossoms and leaves are perfect for decorating this delicious cake.

FLAN TRADITIONAL CARAMEL CUSTARD
SERVES 8

Although every Mexican cookbook seems to have a version of flan, this is one of my most requested recipes. Our regional fare wouldn't be complete without it. This version is very rich, and is lovely when served with coffee and fresh fruit.

Flan must be baked in a water bath. To accomplish this, you need a pan large and deep enough to hold the casserole. Make sure you have a baking pan that is big enough before you begin this recipe. Speaking from experience, it is no fun to discover that you don't have the right size pan when your flan is ready for the oven.

CARAMEL

1 cup sugar

5 drops lemon juice

CUSTARD

4 eggs

4 egg yolks

3 cups whole milk

1 cup heavy cream

1 teaspoon vanilla extract

PREHEAT the oven to 350°F. In a 1-quart saucepan, stir together the sugar, ½ cup water, and the lemon juice, and cook on medium heat until the mixture boils. Allow the mixture to bubble and cook until it turns amber in color, about 10 minutes, or between 320° and 356°F on a candy thermometer. Remove the mixture from the heat and pour into a 2½-quart round casserole or soufflé dish. Set aside and allow to cool.

WHISK together the eggs and egg yolks in a large bowl until thick and form a thick ribbon. In a separate 2-quart saucepan, scald the milk and cream (heat until it is on the verge of boiling). Remove from the heat. Using a whisk, whip the eggs continuously while drizzling in a small amount of the hot milk mixture. Continue to add small amounts of the milk mixture while whisking the eggs until you have added about a cup of milk. Pour the milk and egg mixture into the saucepan and whisk until well combined. Add the vanilla and whisk until well combined.

POUR the flan mixture into your prepared casserole (you can strain the mixture at this point if it contains filaments of cooked egg). Meanwhile, fill a teakettle with water and bring to a boil to prepare the water bath.

LAY a small dishtowel in the bottom of the pan (this will insulate the casserole from the metal pan) and place the pan on an oven rack, then place the casserole in the pan. Pour boiling water into the outer pan (*not* into the flan!). You need at least 1 inch of water around the casserole for a good result. Carefully push the oven rack back into the oven without splashing any water into the flan, and close the oven door. Bake the flan for 50 to 60 minutes, until an inserted knife comes out clean.

REMOVE the casserole carefully from the water bath and allow the flan to cool completely. Before serving, loosen the edges of the flan from its dish, and invert onto a serving platter. Pour over any remaining liquid caramel that remains in the baking dish. Serve at room temperature or chilled, topped with a generous amount of the liquid caramel.

❖ **TO MAKE THE FLAN IN INDIVIDUAL CUSTARD CUPS,** follow the recipe exactly as described above, pour the custard into eight ½-cup custard cups, and reduce the cooking time to 20 minutes.

❖ **TO MAKE FLAVORED FLANS,** add 1 teaspoon extract such as orange or maple. Adding 1 tablespoon of instant coffee makes a delectable coffee flan.

ARROZ CON LECHE RICE WITH MILK

SERVES 8

On the ranch, lunch would be brought out to wherever the cowboys were working. Sometimes I would go along with my dad so I could help with important jobs, such as counting the cattle. In the shade of a mesquite tree, the camp cook would unload a huge pot of hot carne guisada, *or beef stew; a stainless steel bowl filled with homemade flour tortillas kept warm by torn but clean kitchen towels; and a pan of garlicky* sopa de fideo, *our favorite noodle soup. Some days they would also bring along a pot of* arroz con leche—*warm rice pudding flecked with freshly ground cinnamon. Surrounded by incessant mooing, I would happily sit in the cool, blowing grass spooning up every last grain from my warm tin cup and chewing on the cinnamon sticks that remained.*

6 cups whole milk

1 cup rice

2 sticks cinnamon (Mexican if possible; see page 29)

1½ cups sugar

Freshly ground cinnamon (Mexican if possible; see page 29)

BRING the milk, rice, and cinnamon sticks to a boil in a 4-quart saucepan. Reduce to a simmer and cook until the rice is tender, about 30 minutes. Stir the milk every minute or two to make sure the rice is not sticking to the bottom of the pan. Once the milk has thickened and the rice is tender, add the sugar and cook for another 5 minutes. Remove from the heat. The arroz con leche will continue to thicken as it cools. Serve either warm or chilled, topped with cinnamon.

PEPITORIA PUMPKIN SEED BRITTLE

MAKES ABOUT 2 POUNDS

This is my grandmother's recipe. I make this every Christmas to give as gifts. The pumpkin seeds have a distinctive, nutty flavor. They expand when they are roasted in the oven, causing them to develop a hollow center, which adds a bit of crunchiness when they are eaten.

1½ cups raw, unsalted, shelled pumpkin seeds
1 cup sugar
1½ cups light corn syrup

PREHEAT the oven to 350°F. Toast the pumpkin seeds on a baking sheet in the oven for about 8 minutes, until they start to pop. Set aside, but keep warm.

BUTTER a second large baking sheet thoroughly, preferably one with raised sides (e.g., 16 x 10 x 1 inch). In a 2-quart saucepan, combine the sugar, corn syrup, and ½ cup water. Mix well and bring to a simmer. Stir the mixture as it begins to boil. Boil until the mixture turns amber in color and reaches the hard-crack stage, or 300°F on a candy thermometer. Add the pumpkin seeds quickly, stirring well. As quickly as possible, pour the mixture onto the prepared pan. Spread out, using a greased spatula to press down mounds to a thin layer. Allow to cool completely. Break into pieces, and store in an airtight container.

LECHE QUEMADA MILK FUDGE

MAKES 1 POUND

1¾ cups sugar

4 cups whole milk

2 teaspoons vanilla extract

½ cup chopped pecans

BUTTER a 4 x 8-inch loaf pan. Combine the sugar and milk in a heavy 4-quart saucepan. Bring to a boil, lower the heat, and cook at a gentle boil, stirring continuously, until the mixture is thick enough that you can see the bottom of the pan when you stir the candy, about 1 hour. Make sure your mixture is stiff and well cooked, but not burned. Remove from the heat, add the vanilla extract, and stir to combine well.

POUR the leche quemada into the prepared pan. Press the pecans onto the top of the candy while still hot. Allow to cool, then cut into pieces.

SWEET AND HUMBLE REGIONAL CANDIES

MANY OF THE OLD-TIME DESSERTS of the Wild Horse Desert were candies. As few homes had ovens, most of the baked goods described in this chapter would originally have been available only in big *haciendas* or from local bakeries.

Candies were a sweet that could easily be made on the stovetop. Any available starchy base, such as beans, barrel cactus, sweet potatoes, or pumpkins, was used to make these candies, allowing for economy with precious sugar stores. While researching this book I came across many recipes for *dulce de frijol*. It is made exactly the same as *leche quemada*, but with beans added. The beans are initially cooked with cinnamon and water, drained, then puréed and strained to remove the skins. The bean paste is then combined with milk and sugar, and stirred constantly until it renders milk fudge. The addition of beans to milk fudge would have stretched not only sugar supplies but milk supplies as well.

Other popular economizing candies were made from the viznaga cactus, known in English as the "horse crippler." It is a wretchedly thorny squat barrel of a plant, and it had to be split and peeled before it was made into something edible. Another candy base was made with the wild chilecayota gourd, a relative of the cucumber and melon family. Pumpkin and sweet potatoes, as well as the viznaga and chilaecayota, have followed the same preparation for centuries to turn them into popular candies. First, they are peeled and cut into 3-inch chunks. The pieces are then placed in an earthen pot, covered with water and lime (calcium oxide), and allowed to soak overnight. The lime gives the resulting candy a firmer texture. In the morning, the pieces are rinsed and then boiled in a solution of sugar and water. The resulting candy is a crystallized hunk of *calabazate* (pumpkin), *viznaga* (barrel cactus), or *camote* (sweet potato), which is eaten and served in its chunky form.

SEMITAS ANISE BREAD
MAKES 2 LARGE SEMITAS

Semitas *(also spelled* cemitas*)* *are found all over Mexico and are prepared with differing flavors and various degrees of leavening. Semitas are traditionally served in the spring. Because the population of the Wild Horse Desert is over 80 percent Roman Catholic, many associate semitas with Easter, but it is actually a Passover food. Some believe the origin of* pan de semita, *or "Semitic bread," was unleavened Passover bread made by Sephardic Jews who emigrated to northern Mexico.*

The Jews who originally made semitas followed kosher dietary rules. Therefore, the fat in semitas should be either butter or olive oil, as opposed to the ever-present lard used in most traditional pastries of this region. For a completely authentic semita, omit the baking powder in this recipe to produce a traditional Passover unleavened bread.

Usually, semitas are purchased at bakeries and are rarely made at home. Recipes for this pastry are difficult to find; I found only two during my research. One had yeast, the other used vegetable shortening, neither of which were in keeping with the true history of semitas. So the recipe below is one that I fashioned from memory, and from my historical research. My husband remembers the ones he would buy on the way to their family's ranch near El Porvenir in Tamaulipas, in northern Mexico. The semitas were baked in an outdoor earthen oven, fired by mesquite wood. He says that they were the true semita, and that the recipe below is exactly as he remembers them—firm, flat, and flavored with spices.

SYRUP

8 ounces piloncillo (unrefined sugar; see page 26)

2 sticks cinnamon (Mexican if possible; see page 29)

2 pieces star anise

BREAD

4 cups all-purpose flour

1 teaspoon baking powder

½ cup olive oil

1 teaspoon anise seed

2 tablespoons chopped pecans

Extra-virgin olive oil

COMBINE the piloncillo, 1 cup water, the cinnamon, and star anise in a 1-quart saucepan. Bring to a boil and remove from the heat. Stir until the piloncillo dissolves. You should have about $1\frac{1}{2}$ cups of syrup. Let the syrup cool, then strain out the whole spices.

COMBINE the flour, baking powder, olive oil, sugar syrup, the anise seed, and pecans in a large bowl. Knead with your hands until the dough is smooth, about 5 minutes, adding more flour as necessary so the dough does not stick. Allow the dough to rest for at least 20 minutes.

PREHEAT the oven to 350°F. Divide the dough in half. On a floured surface, roll half of the dough to an oval $\frac{1}{4}$ inch thick, about 12 inches long. Rub the surface of the dough with a little extra-virgin olive oil. Place the dough on an ungreased cookie sheet. Roll out and prepare the other half of the dough in the same fashion. Bake the semitas for 15 to 20 minutes. Remove from the oven and cool on wire racks.

SEMITAS CHORREADAS FILLED SEMITAS

MAKES 8 SEMITAS CHORREADAS

These semitas *are made fluffier* than the prior recipe to allow for the filling. This version is similar to the semitas seen in central Mexico. The term chorreada means "dribbling" or "flowing," referring to the spiced piloncillo center. We always buy these when we are visiting family in Saltillo, Coahuila, in northern Mexico. The warm sugary center oozes out of the roll as we break them apart, spilling sticky pecans over our fingers. Sometimes we are very naughty and have them for dinner, accompanied by a cup of Mexican hot chocolate.

TEA

1 piece star anise

3 whole cloves

½ stick cinnamon (Mexican if possible; see page 29)

BREAD

4½ to 5 cups all-purpose flour

1 teaspoon salt

2 packages active dry yeast

½ cup granulated sugar

½ cup heavy cream

⅓ cup butter, melted

2 eggs

2 teaspoons anise seed

FILLING

1 pound piloncillo (unrefined sugar; see page 26)

1 piece star anise

1 stick cinnamon (Mexican if possible; see page 29)

2 whole cloves

¾ cup chopped pecans

COMBINE 1 cup water with the star anise, whole cloves, and cinnamon in a 1-quart saucepan. Bring to a boil, reduce the heat, and simmer for 3 to 5 minutes. Remove from the heat. (Make sure you end up with at least ½ cup of tea. If you have less, just add a little water.) Allow the liquid to cool completely, then strain out the whole spices.

COMBINE 2 cups of the flour, the salt, yeast, and sugar in the bowl of an electric mixer. Set aside.

COMBINE ½ cup of the anise tea, the cream, and butter in a 1-quart saucepan and heat to between 105° and 115°F. Add the warm liquid to the flour mixture in the electric mixer bowl. Start the electric mixer and add the eggs, anise seed, and enough of the remaining flour to make a stiff dough. Knead dough for 5 to 8 minutes in the mixer, using a dough hook.

REMOVE the dough from the mixer and place in a greased bowl. Place the bowl in a warm place and allow dough to rise in a warm, draft-free environment for 1 hour, or until doubled in bulk.

GREASE a 9 x 9-inch baking pan. Combine the piloncillo, $\frac{2}{3}$ cup water, the star anise, cinnamon, and cloves in a 2-quart saucepan. Bring the mixture to a boil over high heat—you can break up the piloncillo (try using a potato masher) to help it dissolve faster. Boil the filling until it reaches 230°F on a candy thermometer (almost at the softball stage). Remove the pan from the heat. While the mixture is still hot, remove all of the whole spices with a slotted spoon. Add the pecans, stirring well to distribute evenly. Pour the hot syrup onto the baking pan. The mixture will crystallize as it cools. When the mixture is cool, break it up into small chunks, about 1 inch.

AFTER THE DOUGH HAS RISEN for the first time, punch it down and allow to rest for 15 minutes. Divide the dough into 8 equal portions. Stretching the dough a bit, fashion each portion into a small cup, about 5 inches in diameter. Fill the cups with a few chunks of the filling. Gather the edges of the cups over the filling and pinch to seal well. Make sure the dough is not too thin at the seams. Place the 5-inch round filled buns seam side down on a greased baking sheet and allow to rise in a warm, draft-free environment for about 1 hour, or until doubled in bulk. Preheat the oven to 350°F.

BAKE the buns for 20 to 25 minutes, until golden brown. Remove from the oven and cool the semitas on wire racks. Serve while they are still warm.

NOTE: You can also let the piloncillo mixture cool in the same pan in which it was cooked; just reheat the pan briefly to melt the sides and release the hardened mixture.

ROSCA DE REYES BREAD OF THE KINGS

SERVES 24

Making Rosca de Reyes is a great old tradition that you can bring back to life with your family. The bread is delicately sweet, and delicious with coffee or a good cup of hot chocolate for dunking.

BREAD DOUGH

6 to 7 cups all-purpose flour

¾ cup sugar

2 packages active dry yeast

1 teaspoon salt

½ cup milk

½ cup butter

3 eggs

3 egg yolks

2 tablespoons orange flower water

TOPPING DOUGH

6 tablespoons margarine, softened

½ cup confectioners' sugar

2 egg yolks

¾ cup all-purpose flour

Crystallized fruit in Christmas colors (cherries, pineapple, figs, etc.)

1 small baby doll, 1 to 2 inches long (see "King Cake Tradition")

COMBINE 2 cups of the flour with the sugar, yeast, and salt in the bowl of an electric mixer. Set aside.

HEAT the milk, ½ cup water, and the butter in a 1-quart saucepan until the butter is melted and the liquid reaches a temperature between 105° and 115°F. Add the liquid to the flour mixture and begin to mix with the paddle attachment of the electric mixer. Add the eggs, egg yolks, and orange flower water as the mixer continues to run. Add enough of the remaining flour to form a stiff dough. Turn off the mixer and switch the beaters to the dough hook attachment. Turn the mixer back on and knead the dough for 5 to 8 minutes, adding small amounts of flour as needed so that the dough is not sticky. Transfer the dough to a greased bowl, cover, and allow to rise in a warm, draft-free environment for 1 hour, or until doubled in bulk.

PUNCH the dough down and allow to rest for 5 to 10 minutes. Make a large round patty of the dough about 12 inches in diameter. Press a hole in the center to make a doughnut shape. Stretch the doughnut to make an oval ring with a large hole in the center. (The rosca somewhat resembles the shape of a horseracing track!) The ring sides should be 4½ to 5 inches thick. Place the bread on a greased pan and allow to rise in a warm, draft-free environment for another hour, until doubled in bulk.

MAKE THE TOPPING: Combine all the ingredients and mix into a soft dough. Set aside. Preheat the oven to 350°F.

DECORATE the top of the rosca with the topping, rolling it out to make circles and stripes and pressing them lightly onto the rosca. Decorate with the crystallized fruit, then bake for 30 minutes, or until brown. Remove from oven and allow to cool completely. Before serving, make a slit underneath the rosca with a knife. Press the baby doll up into the rosca.

KING CAKE TRADITION

JANUARY 6 is the Feast of the Epiphany, the day when the Three Wise Men arrived in Bethlehem to adore the Baby Jesus. Traditionally, Rosca de Reyes, or "The Bread of the Kings," is eaten with family and friends on the Epiphany. Whoever is served the slice of bread with the hidden Baby Jesus inside is obligated to host a party on February 2, the Feast of the Purification. Jewish women went through a ceremony of purification 40 days after the birth of a son, and Mary, in compliance with the purification ritual, took her son to the temple on the 40th day after His birth. Both Mary's purification after birth and Jesus' first appearance in a temple occurred on February 2. The Feast of the Purification (or Presentation) is known in Europe as Candlemas, which became a day on the calendar when people looked forward to the first signs of spring. Eventually, predicting the onset of spring became Groundhog Day.

PAN DE HUEVO EGG BREAD

SERVES 8

You may notice that this recipe is almost identical to the prior recipe for Rosca de Reyes. *This bread base is called* pan de huevo, *or "egg bread," and derives its rich flavor, color, and texture from eggs.*

6 to 7 cups all-purpose flour
¾ cup sugar
1 teaspoon salt
½ cup milk

½ cup butter
2 packages active dry yeast
3 whole eggs
3 eggs, separated

PLACE 5 cups of the flour in a large mixing bowl. Stir in the sugar and salt, and set aside.

HEAT the milk, ½ cup water, and the butter in a small saucepan over low heat until the liquid reaches 100° to 110°F on a thermometer. Add the yeast and stir until completely dissolved. Pour the milk mixture over the flour and stir until well combined. Add the whole eggs and the yolks, reserving the whites, and mix well. The dough will be sticky at first. Add more flour, ½ cup at a time, until the dough is too stiff to stir.

TURN the dough out onto a floured surface and knead with your hands for approximately 10 minutes, until the dough is smooth and elastic, flouring the surface if the dough becomes sticky. Continue to knead until the dough no longer sticks to your hands or to the counter surface. Place the dough in a greased bowl, cover, and allow it to rise in a warm (about 85°F), draft-free environment for 1 hour.

PUNCH the dough down and allow to rest for 15 minutes. Extract a baseball-size portion of the dough. Divide the remaining dough into 8 equal pieces and form each into a round, domed patty (like a hamburger bun). Place the dough patties on a greased baking sheet.

DIVIDE the baseball-size piece of dough in half and roll one half to form a long dough snake, about ½ inch thick. Divide this snake into 8 small strips. Roll out the other half and divide in the same fashion. Position 2 strips of dough on top of each patty, forming a cross. Cover and allow the decorated bread to rise for 1 hour.

PREHEAT the oven to 350°F. Gently stir together the reserved 3 egg whites with 1 tablespoon of water to make an egg wash. Brush the egg wash onto the outer surface of the dough patties. Bake the pan de huevo for 25 to 30 minutes, until golden brown. Remove from oven and cool the pan de huevo on wire racks before serving.

ONE BASE, MANY BREADS

MANY OF THE FAMOUS BREADS of Mexico use the same bread base but are shaped differently. Change the bread's topping or decoration, and you change the name of the bread, even without changing the recipe. Pan de Huevo is usually identified by a simple decorative cross made of dough that is added to the top. Change the top decorations to bone-shaped dough pieces and serve it at the end of October, and it is called *pan de muerto,* or "bread of the dead"—traditional in Day of the Dead celebrations. The sugar topping and distinctive shell markings used in the recipe that follows result in *Conchas.* Even our *semita* recipe bears a striking resemblance to this recipe, having the simple addition of an anise-flavored tea and anise seeds.

CONCHAS SHELL-SHAPED BREAKFAST ROLLS

SERVES 8

Conchas, *round sugar-topped buns,* are probably the most popular bread seen in
*Mexican bakeries. Traditionally, the topping is colored pastel pink, yellow, or brown (using
cocoa), or is left white. Dunking conchas in frothy hot chocolate is a must.*

1 recipe Pan de Huevo (see page 258)

6 tablespoons vegetable shortening

½ cup confectioners' sugar

2 egg yolks

¾ cup all-purpose flour

OPTIONAL TOPPING COLORINGS

3 to 4 drops yellow food coloring

3 to 4 drops red food coloring

1 tablespoon cocoa

FOLLOW the recipe for making Pan de Huevo, bringing the dough through the second rising.

COMBINE the shortening, sugar, egg yolks, flour, and one of the optional topping
colorings in a small bowl. Press the mixture with the back of a fork to combine
the ingredients. When the dough is well combined, divide it into 8 portions. With
your fingers, press out a small patty and lightly press that patty onto a portion
of dough. Using a dull table knife, score the top of the dough. Continue to make
the toppings. Bake as directed in the recipe for Pan de Huevo.

CAPIROTADA LENTEN BREAD PUDDING

SERVES 8

This spiced bread pudding is a substantial dish, traditionally made during the Lenten fasting season. Originally, capirotada was a meat and potato layered dish that can be traced back to medieval times. It is believed that the name capirotada comes from the word capirote, a pointed, hooded cloak usually worn by the pilgrims during their Easter parades in Mexico and Latin America.

Here is one of the best recipes for capirotada I have ever made. My mother-in-law thinks it is great, which is a powerful endorsement. Her next-door neighbor, Nohemi Vela, gave me the recipe. Mrs. Vela is a strong Catholic woman with a big family and a loving heart. Her recipes are hearty and authentic to the region, and the servings as generous as the woman herself.

What differentiates capirotada from regular bread pudding is the depth of spices, the mixed fruit, the cheese, and the piloncillo—the raw, cone-shaped sugar from Mexico. Mrs. Vela's addition of the black peppercorns and onions is pure genius: It gives this pudding a pleasing bite.

Make sure you have a metal tea ball available to infuse the fruit and tea mixture with the heady essence of the whole anise and cloves. The aroma is divine.

CASO COOKERY

MRS. VELA AND I like to use our traditional *caso* for baking this dish. *Caso* simply means "big pot." They are handmade clay pots with lids that hold about 12 quarts. Casos are big and fragile, and hard to find outside Mexico or its border regions (see "Olla Cookery," page 187). You can substitute a large ceramic casserole, Dutch oven, or even a stockpot with an ovenproof lid—just make sure that the baking dish you choose is very deep. If you do have a large caso, you can easily double, even quadruple the recipe (I do!). Of course, this would increase your cooking time, but use the same test for doneness as indicated above: just make sure that all the tea is absorbed by the bread before you remove it from the oven. Even when I make a quadruple batch, the baking time is never more than 90 minutes.

CAPIROTADA, CON'T.

1 (8-ounce) loaf day-old French bread, sliced into 1-inch-thick slices

FRUIT AND SPICE TEA

½ teaspoon anise seeds

½ teaspoon whole black peppercorns

4 pieces star anise

2 sticks cinnamon (Mexican preferred; see page 29)

8 ounces piloncillo (unrefined sugar; see page 26), or ¾ cup packed brown sugar

¼ cup granulated sugar

½ cup pitted prunes, snipped in half

½ cup raisins

½ cup butter

2 green onions

1 teaspoon ground cinnamon

¾ cup pecans, roughly chopped

8 ounces cheese, thinly sliced (preferably Colby or Monterey Jack)

PREHEAT the oven to 375°F.

TOAST the bread on an ungreased cookie sheet under a broiler until golden on each side. Set aside.

BRING 1 quart of water to a boil in a large pot. Place the anise seeds and whole peppercorns in a metal tea ball and add to the water. Add the remaining spices, piloncillo, and sugar. Boil for 10 minutes.

ADD the prunes to the boiling tea and boil for 5 minutes. Add the raisins and boil for 5 minutes more. Remove the tea from the heat; remove the fruit with a strainer and reserve.

MELT the butter in a deep 6-quart casserole (see "Case Cookery," page 263). Add the green onions and cinnamon, and sauté for a minute or two. Add the bread slices and toss them with the green onions and butter to cover evenly on both sides. When all the bread has been coated, remove the green onions and discard. Remove the bread to a bowl.

ARRANGE the ingredients in layers in the casserole, starting with a single layer of bread. Cut smaller pieces of bread to fill large gaps. Pour about a quart of the tea syrup over it, soaking the bread well. Place a few cooked prunes and raisins over the bread. Add a layer of pecans, then cheese. Keep in mind that you will need even amounts of fruit and tea for each layer of bread. Continue layering your capirotada with bread, tea, fruit, pecans, and cheese until the ingredients are finished, topping the bread pudding with a layer of cheese. You should have 3 to 5 layers. Pour over any remaining tea. Cover the baking dish with lid or aluminum foil.

BAKE the bread pudding for 1 hour. To test for doneness, tilt the baking dish to see if any liquid is visible. If so, continue baking until all the liquid is absorbed by the bread. Serve warm.

❖ **VARIATION**: Mrs. Vela and I are especially fond of using orange-scented prunes for this recipe, which you can find in the dried fruit section of the grocery store. Coconut, peanuts, Mexican pine nuts (piñon), and even apples and peaches are some of the imaginative, personal touches cooks add to this traditional dish.

BIBLIOGRAPHY

Aguirre, Francisco Ramos. *Los Viejos Sabores del Nuevo Tamaulipas*. Privately printed, 1998.

Aidells, Bruce, and Denis Kelly. *The Complete Meat Cookbook*. Boston: Houghton Mifflin, 1998.

Allen, John Houghton. *Song to Randado*. Dallas: Kaleidescope Press, 1935.

Amberson, Mary Margaret McAllen, James A. McAllen, and Margaret H. McAllen. *I Would Rather Sleep in Texas*. Austin, Tex.: Texas State Historical Association, 2003.

Baker, Samuel White. *The Nile Tributaries of Abyssinia and the Sword Hunters of the Hamran Arabs*. London: Macmillan, 1867. Available at www.congocookbook.com.

De Moral, Paulina, and Alicia Siller V. *Recetario Mascogo de Coahuila*. Mexico City, Mexico: Conaculta, 2000.

De Rubio, Vicenta T. *Manual de Cocina Michoacana*. Michoacan, Mexico: Zamora, 1896.

El Mejor Libro de Cocina. Mexico City, Mexico: Simon Blanquel, 1864.

Everitt, James H., and D. Lynn Drawe. *Trees, Shrubs and Cacti of South Texas*. Lubbock, Tex.: Texas Tech University Press, 1993.

Flandarin, Jean-Louis, and Massimo Montanari, eds. *Food: A Culinary History*, trans. Albert Sonnefeld. New York: Columbia University Press, 1996.

Ford, John Salmon, ed. *Rip Ford's Texas,* ed. Stephen Oates. Austin, Tex.: University of Texas Press, 1963, 1987.

Fussell, Betty. *The Story of Corn*. Albuquerque, N.M.: University of New Mexico Press, 2004.

Garza, Lucy. *South Texas Mexican Cookbook*. Austin, Tex.: Eakin Press, 1982.

Grant, U. S. *Personal Memoirs: Selected Letters 1839–1865*. New York: Library of America, 1990.

Herbst, Sharon Tyler. *The New Food Lovers Companion,* 2nd ed. Woodbury, N.Y.: Barron's Educational Series, 1995.

Horgan, Paul. *Great River: The Rio Grande in North American History*, Vols. 1–2. Toronto: Rinehart and Company, 1954.

Ibaldi, Bertha Young. *A Childhood History of Santa Anita*. Unpublished manuscript, 1996.

Iturriaga, Jose N. *Las Cocinas de Mexico,* Vols. 1–2. Mexico City, Mexico: Fondo de Cultura Economica, 1998.

Kilman, Ed. *Cannibal Coast.* San Antonio, Tex.: Naylor Company, 1959.

Kurlansky, Mark. *Salt: A World History.* New York: Walker and Company, 2002.

La Cocina Familiar en el Estado de Tamaulipas, 2nd ed. Mexico City, Mexico: Editorial Oceano de Mexico, S.A. de C.V., 2001.

La Cocinera Poblana. Mexico City, Mexico: Herrero Hermanos Sucesores, 1921.

Latorre, Dolores L. *Cooking and Curing with Mexican Herbs.* Austin, Tex.: Encino Press, 1977.

Life Application Bible: New International Version. Wheaton, Ill.: Tyndale House, 1991.

Martinez, Maximino. *Las Plantas Medicinales de Mexico.* Mexico City, Mexico: Libreria y Ediciones Bota, S.A de C.V., 1967, 1996.

McAllen, Margaret H. Sabores. "The Lifetime Recipes," ed. Mary Margaret McAllen Amberson. Unpublished manuscript, 1995.

Mesquite Country: Tastes and Traditions from the Tip of Texas. Edinburg, Tex.: Hidalgo County Historical Museum, 1996.

Miller, Mark. *The Great Chile Book.* Berkeley, Calif.: Ten Speed Press, 1991.

Ortiz, Lie. Horacio Alvardo. *Nuestros Platillos Panes y Postres.* McAllen, Tex.: privately printed, 1993.

Pilcher, Jeffrey. *Que Vivan los Tamales!* Albuquerque, N.M.: University of New Mexico Press, 1998.

Rivera, Mariano Galvan. *Nuevo Cocinero Mexicano en Forma de Diccionario.* Mexico City, Mexico: I. Cumplido, 1845.

Robertson, Brian. *Wild Horse Desert: The Heritage of South Texas.* Edinburg, Tex.: New Santander Press, 1985.

Saldivar, Gabriel. *Historia Compendiada de Tamaulipas.* Mexico City, Mexico: La Academia Nacional de Historia y Geografia, 1945.

Salinas, Martin. *Indians of the Rio Grande Delta.* Austin, Tex.: University of Texas Press, 1990.

Sanchez de Pineda, Dolores and Luz Olivia Pineda Sanchez. *Comida Tradicional de San Cristobal de las Casas.* Mexico City, Mexico: privately printed, 1988.

Sands, Kathleen Mullens. *Charreria Mexicana–An Equestrian Folk Tradition.* Tucson: University of Arizona Press, 1993.

SantaMaria, Francisco J. *Diccionario de Mexicanismos.* Sexta Edicion. Mexico City, Mexico: Editorial Porrua, 2000.

Simon, John Y., ed. *The Papers of Ulysses S. Grant,* Vol. 1. Carbondale: Southern Illinois University Press, 1967.

Solis, Janet Long. *El Placer del Chile.* Mexico City, Mexico: Editorial Clio, Libros y Videos, S.A de C.V., 1998.

Texas State Historical Association (in partnership with the College of Liberal Arts and the General Libraries at the University of Texas at Austin). *Handbook of Texas Online,* http://www.tsha.utexas.edu.

Toussaint-Samat, Maguelonne. *History of Food,* trans. Anthea Bell. London: Blackwell, 1992, 1994. [Original French. Paris: BORDAS, 1987]

Tweedie, Alec. *Mexico As I Saw It.* London: Thomas Nelson and Sons, 1911.

Vela Family Members. *La Cocina de los Vela.* Hidalgo County, Tex.: Privately printed, 1984.

Vela Family Members. *La Cocina Moderna de los Vela.* Hidalgo County, Tex.: Privately printed, 1993.

Velaquez de Leon, Josefina. *Cocina de San Luis Potosi.* DeLeon, Mexico: Academia de Cocina Velaquez De Leon, 1957.

Von Mentz de Boege, and Brigida Margarita. *Mexico en el Siglo XIX, Visto por los Alemanes.* Mexico City, Mexico: Universidad Autonoma de Mexico, 1982.

Yturbide, Teresa Castello. *Presencia de La Comida Prehispanica.* Mexico City, Mexico: Fomento Cultural Banamex, 1986.

Zurita, Ricardo Mendoza. *Enciclopedico de Gastonomia Mexicana.* Mexico City, Mexico: Editorial Clio, Libros y Videos, S.A de C.V., 2000.

INDEX

Bruns   Eggs 8   Syr butter

4 stks

Flour	Sugar	Egg	Butter	Chocolate	~~Enoth~~
Brownies 2 cups	6 cup	8	7 sticks	1 1/4 cup	3/4 cup
Syrup 4 cup	1 t	2	2 Sticks	0	0
Fudge	3 1/2	2	1/2	1 pound	1 1/2
Walnuts 4	~~4~~ 2	2	4	2 cup	
Cake cone					
Bak 0	0	0	0	0	0